HARDEN'S

London
Restaurants
1998

Where to buy Harden's guides

Harden's guides are on sale in most major bookshops
in the UK, and many major bookshops in the US.
In case of difficulty, call Harden's Guides on
0171-839 4763.

**Customised editions –
the ideal corporate gift**

Harden's London Restaurants is available in specially
customised corporate gift formats. For information,
please call 0171-839 4763.

To register for Updates and the Survey
- **return the reply-paid card or**
- **send an e-mail to mail@hardens.com**
   Don't forget to include your postal address.

© Harden's Guides, 1997

ISBN 1-873721-14-5

British Library Cataloguing-in-Publication data:
a catalogue record for this book is available from
the British Library.

Printed and bound in Finland by
Werner Söderström Osakeyhtiö

Harden's Guides
29 Villiers Street
London WC2N 6ND

Distributed in the United States of America by
Seven Hills Book Distributors,
49 Central Avenue, Cincinnati, OH 45202

CONTENTS

RATINGS & PRICES

Ratings

Our rating system is unlike those found in other guides (most of which tell you nothing more helpful than that expensive restaurants are, as a general rule, better than cheap ones).

What we do is to compare each restaurant's performance with other restaurants in the same price-bracket.

This system has the advantage that it helps you find – whatever your budget for any particular meal – where you will get the best "bang for your buck".

The following qualities are assessed:

F — Food
S — Service
A — Ambience

The rating indicates that, *in comparison with other restaurants in the same price-bracket*, performance is ...

❶ — Exceptional
❷ — Very good
❸ — Good
④ — Mediocre
⑤ — Disappointing

Prices

The price shown for each restaurant is the cost for one (1) person of an average three-course *dinner* with half a bottle of house wine and coffee, any cover charge, service and VAT. Lunch is often cheaper. With BYO restaurants, we have assumed that two people share a £5 bottle of off-licence wine.

Telephone numbers – only '0181' numbers are prefixed; all others are '0171' numbers.

Map reference – shown immediately after the telephone number.

Last orders time – the first entry in the small print (Sunday may be up to 90 minutes earlier).

Opening hours – unless otherwise stated, restaurants are open for lunch and dinner seven days a week.

Credit and debit cards – unless otherwise stated, Mastercard, Visa, Amex and Switch are accepted.

Dress – where appropriate, the management's preferences concerning patrons' dress are given.

Smoking – cigarette smoking restrictions are noted. Pipe or cigar smokers should always check ahead.

Special menus – if we know of a particularly good value set menu we note this (eg "set weekday L"), together with its formula price (FP) calculated exactly as in 'Prices' above. Details change, so always check ahead.

FROM THE EDITORS

This is the seventh edition of our annual guide, designed to help you find the right London restaurant for any particular occasion and then, as briefly as possible, to tell you everything you need to know about it.

The Survey

Once again this year, the guide has been compiled with the benefit of a much-enlarged survey. This year over 2,750 people participated (over 80 per cent more than last year). We are very grateful to all who did so, and also to those who have helped enlarge the survey by introducing friends and colleagues.

Reporters eat out, on average, 3.5 times a week. Thus the survey reflects the experiences of some 500,000 meals eaten in the preceding 12 months.

Whose views?

We have ourselves visited every restaurant, or chain, listed in this book – always anonymously and at our own expense. But, for the most part, we use these personal experiences only to help you to interpret and explain the results of the survey – we do not seek to superimpose our personal views. Rather, we seek from our informed starting-point, to analyse and comment on the views and ratings from our 'reporters'. In the rare cases we feel that we can add something by noting our dissent from the general view, we do so in the text. The numerical ratings reflect the survey results.

The survey however can provide no useful information on the 'hot' summer openings (upon which we receive little or no commentary), and it is of only limited assistance where there has been a recent major chef or ownership change. In these cases, our own opinions are, of necessity, more to the fore, and, in these cases only, any numerical rating reflects our personal opinions alone.

We believe that it is this pragmatic combination of the views of thousands of people with the impressions from our own personal visits which enables the production of an up-to-date guide of unequalled reliability.

Please help us to make the next edition even more accurate. If you register for the free updates (by returning the reply-paid card at the back of the book) you will be invited, in the summer of 1998, to take part in our next survey. **If you take part in the survey, you will, on publication, receive a complimentary copy of *Harden's London Restaurants 1999*.**

Richard Harden   **Peter Harden**

SURVEY – MOST MENTIONED

These are the restaurants which were most frequently mentioned by reporters. (Last year's position is given in brackets. An asterisk* indicates a first appearance in the list of a recently opened or re-launched restaurant.)

1   Oxo Tower*
2   Mezzo (1)
3   Quaglino's (2)
4   The Ivy (3)
5   Bank*
6   Le Pont de la Tour (4)
7   Aubergine (9)
8   Le Palais du Jardin (13)
9   The Criterion (7)
10 Le Caprice (8)

11 Blue Elephant (17=)
12 Bibendum (5)
13 Livebait*
14 L'Odéon (6)
15 The River Café (14)
16 Wagamama (22)
17 Vong (24)
18 L'Oranger (-)
19 Coast (11)
20 La Tante Claire (16)

21 The Fifth Floor (19)
22 Bluebird*
23 Kensington Place (12)
24 The Collection*
25 The Avenue (20)
26 Chutney Mary (40)
27 Atlantic Bar & Grill (23)
28= Rules (10)
28= Belgo Centraal (15)
30= The People's Palace (32=)

30= Marco Pierre White (see Oak Room) (21)
32 Nobu*
33 Maison Novelli*
34 The Sugar Club (-)
35 Andrew Edmunds (-)
36 Simpsons-in-the-Strand (25)
37 Café Fish (-)
38 Café Spice Namaste*
39= Le Gavroche (32=)
39= The Square (-)

SURVEY – NOMINATIONS

Ranked by the number of reporters' votes for:

Best meal of the year

 1 Aubergine (1)
 2 La Tante Claire (2)
 3 The River Cafe (8)
 4 Bibendum (3)
 5= Le Gavroche (5)
 5= The Ivy (10)
 7 L'Oranger (-)
 8 Le Pont de la Tour (6)
 9 Chez Nico at Ninety (7)
10 Marco Pierre White (see Oak Room) (4)

Favourite

 1 The Ivy (1)
 2 Le Caprice (2)
 3 Le Palais du Jardin (7)
 4 Aubergine (3)
 5 The River Café (8)
 6= Oxo Tower*
 6= Quaglino's (-)
 8 Kensington Place (10)
 9 Bibendum (5)
10 Le Pont de la Tour (6)

Best for business

 1 Le Pont de la Tour (1)
 2= Savoy Grill (2)
 2= The Ivy (3)
 4 Oxo Tower*
 5 Bank*
 6 City Rhodes*
 7 Quaglino's (-)
 8 The Square (4)
 9 L'Odéon (-)
10 Le Caprice (5)

Best for romance

 1= La Poule au Pot (1)
 1= Julie's (2)
 3 Andrew Edmunds (8=)
 4 Aubergine (6)
 5 Launceston Place (3)
 6 The Blue Elephant (5)
 7 The Ivy (-)
 8= The Criterion (8=)
 8= Oxo Tower*
10 Le Caprice (8=)

SURVEY – HIGHEST RATINGS

Rankings are determined from reporters' average ratings:

Money no object (£50+)

Food	Service
1 Aubergine	1 Connaught
2 La Tante Claire	2 La Tante Claire
3 Pied à Terre	3 Dorchester Grill
4 Tatsuso	4 Claridges Restaurant
5 Chez Nico	5 Aubergine

Expensive (£40-£49)

Food	Service
1 City Rhodes	1 Le Caprice
2 Matsuri	2 Clarke's
3 L'Oranger	3 The Ivy
4 Clarke's	4 Matsuri
5 The River Café	5 L'Oranger

Upper mid-price (£30-£39)

Food	Service
1 Chinon	1 Oslo Court
2 Chez Bruce	2 Quincy's
3 Bibendum Oyster Bar	3 Chezmax
4 Zafferano	4 Vasco & Piero's Pavilion
5 Jason's	5 Assaggi

Lower mid-price (£20-£29)

Food	Service
1 Mandarin Kitchen	1 Tandoori Lane
2 Royal China W2	2 La Pomme d'Amour
3 Toff's	3 Soulard
4 Chez Liline	4 Emile's
5 Inaho	5 Leonardo's

Budget (£19 or less)

Food	Service
1 Kastoori	1 Mandalay
2 Bedlington Café	2 Rasa
3 Rasa	3 Costa's Grill
4 Shree Krishna	4 Kastoori
5 Porchetta Pizzeria	5 Tokyo Diner

Ambience	Overall
1 The Ritz	1 Aubergine
2 Blakes Hotel	2 La Tante Claire
3 Café Royal Grill Room	3 Pied à Terre
4 Aubergine	4 Connaught
5 Savoy River Restaurant	5 Dorchester Grill

Ambience	Overall
1 Blue Elephant	1 Le Caprice
2 Julie's	2 The Ivy
3 The Ivy	3 Blue Elephant
4 Launceston Place	4 Clarke's
5 Le Caprice	5 Launceston Place

Ambience	Overall
1 Momo	1 Chez Bruce
2 Sale e Pepe	2 L'Aventure
3 Odin's	3 Oslo Court
4 La Poule au Pot	4 Odin's
5 L'Aventure	5 Chezmax

Ambience	Overall
1 Sarastro	1 Soulard
2 Naked Turtle	2 Tandoori Lane
3 Andrew Edmunds	3 La Pomme d'Amour
4 Café Bohème	4 Pizza Metro
5 Ffiona's	5 Ffiona's

Ambience	Overall
1 Gordon's Wine Bar	1 Iznik
2 Troubadour	2 Rasa
3 Bar Italia	3 Costa's Grill
4 Pucci Pizza	4 Kastoori
5 Iznik	5 Gordon's Wine Bar

SURVEY – HIGHEST RATINGS

Highest average ratings by cuisine

These are the restaurants which received the best average food ratings, listed by cuisine. (A few equally deserving restaurants are excluded because they are too little known to generate a sufficient number of reports.)

Each section is divided into '£30 and over', and 'under £30'. Within each section, restaurants are ranked by rating.

Modern British

£30 and over
1 Chez Bruce
2 City Rhodes
3 The Square
4 Clarke's
5 Halcyon Hotel
6 Le Caprice
7 The Sugar Club
8 The Ivy
9 The Stepping Stone
10 Stephen Bull

Under £30
1 The Chelsea Ram

Traditional British

£30 and over
1 Dorchester Grill
2 Connaught

Under £30
1 Fox & Anchor

East/West

£30 and over
1 Nobu
2 Vong

Steaks & Grills

£30 and over
1 Hope & Sir Loin

Under £30
1 Popeseye

Vegetarian

Under £30
1 The Gate
2 Carnevale

French

£30 and over
1 Aubergine
2 La Tante Claire
3 Pied à Terre
4 Chinon
5 Chez Nico at Ninety
6 Le Soufflé
7 Le Gavroche
8 L'Oranger
9 Chezmax
10 Capital Hotel
11 Four Seasons W1
12 Oslo Court

Italian/Mediterranean

£30 and over
1 Al San Vincenzo
2 Zafferano
3 The River Café
4 Assaggi
5 Del Buongustaio
6 Enoteca Turi

Under £30
1 Vegia Zena
2 Porchetta Pizzeria

Pizza

Under £30
1 Pizza Metro
2 Porchetta Pizzeria
3 Eco
4 Pizzeria Castello

Fish & chips

Under £30
1 Toff's
2 Two Brothers
3 Seashell

Fish & seafood

£30 and over
1 Bibendum Oyster Bar
2 Jason's
3 The Lobster Pot
4 Livebait
5 Poissonnerie de l'Avenue
6 Zilli Fish

Under £30
1 Chez Liline

Greek

Under £30
1 Costa's Grill

Russian

£30 and over
1 Kaspia

Persian

Under £30
1 Alounak

Tunisian

Under £30
1 Laurent

Turkish

Under £30
1 Iznik

Snacks

Under £30
1 Brick Lane Beigel Bake
2 Seattle Coffee

Thai

£30 and over
1 Blue Elephant

Under £30
1 Bedlington Café
2 Tui

Chinese

£30 and over
1 Dorchester, Oriental
2 Mao Tai
3 Fung Shing
4 Ken Lo's SW1

Under £30
1 Mandarin Kitchen
2 Royal China W2
3 Golden Dragon

Japanese

£30 and over
1 Tatsuso
2 Matsuri

Under £30
1 Inaho
2 Café Japan
3 Moshi Moshi Sushi
4 Ikkyu

Indian

£30 and over
1 Tamarind
2 Bombay Bicycle Club

Under £30
1 Kastoori
2 Rasa
3 Shree Krishna
4 Gopal's of Soho
5 Lahore Kebab House
6 Tandoori Lane
7 Cafe Spice Namaste
8 Diwana Bhel Poori House
9 Mandeer

Burmese

Under £30
1 Mandalay

TOP SPECIAL DEALS

Menus are included in the following lists which give you the chance to eat in the restaurants concerned at a significant discount compared to the evening à la carte prices.

The price in brackets is calculated in accordance with our formula (ie three courses with house wine, coffee and tip).

Special menus are by their nature susceptible to change – please call ahead to check that they are still available.

Weekday lunch

Chez Nico *(£53)*
Oak Room MPW *(£51)*
Connaught *(£43)*
Dorchester, Oriental *(£40)*
Le Gavroche *(£40)*
The Ritz *(£38)*
Capital Hotel *(£37)*
Interlude *(£36)*
Café Royal Grill *(£35)*
Aubergine *(£35)*
Leith's *(£35)*
La Tante Claire *(£35)*
The Halkin *(£34)*
Four Seasons *(£34)*
Santini *(£32)*
Nobu *(£31)*
Sheekey's *(£29)*
Chavot *(£28)*
Clarke's *(£27)*
The Criterion *(£27)*
Turner's *(£27)*
Mezzo *(£26)*
Salloos *(£26)*
Quaglino's *(£25)*
Al Bustan *(£25)*
Bentley's *(£25)*
La Porte des Indes *(£25)*
Aykoku-Kaku *(£24)*
Bombay Brasserie *(£24)*
English House *(£24)*
La Poule au Pot *(£24)*
Bank *(£23)*
Drones *(£23)*
First Floor *(£23)*
Orsino *(£23)*
Kensington Place *(£23)*
English Garden *(£23)*
Lobster Pot *(£22)*
Montpeliano *(£22)*
Motcomb's *(£22)*

Café du Jardin *(£21)*
Wódka *(£21)*
Stratford's *(£20)*
Veeraswamy *(£20)*
192 *(£20)*
Miyama *(£20)*
Gresslin's *(£19)*
Joe Allen *(£19)*
Odette's *(£19)*
Le Suquet *(£19)*
La Bouchée *(£18)*
Mezzonine *(£18)*
Beach Blanket
  Babylon *(£18)*
Lou Pescadou *(£18)*
Naked Turtle *(£18)*
Palio *(£18)*
Ajimura *(£17)*
Chezmax *(£17)*
Jindivick *(£17)*
Café Lazeez *(£17)*
La Cage Imaginaire *(£17)*
Phoenicia *(£17)*
Le Bouchon Bordelais *(£16)*
Busabong Tree *(£16)*
Caravan Serai *(£16)*
Le P'tit Normand *(£16)*
Singapore Garden *(£16)*
Phoenix *(£16)*
Café des Arts *(£15)*
Ikkyu *(£15)*
Bonjour Vietnam *(£14)*
Inaho *(£14)*
Isfehan *(£14)*
Lemonia *(£14)*
Pasha *(£14)*
Toff's *(£14)*
Café de la Place *(£13)*
Vegia Zena *(£13)*
Bu San *(£12)*
Woodlands *(£12)*

Khyber Pass *(£11)*
Le Sacré-Coeur *(£11)*
Le Shop *(£11)*
Haandi *(£10)*
Galicia *(£10)*
Mandeer *(£9)*

Pre/post theatre
(and early evening)

Café Royal Grill *(£35)*
Le Pont de la Tour *(£31)*
Sheekey's *(£29)*
Christopher's *(£26)*
Quaglino's *(£25)*
L'Odéon *(£25)*
Mezzo *(£24)*
Bank *(£23)*
Café du Jardin *(£21)*
Luigi's *(£21)*
Stratford's *(£20)*
Manzi's *(£20)*
Ajimura *(£19)*
La Bouchée *(£18)*
L'Estaminet *(£18)*
Chezmax *(£17)*
Jindivick *(£17)*
Boudin Blanc *(£17)*
Mezzonine *(£16)*
Café des Arts *(£15)*
Mon Plaisir *(£15)*

Sunday lunch

Connaught *(£48)*
Le Soufflé *(£36)*
English Garden *(£27)*
Mezzo *(£26)*
Blue Elephant *(£26)*
La Porte des Indes *(£25)*
Kensington Place *(£25)*
Bombay Brasserie *(£24)*
The Ivy *(£23)*
Maggie Jones's *(£22)*
Basil St Hotel *(£20)*
Phoenicia *(£19)*
Phoenix *(£19)*
Galicia *(£11)*

WHERE'S THE BEEF?

Ten years ago, London was very clearly backwards in terms of restaurants. The ensuing revolution is history. Part of the story to which too little attention has been given, though, is the rôle which Big Business – the provider of much of the capital needed to fund such an explosion in the number of eateries – has carved out for itself, and the effect this has had on the restaurant landscape.

The quality end of the market is now dominated, in a way which is probably unprecedented, by a small group of large operators. They have brought a lot of style, a lot of marketing pizazz, and a lot of excitement into the business. Their very presence has provided the opportunity for many more trainees to join the quality catering trade – the long-term effect of this on dining out in England (not just in London) may be profound.

But what sort of value do they currently offer? If you look at the top 100 survey ratings set out on pages 12 and 13 (determined by the votes of 2,750 reporters), what is most striking is the virtual absence of Big Business restaurants. The two highest profile operators manage a lonely single representative apiece – and those both 'special cases'! Conran's champion is Bibendum Oyster Bar (which does little cooking) and Groupe Chez Gérard has Livebait (which it acquired only recently).

This is no statistical peculiarity – it is a reflection of the fact that the Big Business restaurants in London are, with few exceptions, offering mediocre value for money. Despite their vast economies of scale – for example in purchasing – they are succeeding in selling an inferior product for a higher price than much of their less amply funded competition. That's the power of marketing!

The leading figures in the hospitality industry are prone nowadays to telling us that London is the culinary centre of the universe. Therein lies a certain irony. Because what really makes London eating more and more interesting is the growing number of: 1) places of real culinary achievement; and 2) interesting ethnic restaurants. What these two types of restaurant have in common is that Big Business is almost invariably not involved.

What Big Business continues to fail to do is what, in our view, it most particularly *ought* to be doing – providing places where ordinary people can enjoy European cooking of good quality at reasonable prices somewhere not too far removed from the centre of town. London still fails – and comparisons with New York or Paris are, in this regard, stark – to meet this demand. When it finally succeeds, the panjandrums of the trade will truly be able to claim that dining out in London has come of age.

THE RESTAURANT SCENE

A change in the air?

The story "Capital's Restaurants Boom" has run so long that it's no longer news. As recently as last year, large new openings seemed the talk of the town. And yet the arrival, just before we went to press, of La Belle Epoque, an 800-seater said to be Europe's largest restaurant complex, provoked scant interest.

For the first time since our initial review in 1991 it appears that the London restaurant business is no longer riding an "up only" escalator. This year we note 90 openings (listed on page 20) – practically the same as the record-breaking number of last year (89). But we also list 58 closings (see page 21) – almost twice as many as last year's record figure, and far higher than the figure recorded at any time during the recession.

It isn't that the market has stopped growing. It does seem, though, that market capacity is finally catching up with demand. As a result, the business is becoming more competitive, with marginal places – in particular new ventures which miss their mark, or old formulas which now seem passé – falling more rapidly by the wayside.

It may be the sign of a market at its peak that in the last year a number of 'old hands' have perceived a good opportunity to sell out – Anna left Anna's Place, Boyd Gilmour quit Boyd's, Magno departed from Magno's Brasserie, and the Ttofalli family's sold Toff's.

Sir Terence Conran has also noted a major turning-point. He has said that no further mega-brasseries – a phenomenon for which he is almost single-handedly responsible – are planned. Another man adept at sniffing out a change in the air, Antony Worrall Thompson, is also predicting a major change move away from gigantism, in favour of smaller, more personal ventures.

The 'top ten' notable newcomers

In each edition of the guide, we present what appear to us to be the ten most significant openings of the past twelve months. This year, our selection is as follows:

Belair House	Momo
La Belle Epoque	Nobu
Bistrot 2 Riverside	Putney Bridge
Bluebird	Stephen Bull WC2
City Rhodes	Zilli Fish

As last year, two of the most original new ventures have foreign backing – Momo from Paris and Nobu from New York. Many home-grown ventures still seem stuck in a rather 'samey' groove, but first inklings of projects in the pipeline give hope that next year may be a little different.

OPENINGS

Abbaye
Anonimato
Aquarium
L'Arte
Bar
Bar Japan
Beirut Express
Belair House
La Belle Epoque
Bistrot Soho
Bistrot 2
Bluebird
Blythe Road Restaurant
The Brook
Cactus Blue
Café 206
Café de Paris
Café Indiya
Café Latino
Capital Radio Restaurant
Caravaggio
The Chapel
Chavot
Chelsea Restaurant
Chelsea Square
Chor Bizarre
La Ciboulette
Circus
City Rhodes
Coq d'Argent
Fisk
Four Regions
Gabriel
Gecko
Ghillies
Goolies
Grissini
Hornimans
Jindivick
Justin de Blank
Ken Lo's Memories of
   China W8
The Little Bay SW1
Lola's
Mesclun
Momo
Monsieur Max
Moro
MPW
Nobu
Novelli EC1
Novelli W8
Oceana

On The Rise
1 Lawn Terrace
Oak Room
   Marco Pierre White
Opus 70
Orrery
Osteria del Parco
Parson's Nose
Pasha SW7
Polygon Bar & Grill
Putney Bridge
Rainforest Café
Redmond's
S Bar
Sabatino
Searcy's Brasserie
Simply Nico Chelsea
Soho Spice
South
La Spighetta
Sri India
Stephen Bull WC2
Stone Mason's Arms
Sushi Wong
t'su
Townhouse Brasserie
Tuscan
Uno
Vama
The Vine
The White Onion
Wok Wok
Woz
Yo! Sushi
Yoshino
Zilli Fish
Zinc
Zucca
Zujuma's

CLOSINGS

Al Basha
All Saints
Alwaha
The Ark
L'Artiste Assoiffé
B Square
The Bank SW11
Big Night Out
Blenheim Bis
Brady's SW6
Brahms
Brasserie Highgate
Bruno Soho
Cappadoccia
Cento 50
Chiaroscuro
China Court
Christoph's
F Cooke & Sons
Delicious Blue
The Establishment
Euten's
Exxo
La Fenice
Fulham Road
Garbo's
La Giara
The Heights
Hollihead
Hoults
Irving's
Karahi
Kassoulet
Lobster Trading Co
Marché Mövenpick W1
Le Mesurier
Mon Petit Plaisir
Nineteen
Oliver's Island
Parks
Parsons
Pélican E14
Princess of Wales
R Bar
Red SW3
Restaurant Marco Pierre
   White SW1
Rock Island Diner
Scandinavian Restaurant
Sol e Stella
South Bank Brasserie
Stamford
Tabac

La Truffe Noire
Twenty Trinity Gardens
Walton's
Wolfe's SW3
Wynkyn de Worde
Young Turks

DIRECTORY

Comments in "double quotation-marks" were made by reporters.

Establishments which we judge to be particularly notable have their NAME IN CAPITALS.

A Tavola NW8 £28 ④④❷
7 St John's Wood High St 586 4776 8–3A
*"Very rustic" St John's Wood Italian whose supporters think it
"sadly underused" – perhaps that's because it's "pricey",
and service can jar. / 10.30 pm; no credit cards.*

Abbaye EC1 £26 ❸④④
55 Charterhouse St 253 1612 9–2A
*We're with those who say that this Smithfield newcomer is
"not as good as Hubble & Co", which it replaced; the beer
and mussels fare is "standard", and little is made of the
potentially interesting site. / 10.30 pm; closed Sat & Sun;
no smoking area.*

The Abingdon W8 £32 ❸❸❸
54 Abingdon Rd 937 3339 5–2A
*This "very pleasant" Kensington "haunt", in a quiet back
street location, is praised for its good bar, "mellow booths"
and "stylish" and "relaxed" atmosphere; the modern British
cooking is "consistent". / 11 pm.*

L'Accento Italiano W2 £28 ❸④❸
16 Garway Rd 243 2201 6–1B
*"Noisy" and "crowded" Bayswater local, offering rather hit-
and-miss, "rustic" Italian cooking. / 11.30 pm; no Amex; smart casual.*

Adams Café W12 £21 ❷❷④
77 Askew Rd 0181-743 0572 7–1B
*By day it's a greasy spoon, at night this "cheery, charming
and different" Shepherds Bush local turns north African,
with "great cous-cous" the special attraction; "BYO is a
major plus". / 11 pm; D only.*

Afghan Kitchen N1 £12 ❸④❸
35 Islington Gn 359 8019 8–3D
*"Delicious", "different" cooking at "very cheap" prices puts
this tiny Islington Green café on the map; the service – "Earth
to waitress, do you read me?" – has few fans. / 11.30 pm; closed
Mon & Sun; no credit cards.*

Ajimura WC2 £34 ❸④⑤
51-53 Shelton St 240 9424 4–2C
*Britain's longest-established Japanese is now often overlooked,
and as a result it has "no ambience"; some still think it "good
value", though, and it has a handy Covent Garden location.
/ 10.30 pm; closed Sat L & Sun; no Amex & no Switch; no smoking area; set
weekday L £17(FP), pre-th. £19(FP).*

Al Bustan SW1   £ 39   ❷❷④

27 Motcomb St   235 8277   2–4A

"Huge portions of authentic Lebanese food" and pleasant service combine to make this discreetly located Belgravian a "very, very good" place of its type; it's a shame that the ambience is so low-key. / 11 pm; no Switch; smart casual; set weekday L £25(FP).

Al Hamra W1   £ 38   ❸④❸

31-33 Shepherd Mkt   493 1954   3–4B

"In the lively setting of Shepherd Market", this smart Lebanese boasts pavement tables "among the best in London", and cooking which is consistently "good, but expensive"; the famously iffy service was better this year, and a recent (much needed) refit suggests something of a new broom. / 11.30 pm; no Switch.

Al San Vincenzo W2   £ 40   ❶❷④

30 Connaught St   262 9623   6–1D

"Consistently excellent, in its funny way", the Borgonzolo family's "miniature" Bayswater restaurant is proclaimed the "best Italian in London" by its (necessarily) limited following; even fans admit it's "hardly a party place". / 10 pm; closed Sat L & Sun; no Amex & no Switch.

Al Sultan W1   £ 31   ❸④④

51-52 Hertford St   408 1155   3–4B

Smart Shepherd Market yearling, whose "variable" Lebanese fare can be "very enjoyable"; however, sometimes "arrogant" service and the rather anodyne furnishings can make it underpopulated. / 11.30 pm.

Al's EC1   £ 19   ❸⑤❸

11-13 Exmouth Mkt   837 4821   8–4D

Funky and "relaxed" all-day Clerkenwell café whose ragbag of breakfast and other grub is "great for hangovers"; service is "slow and forgetful". / Midnight, Wed–Sat 1.30 am (bar 3 am).

Alastair Little W1   £ 40   ❸④⑤

49 Frith St   734 5183   4–2A

"Very disappointing" remains the verdict on this once path-breaking modern British Soho restaurant; the cooking can hit the spot – sometimes – but service is "very poor", and its bare café-like premises are devoid of atmosphere. / 11 pm; closed Sat L & Sun.

Alastair Little, Lancaster Road W11 £36 ❸❸④
136a Lancaster Rd   243 2220   6–1A
*On a good day, you get "interesting" cooking at this famous
modern British chef's "cramped" and "spartan" Notting Hill
yearling; it's a perfectly competent neighbourhood place –
given Little's fame, you might hope for more. / 11 pm; closed Sun.*

Alba EC1 £29 ❸❸④
107 Whitecross St   588 1798   9–1B
*"An Italian treat" with "good seasonal ingredients", say loyal
fans of this "airy", but characterless spot in the "otherwise
desolate" area by the Barbican; it's "not cheap however",
and some complain of "bland" food. / 11 pm; closed Sat & Sun.*

Albero & Grana SW3 £45 ④④❷
89 Sloane Ave   225 1048   5–2C
*"Relaxed", "Mediterranean cool" Brompton Cross Hispanic,
which is less frenetic these days than it was of old; the quite
serious, contemporary cooking can be "superb", but is not
reliably so. / 11 pm; smart casual.*

Albero & Grana Tapas Bar SW3 £24 ❷④❷
89 Sloane Ave   225 1048   5–2C
*"It can be a bit of a scrum" and "too smoky", but this still
stylish bar makes an "entertaining" rendezvous and dishes up
affordable, quality grub. / Midnight; D only ex Sat, when open all day.*

Alfred WC2 £32 ❸④④
245 Shaftesbury Ave   240 2566   4–1C
*It "scores on informality", but the setting at this 60's kitchen-
like Bloomsbury site has never been up to much; sadly the
"interesting", "traditional British" cooking seems to be going
the same way. / 11.30 pm; closed Sat L & Sun.*

Ali Baba NW1 £18 ❷❷④
32 Ivor Pl   723 5805   8–4A
*"Real, family-made Middle Eastern food" at "super value"
prices makes it worth seeking out this brightly-lit dining room,
behind a take-away near Marylebone station; BYO. / 11.30 pm;
no credit cards.*

All Bar One £ 24 ③④③

289-293 Regent St, W1   636 6554   3–1C
3-4 Hanover St, W1   495 2216   3–2C
36-38 Dean St, W1   287 4641   4–2A
48 Leicester Sq, WC2   839 0972   4–4A
587-591 Fulham Rd, SW6   385 6668   5–4A
197-199 Chiswick High Rd, W4   0181-742 3339   7–2A
1 Liverpool Rd, N1   278 5906   8–3D
1-3 Hampstead Ln, N6   0181-340 6555   8–1B
60 St John's Wood High St, NW8   722 6144   8–3A
42 Mackenzie Walk, E14   512 3435   1–3D
103 Cannon St, EC4   512 9495   9–3C
44-46 Ludgate Hl, EC4   248 1356   9–2A
*"A winning concept" – this growing chain "pleasantly
surprises" with its "commendable", "well priced" fare and its
"wine bar atmosphere"; the younger crowd says it's "a good
place to mingle", so fogies may find noise-levels "atrocious".
/ Mon-Thu 10 pm, Fri-Sun 9 pm; Hanover St, City and E14 branches close part
of weekend; no booking.*

Alma SW18 £ 22 ③④③

499 Old York Rd   0181-870 2537   10–2B
*"Victoriana heaven" Wandsworth boozer whose rear
restaurant offers improving, "very tasty", if "variable", fare;
"too many rugby shirts" can be a problem. / 10.30 pm.*

Alounak W14 £ 19 ❶③③

10 Russell Gdns   603 1130   7–1D
*We miss the Portakabin that used to house this Olympia
Persian; it now has 'proper' premises nearby (formerly Uma,
RIP), but the "down to earth" grub remains "amazingly cheap
and very tasty", and you can still BYO. / Midnight; no credit cards.*

L'Altro

75 Beak St, W1   287 1840   3–2D
4 Sydney St, SW3   352 3433   5–2C
294 Fulham Rd, SW6   795 0048   5–3B
210 Kensington Pk Rd, W11   792 1066   6–1A
108 Heath St, NW3   794 9919   8–1A
*This Italian chain that specialises in seafood was sold as we
were going to press; only the tiny, theatrically designed
Notting Hill original (once of considerable ambition) has
what could be described as a following. / 11.30 pm.*

Anarkali W6 £ 25 ③④④

303-305 King St   0181-748 1760   7–2B
*"Still first-rate after 25 years", say fans of this "sombre"
Hammersmith Indian, with its sinister black-tinted windows;
our experience – on a day when nearly all the specials were
'off' – was of cooking that never lived up to its promise.
/ 11.30 pm; .*

Andrew Edmunds W1   £ 24   ❸❷❶

46 Lexington St   437 5708   3–2D

"Candlelit, shadowy and perfect", this "offbeat" Soho townhouse, with its "'mesmerising atmosphere", has a following quite disproportionate to its size – the seating is less "squashed" upstairs; the simple but "imaginative" modern British food is "reliable" and "inexpensive", and the wine list "always has interesting bottles at sensible prices"; "book". / 10.45 pm.

Anglesea Arms W6   £ 23   ❷⑤❸

35 Wingate Rd   0181-749 1291   7–1B

"Slow", "harassed" service "lets down a good package" at this trendy Brackenbury Village pub, where Dan Evans's accomplished and inexpensive modern British nosh "rarely disappoints". / 10.30 pm; no Amex; no booking.

Anglo Asian Tandoori N16   £ 19   ❸❸❸

60-62 Stoke Newington Ch St   254 9298   1–1C

"Tacky" it may be, but this low-lit, quite romantic Stoke Newington Indian provides "good food" at modest cost. / 11.45 pm, Fri & Sat 12.30 am; no Switch.

Anna's Place N1   £ 31   ❸❷❷

90 Mildmay Pk   249 9379   1–1C

"Lovely surroundings and atmosphere" still make this cosy Islington townhouse a popular choice; Anna has now quit the scene, though, and it is too early to say whether sliding ratings for the Scandinavian fare reflect the dying days of the old régime, or the teetering steps of the new. / 10.45 pm; closed Mon & Sun D; no credit cards.

Anonimato W10   £ 31   ❷❶❸

12 All Saints Rd   243 2808   6–1B

The "innovative", "globe-trotting" cooking and "attentive and friendly, but not overbearing" staff are highly praised at this "laid back" Portobello newcomer (on the site of All Saints, RIP); "they need to sort out some PR to get the number of covers up". / 11 pm; D only Mon-Fri; no Amex.

Antipasto e Pasta SW4   £ 30   ❸❷❸

31 Abbeville Rd   0181-675 6260   10–2D

"A bit pricey", it may be, but you "usually have to book" for the "exceptional pastas" (and so on) offered by this stylish and "consistent" Clapham Italian. / 11.30 pm.

The Apprentice SE1   **£ 26**   ❷④⑤
31 Shad Thames   234 0254   9–4D
*"Incompetent, but willing (and sometimes hilarious)" service
plus "consistently good" modern British cooking makes this
Tower Bridge-side chefs' school a "super value", "unusual
choice" – even worth braving the "icy" setting for.* / 8.15 pm;
closed Sat & Sun; no Amex; no smoking area.

Aquarium E1   **£ 35**   ❸④❸
Ivory Hs, St Katharine-by-the-Tower   480 6116   1–2D
*"Fresh", "keenly flavoured" and "different" fish dishes are
creating a ripple of interest in this "loud and stylish" new
St Katharine's Dock restaurant (site of the disastrous M Fish,
RIP) – a "brilliant summer location"; a minority think it "odd
and expensive".* / 11 pm; closed Mon D & Sun L; closed Sun.

Arcadia W8   **£ 35**   ④❷❷
35 Kensington High St   937 4294   5–1A
*The Anglo/French cooking may not excite, but some find a
"great atmosphere" at this comfortable standby, just off
Kensington High Street; pluses include staff who make you
"always welcome", set meals which usually offer "very good
value" and "parrots".* / 11 pm; closed Sat L.

Archduke Wine Bar SE1   **£ 26**   ❸❸❸
Arch 153, Concert Hall Appr.   928 9370   2–3D
*A recent (much overdue) revamp has brightened up this large,
railway-arch wine bar/restaurant, long-famed as a useful
rendezvous for the South Bank Centre; it boasts an
"interesting, good value wine list".* / 11 pm; closed Sat L & Sun.

Arisugawa W1   **£ 35**   ❷④④
27a Percy St   636 8913   2–1C
*"Good" cooking is the prime virtue of this professional and
comfortable, but dull, basement Japanese, just off Tottenham
Court Road.* / 10 pm, Sat 9.30 pm; closed Sat L & Sun.

Arkansas Café E1   **£ 15**   ❷❸④
Unit 12, Old Spitalfield Market   377 6999   9–1D
*"The best BBQ steak, burgers and ribs in town", proclaim
fans of this simple Spitalfields Market café, where chef-patron
Bubba is much in evidence; service is "personal and friendly",
but slow.* / L only.

L'Arte W1   **£ 24**   ❶❸④

126 Cleveland St   813 1011   2–1B
*Displaced from the West End (where it was the Arts Theatre
Café) to the fringe of Fitzrovia, this "interesting" modern
Italian newcomer boasts "terrific" cooking using "very fresh
ingredients"; the setting is rudimentary.* / 11 pm; closed Sat L
& Sun.

L'Artiste Musclé W1   **£ 21**   ④❷❷

1 Shepherd Mkt   493 6150   3–4B
*This "intimate", "little bistro, like you find in France"
(picturesquely situated on a corner of Mayfair's Shepherd
Market) is useful for "easy and quick" meals; the cooking is
"very plain".* / 11 pm; winter closed Sun L

Ashtons EC3   **£ 39**   ④④❸

13-15 Leadenhall Mkt   929 2022   9–2D
*This agreeable "Leadenhall Market eyrie" seafood parlour
would not rate a mention outside the Square Mile; some do
like its "French-ish" food, but others say it's "not all it's
cracked up to be" and "far too pricey".* / L only; closed Sat & Sun.

Ask! Pizza   **£ 18**   ❸❸❸

160-162 Victoria St, SW1   630 8228   2–4B
121-125 Park St, W1   495 7760   2–2A
48 Grafton Way, W1   388 8108   2–1B
345 Fulham Palace Rd, SW6   371 0392   10–1B
1 Gloucester Arcade, SW7   835 0840   5–2B
145 Notting Hill Gt, W11   792 9942   6–2B
219-221 Chiswick High Rd, W4   0181-742 1323   7–2A
Bus' Design Ctr, Upper St, N1   226 8728   8–3D
216 Haverstock Hill, NW3   433 3896   8–2A
*"A poor imitation of PizzaExpress", cry critics of this
pizza/pasta chain, many of whose "light and airy" premises
do, indeed, seem rather similar to those of its famous
competitor; the majority, though, approve the "reliable" and
"reasonable" food, and vote them useful standbys, especially
with kids.* / 11.30 pm.

Assaggi W2   **£ 35**   ❶❶❸

39 Chepstow Pl   792 5501   6–1B
*"Unusual, delicious Italian food" (from a "limited" menu)
enhanced by "attentive, friendly service" has made this
Bayswater yearling a foodie shrine; the bright, cheery setting
over a pub is a touch "uncomfortable" though, and we are
with those who find prices "a fraction higher than is justified".*
/ 11 pm; closed Mon & Sun D.

Atelier W1   **£ 37**   ❸❸④

41 Beak St   287 2057   3–2D

"Fresh" and *"interesting"* modern British cooking and *"welcoming"* service win approval for this *"airy"* *"oasis of calm"* in Soho; the local ad-world following inflates lunch prices, but in the evening (when it can be *"empty"*) there's a bargain prix-fixe. / 10.45 pm; closed Sat L & Sun.

Atlantic Bar & Grill W1   **£ 40**   ④⑤❷

20 Glasshouse St   734 4888   3–3D

If you make it past the aggressive door policy, stick to the *"great bar"* in this vast and *"glamorous"* basement, near Piccadilly Circus; the *"snotty"* restaurant – with its *"consistently atrocious"* service and *"dull and lifeless"* food – is *"cashing in without caring"*. / 11.30 pm, bar food until 2.30 am; closed Sat L & Sun L.

Atrium SW1   **£ 40**   ④⑤④

4 Millbank   233 0032   2–4C

"Strange", *"dull"* modern British cooking, which is *"very expensive for what it is,* and *"slow"* service do little to stop this airy spot – uniquely convenient for the Westminster media centre – from being *"full of BBC types and politicos"*. / 10 pm; closed Sat & Sun; no smoking area.

Au Bon Accueil SW3   **£ 25**   ④❶❷

19 Elystan St   589 3718   5–2C

"Unchanging and reliable", this *"very civilised"* Chelsea Green Franco-Italian *"lives up to its name"*; the cooking may be *"unimaginative"*, but the generation which comes here has, by and large, outgrown the pursuit of excitement. / 11.30 pm; closed Sat L & Sun; no Switch.

Au Jardin des Gourmets W1   **£ 35**   ④❷❸

5 Greek St   437 1816   4–2A

Large, but often overlooked, this Soho old-timer offers a *"classic"* formula of *"traditional"* French cooking in bourgeois comfort; it all now seems rather passé, and – not for the first time – a revamp is promised as we go to press. / 11.15 pm; closed Sat L & Sun; smart casual; no smoking area.

AUBERGINE SW10   **£ 58**   ❶❷❷

11 Park Wk   352 3449   5–3B

"Excellent, excellent, excellent" – *"just a superb experience"*; it's *"worth the four-month wait"* to sample Gordon Ramsay's *"simply brilliant"* modern French cooking – once again reporters' top gastronomic choice; there is the odd reservation about *"OTT"* service, but, overall, the verdict stands – *"pretty well perfection"*. / 11 pm; closed Sat L & Sun; set weekday L £35(FP).

Aurora W1 £19 ❷❸❷

49 Lexington St   494 0514   3–2D

"Healthy" lunchtime fare leaves the fashionably skinny clientèle of this "very relaxing", "homely" café with space for the "great cakes and coffee"; it makes "a perfect place to hide in Soho", with an unusually nice courtyard. / 4 pm, snacks till 7 pm; closed Sun; no Amex.

L'Aventure NW8 £37 ❷❷❶

3 Blenheim Ter   624 6232   8–3A

This "very French" and "romantically discreet" St John's Wood restaurant du quartier is "a model of its kind"; summer dining on the "beautiful" terrace comes particularly recommended. / 11 pm; closed Sat L and, in Winter, Sun; no Switch.

The Avenue SW1 £41 ④④❸

7-9 St James's St   321 2111   3–4D

The "light, airy and spacious" setting of this "very New Yorkish" St James's yearling is widely voted its chief attraction (although its rather "functional" feeling perhaps suits it best to business); the modern British cooking scores hits and misses, and service can get "hassled". / 11.45 pm, Fri & Sat 12.30 am.

Aykoku-Kaku EC4 £43 ❸④④

9 Walbrook   248 2548   9–3C

"Good value set lunches" (served in a separate room) are the highlight at this City Japanese; it's "a tad overpriced", and the dated basement setting "leaves a little to be desired". / 10 pm; closed Sat & Sun; no booking for lunchtime refectory; set weekday L £24(FP).

Babe Ruth's E1 £26 ④④❸

172-176 The Highway   481 8181   1–2D

At its best this Docklands sports-bar yearling provides "good American fun" and "mammoth portions of fairly tolerable food" that "keep the kids happy"; it's "pricey", though, and really could be better. / Mon-Thu 11.30 pm, Fri & Sat 12.30 am; no smoking area; no booking.

Bah Humbug SW2 £21 ⑤❸❶

St Matthew's Peace Garden   738 3184   10–2D

It's the "dark, gothic" air of this Brixton church crypt – "all candles and jumbled furniture" – which is its special attraction; the food (mainly veggie) and service "could try harder". / 10.30 pm; D only Mon-Fri, Sat & Sun open L & D; no Amex.

Bahn Thai W1 £ 29 ③⑤⑤
21a Frith St   437 8504   4–2A
*"Good food at a reasonable price" is the sole justification for
the existence of this Soho Thai – the premises "could do
with a refit" and service can be "criminally slow". / 11.15 pm;
smart casual.*

Balans £ 26 ❸❷❸
60 Old Compton St, W1   437 5212   4–3A
239 Old Brompton Rd, SW5   244 8838   5–3A
*"Relaxed" modern hang-outs with a winning package of
"reasonable food, good efficient service and a buzzy
atmosphere"; the original Soho branch – open almost all
hours – is "too gay at night" for some tastes, but the smarter
and more spacious Earl's Court off-shoot has a more
homogeneous appeal. / W1 Mon-Thu 4 am, Fri & Sat 6 am, Sun 1 am –
SW5 1 am; W1 no booking – SW5 Sat & Sun no booking.*

Bangkok SW7 £ 25 ❷❸④
9 Bute St   584 8529   5–2B
*"Practical", "no chic" South Kensington Thai with a devoted
following – "never had even a mediocre meal in over 25
years"; "updated décor is now needed". / 11 pm; closed Sun;
no Amex; smart casual.*

BANK WC2 £ 38 ❸④❸
1 Kingsway   379 9797   2–2D
*"The best of the new mega-brasseries", this colourful modern
British yearling shows a culinary consistency lacked by its
peers; its Aldwych location makes it a popular business venue,
which is also "excellent for breakfast" and a "great meeting
point pre-theatre". / 11 pm; no Switch; set weekday L & pre-th. £23(FP).*

Banners N8 £ 24 ④④❷
21 Park Rd   0181-348 2930   1–1C
*"Trendy Crouch Enders" "overpack" this "casual" and "lively"
joint – "big breakfasts" and brunches are the key features,
but at other times, the "interesting" scoff scores hits and wide
misses. / 11.30 pm, Fri & Sat midnight; no Amex & no Switch.*

The Bar EC4 £ 26 ❸④⑤
8 Crane Court   353 9230   9–2A
*This bar-restaurant – in the thinly provided area around
Fleet Street – surprises with willing (if slow) service and quite
decent modern British grub; let's hope they get lots of custom
so they can afford to refurbish their awful basement premises.
/ L only; closed Sat & Sun.*

FSA

Bar Central   £ 33   ④④❸
316 King's Rd, SW3   352 0025   5–3C
131 Waterloo Rd, SE1   928 5086   9–4A
11 Bridge St, TW9   0181-332 2524   1–4A
*This modish chain of bar-restaurants has not really lived up to
its initial promise; "lively" places they may be, but they are
"overpriced", too, and their ambitious modern British menus
"try hard but do not always deliver".* / SE1 11.45 pm – SW3
11.45 pm, Thu-Sat 12.30 am – Richmond 10.30 pm.

Bar Gansa NW1   £ 18   ❷❸❷
2 Inverness St   267 8909   8–3B
*"Much impromptu salsa-ing and sangria-sharing" plus good
cheap nosh make this Camden Town's "tapas bar par
excellence".* / Midnight; no Amex & no Switch.

Bar Italia W1   £ 5   ④❸❶
22 Frith St   437 4520   4–2A
*"Classic" 24-hour Soho coffee shop – of over 40 years'
standing – that is "still the best place after a night on the
town" (and popular around the clock).* / 4 am, Fri & Sat 24 hours;
no booking.

Bar Japan SW5   £ 18   ❸❸❸
251 Old Brompton Rd   370 2323   5–3A
*"Well priced" Earl's Court newcomer with "decent" Japanese
fare and a "friendly" proprietor.* / 10.45 pm; closed Mon.

Bar Madrid W1   £ 15   ④④❷
4 Winsley St   436 4649   3–1D
*If you are in your early twenties and single, this can be an
extremely "exciting place"; the irrelevant tapas could be
worse.* / 2.30 am; D only; closed Sun; smart casual.

Barcelona Tapas   £ 18   ❷❸❸
1a Bell Ln, E1   247 7014   9–2D
1 Beaufort Hs, St Botolph St, EC3   377 5222   9–2D
*These two City-fringe bars – one in a hard-edged glitzy office
building and the other in a "cramped" cellar – could hardly be
more different, but they both serve "super", "authentic" food.*
/ 10 pm; closed Sat & Sun D.

Basil St Hotel SW3   £ 33   ❸❷❷
8 Basil St   581 3311   5–1D
*"Old-fashioned service, atmosphere and clientèle" abound in
this "lovely" creaky Knightsbridge haven; especially if you stick
to the set menu, the English cooking offers "very good value".*
/ 10 pm; jacket & tie; set Sun L £20(FP).

Battersea Barge Bistro SW8   £ 17   ④❸❷

Nine Elms Ln   498 0004   10–1D

*Quirky Thames-side barge, moored down a lane opposite
New Covent Garden market; it makes a "fun" and cosy
destination, so long as you go with modest culinary
expectations. / 11 pm; closed Sun D.*

Battersea Rickshaw SW11   £ 23   ❸❸❸

1-16 Battersea Sq   924 2450   5–4C

*A "good local Indian without the flock wallpaper", which
consistently pleases the burghers of Battersea. / 11.30 pm.*

Beach Blanket Babylon W11   £ 35   ⑤⑤❷

45 Ledbury Rd   229 2907   6–1B

*"Funky and fun" Notting Hill scene whose "bizarre and
wonderful" design attracts a strong twentysomething
following; "stick to the bar" – the "awful" Mediterranean
food is "far too expensive". / 11 pm; set weekday L £18(FP).*

Beauchamp's EC3   £ 47   ④④④

23-25 Leadenhall Mkt   621 1331   9–2D

*As ever, this Leadenhall Market parlour creates an
unbridgeable 50/50 divide between those (on expenses?) who
say it offers "some of the best fish in the City" and others
who say it's "very poor" and "not value for money". / Mon
& Fri L only, Tue-Thu 9 pm; closed Sat & Sun.*

Bedlington Café W4   £ 19   ❶④④

24 Fauconberg Rd   0181-994 1965   7–2A

*You "must book", as people journey from all over town to dine
at this "basic" Chiswick Thai café (by day a greasy Joe) whose
"cramped and frantic" setting "feels like Bangkok"; the "very
authentic", very spicy grub – at knockdown prices – "is worth
the hassle"; BYO. / 10 pm; no credit cards; no smoking area.*

Beirut Express W2   £ 15   ❷❷❸

112-114 Edgware Rd   724 2700   6–1D

*"A good range of dishes", "relatively low cost" and
"waiters keen to explain the menu" make this new Lebanese
café/take-away (a Maroush group venture) a useful standby.
/ 1.45 am; no credit cards.*

Belair House SE21   £ 37   ❸④❷

Gallery Road, Dulwich Village   0181-299 9788   1–4C

*Dulwich's first decent restaurant occupies an "airy, bright and
spacious" room in a listed Georgian house near the Picture
Gallery (there's also a bar where breakfast is served); the
modern British cooking generally finds favour – especially
"excellent fish dishes" – but it's "pricey", and service can be
"precious" and "chaotic". / 10 pm; closed Sun.*

Belgo £ 29 ④④❷

50 Earlham St, WC2   813 2233   4–2C
72 Chalk Farm Rd, NW1   267 0718   8–2B
"Boy, have those Belgo lads lost their way" – although the
"unusual setting" of these moules, frites and beer emporia
still creates "great atmosphere", many think the formula
"is getting a little stale"; gripes include sometimes "awful"
food, "unfocussed" service and, at Covent Garden, "hot" and
"cramped" conditions. / 11.30 pm.

La Belle Epoque SW3 £ 35 ④④❸

151 Draycott Ave   460 5000   5–2C
Brompton Cross's huge and lavishly furnished new sibling
to the Palais du Jardin comprises a no-booking 'Brasserie',
a slightly more expensive 'Salle' and a grandiose basement
'Oriental' (£66); our early visit to the brasserie was
surprisingly rough-edged in all respects – it's too early to be
sure that the success of Covent Garden can be replicated
here. / Midnight; smart casual.

Bellinis SW13 £ 15 ❸❸❸

2-3 Rocks Ln   0181-255 9922   10–1A
"Well cooked", "solid" pizzas make this cheerful, brightly-
decorated Barnes Italian a superior local. / 11.30 pm.

Belvedere W8 £ 35 ⑤④❷

Holland Hs, off Abbotsbury Rd   602 1238   7–1D
"A woeful waste of a wonderful venue" – this "relaxed",
very romantic rendezvous, with its "great location in Holland
Park", continues to provide modern British cooking which is
too often "tasteless". / 11 pm; closed Sun D.

Ben's Thai W9 £ 20 ❷❸❸

93 Warrington Cr   266 3134   8–4A
"Fun Thai" above an impressive Maida Vale pub (The
Warrington Hotel) which continues to offer "good food,
reasonably priced"; "book early to avoid disappointment".
/ 10 pm; D only; no Amex & no Switch; no smoking area.

Bengal Clipper SE1 £ 33 ❷❸④

Shad Thames   357 9001   9–4D
The "hotel restaurant feel" of this "very large", "posh" and
"comfortable" Indian near Tower Bridge discourages the
following it deserves – dishes are "very authentic" and
"unusual". / 11 pm.

Benihana   £ 45   ④❸④

37-43 Sackville St, W1   494 2525   3–3D
77 King's Rd, SW3   376 7799   5–3D
100 Avenue Rd, NW3   586 9508   8–2A
*Enthusiasts for this international teppan-yaki chain love
"the show" – knife-juggling chefs preparing your meal before
your very eyes; critics damn "outrageously overpriced Yankie
Jap food", and proclaim "a Lloyd Webber performance –
for tourists only". / 10 pm, Fri & Sat Midnight.*

Bentley's W1   £ 41   ❸❸❸

11-15 Swallow St   734 4756   3–3D
*"Comfortable", traditional fish and seafood specialist near
Piccadilly Circus, whose long-time devotees find "good,
reliable" fare; the top-value set meals are no more, however,
and some fear that the place is "becoming preoccupied with
catering for rich tourists". / 11.30 pm; closed Sun; smart casual; set
weekday L £25(FP).*

Beotys WC2   £ 32   ④❶❸

79 St Martin's Ln   836 8768   4–3B
*"My father used to eat here in the '50s – no change since"
is a typical report on this very comfortable, "old-style"
family-run Theatreland bastion, where the "host makes you
feel special" and the solid Franco-Greek food "isn't that bad".
/ 11.30 pm; closed Sun; no Switch.*

Bersagliera SW3   £ 25   ❸❷❸

372 King's Rd   352 5993   5–3B
*"Rowdy, but fun", this "authentic", "good value" Chelsea
Italian delivers "huge" pizzas, good pasta and "the best garlic
bread in town"; some find it "a little too cheerful". / Midnight;
closed Sun; no Amex.*

Bertorelli's   £ 30   ④④④

19-23 Charlotte St, W1   636 4174   2–1C
44a Floral St, WC2   836 3969   4–2D
*These large, mid-range Italians in Covent Garden (a "good
Theatreland standby") and Fitzrovia get a very inconsistent
press; they have their fans, but too many find "worse then
mediocre" standards and "little attention to detail".
/ W1 11 pm, WC2 11.30 pm; WC2 closed Sun; no smoking area.*

Beyoglu SW11   £ 15   ❶❸④

50 Battersea Pk Rd   627 2052   10–1C
*"Tiny" Battersea Turk delivering "ace" food at "low prices";
the setting is a mite "chilly" for some, but the "warm
welcome" is a compensation. / 11 pm; closed Sun; no Switch.*

F S A

BIBENDUM SW3 £ 55 ❸❸❸
81 Fulham Rd 581 5817 5–2C
*"Smooth as a vintage limousine", say deep-pocketed
devotees of Conran's grandest establishment, who acclaim the
"fantastic" atmosphere of its light and airy Brompton Cross
premises; ratings, though, especially for the modern French
food, are on the slide – this is no longer the very special place
it once was. / 10.30 pm.*

Bibendum Oyster Bar SW3 £ 31 ❶❷❷
81 Fulham Rd 589 1480 5–2C
*Oyster-lovers, in particular, vaunt the "excellent selection of
fish and seafood" that is "always fresh and wonderful" at this
fashionable Brompton Cross rendezvous. / 10 pm; no booking.*

Bice W1 £ 42 ⑤④④
13 Albemarle St 409 1011 3–3C
*"Overpriced", "very mid-Atlantic" Mayfair basement Italian –
"a really poor cousin to the NYC location". / 10.45 pm;
closed Sat L & Sun; smart casual.*

Big Easy SW3 £ 28 ④④❸
334 King's Rd 352 4071 5–3C
*Chelsea crab-shack where kids in particular love the "fun"
and "noisy" environment; grown-ups sometimes enjoy it too –
especially when there's live music – though the burgers and
seafood dishes can disappoint. / Midnight, Fri & Sat 12.30 am;
no smoking area; Fri pm & Sat pm, no booking after 7 pm.*

Billboard Café NW6 £ 23 ④❷❸
280 West End Ln 431 4188 1–1B
*Though it's quite well-known, some feel that this
"unpretentious" West Hampstead local's reputation is too
"pumped up", given its "so-so" Italian cooking. / 11.30 pm; Mon-
Fri closed L.*

Bistrot 190 SW7 £ 31 ❸④❷
189-190 Queen's Gt 581 5666 5–1B
*The "very buzzing", "informal" ambience of this South
Kensington townhouse brasserie underpins its popularity,
and, though service can be "lousy", the Mediterranean fare
is "reliable"; brunch is a forte. / 12.30 am; no booking.*

Bistrot 2 Riverside SE1 £ 29 ❷❷❷
Oxo Tower Wharf 401 8200 9–3A
*Our first-day (August '97) visit to this new, second-floor
brasserie boded well – a long, eclectic menu, charmingly
served, in a welcoming, bright environment; the panorama
isn't as spectacular as from the 'Oxo Tower', six floors up,
but the overall package is much more pleasant. / 11.30 pm.*

Bistrot Soho W1 £ 30 ④④④
64 Frith St   734 4545   4–2A
*Bruno Soho is no more, and, physically unchanged, this
oddly-proportioned site now houses a high class, but pricey,
Gallic bistro; service is "perfunctory", however, and
'ingredient X' sadly lacking.* / 11.30 pm; closed Sat L & Sun.

Blah! Blah! Blah! W12 £ 22 ❸④④
78 Goldhawk Rd   0181-746 1337   7–1C
*"Inventive veggie" grub and a "groovy sort of atmosphere"
make this an unusual find on a bleak Shepherd's Bush
highway; some note that the food can be "slow in coming",
and others think the place a bit "dingy"; BYO.* / 11 pm;
closed Sun; no credit cards.

Blakes Hotel SW7 £ 82 ④④❶
33 Roland Gdns   370 6701   5–2B
*"Outrageously, obscenely expensive", but still "romantic,
sexy, and cool" – this South Kensington basement's "unusual"
and "beautifully presented" cooking may "leave you
penniless", but few begrudge the cost.* / Midnight.

Bleeding Heart EC1 £ 28 ❷❷❷
Bleeding Heart Yd, Greville St   242 8238   9–2A
*Even if it's "as cramped as hell", this ancient basement
(hidden off a yard near Holborn) offers "excellent
atmosphere", a "strong", "well priced" wine list and "solid,
old school" French cooking – a highly "reliable" combination
for business or pleasure; in summer, you can eat in the yard.*
/ 10.30 pm; closed Sat & Sun.

The Blenheim NW8 £ 30 ④④④
21 Loudon Rd   625 1222   8–3A
*Some proclaim the virtues of this St John's Wood local as a
"good casual venue"; the "filling" modern British fare is
inconsistent, however, and "overpriced" – "for a glorified
pub".* / 10.45 pm; no smoking area.

BLUE ELEPHANT SW6 £ 43 ❷❷❶
4-6 Fulham Broadway   385 6595   5–4A
*With its bridge, lake and "jungle", Fulham's "grand Thai"
remains London's most impressive ethnic; "who cares if it's
over the top?" – or "wallet-numbingly expensive?" –
gush fans, "it's worth it".* / 12.30 am, Sun 10.30 pm; closed
Sat L; no Switch; smart casual; set Sun L £26(FP).

Blue Jade SW1   **£ 23**   ❸❸④

44 Hugh St   828 0321   2–4B

It's "nothing remarkable", but there's "always a pleasant evening" to be had at this "welcoming" Pimlico back street Thai. / 11 pm; closed Sat L & Sun.

Blue Print Café SE1   **£ 37**   ❸④❷

Design Mus, Butler's Whf   378 7031   9–4D

The "stunning views" (of Tower Bridge) and an "interesting menu" make the Design Museum's "relaxed" modern British café a favourite, though sometimes "awful" service is a perennial complaint; the balcony has been replaced by a "marvellous new conservatory". / 11 pm; closed Sun D.

BLUEBIRD SW3   **£ 36**   ④❸❷

350 Kings Rd   559 1000   5–3C

This "great and spacious", new Chelsea landmark epitomises the strengths and weaknesses of the Conran group; "overpriced", "bland and uninspiring" modern British cooking is served (sometimes "with attitude") in a place "to be seen, but not to eat" – it "could do better". / 11.30 pm.

Blues W1   **£ 29**   ❸❷❷

42 Dean St   494 1966   4–2A

"Brash" and "crowded" it may be, but its many younger fans hail this "lovely", "buzzy" Soho scene; the "varied" modern British menu is "surprisingly edible", but it's the "great staff attitude" which is the key. / 11.30 pm, Thu-Sat midnight; closed Sat L & Sun; set Mon & Tue £18(FP).

Blythe Road Restaurant W14   **£ 28**   ❸❸❷

71 Blythe Rd   371 3635   7–1C

"Good small local", near Brook Green, whose modern British cuisine "has potential"; the "friendly" service "can be slow". / 10.30 pm; closed Sat L & Sun.

Boiled Egg & Soldiers SW11   **£ 16**   ❸④❸

63 Northcote Rd   223 4894   10–2C

This Wandsworth "street café with decent grub" is popular locally for breakfasts and light bites – "don't be put off by the prams and au pairs". / 6 pm; no booking.

Boisdale SW1   **£ 36**   ❸❷❷

15 Eccleston St   730 6922   2–4B

Thanks to its "excellent, clubby atmosphere", this modern British wine bar/restaurant draws a surprisingly "smart" crowd to the environs of Victoria; the management is capable of "insufferable pomposity". / 10.30 pm; closed Sat L & Sun.

Bombay Bicycle Club SW12   £30   ❷❸❸

95 Nightingale Ln   0181-673 6217   10–2C
*"Really fresh", "well above average" Indian cooking ("with a
European twist") makes this "expensive" Wandsworth fixture
south London's top upmarket subcontinental; the take-away
(28 Queenstown Road SW8) is also highly thought of.*
/ 11.30 pm; D only; closed Sun.

Bombay Brasserie SW7   £44   ❷❸❷

Courtfield Clo, Glouc. Rd   370 4040   5–2B
*"Nostalgic" décor that "takes one back to the Raj" still holds
the key to this enormous South Kensington institution's
popularity (with "the conservatory being better than the main
room"); this year, though, the cooking scored much more
consistently than last; for top value, try the daily lunchtime
buffet.* / Midnight; no Amex & no Switch; smart casual; set L £24(FP).

Bombay Palace W2   £30   ❷❷❸

50 Connaught St   723 8855   6–1D
*"Unique", "really delicious" cooking, is vaunted by fans of this
"consistently good" and "polite", but still relatively unknown,
Indian, just north of Hyde Park.* / 11.15 pm; no smoking area.

Bonjour Vietnam SW6   £24   ④⑤④

593-599 Fulham Rd   385 7603   5–4A
*"Huge amounts" of food make this "kitsch" and "noisy"
Fulham oriental – where you can eat as much as you like –
popular with younger party-goers; "the novelty can wear off",
though and, to some, it's just "rubbish".* / 11 pm; set weekday L
£14(FP).

La Bouchée SW7   £28   ④⑤❷

56 Old Brompton Rd   589 1929   5–2B
*The "hearty" Gallic cooking has "gone downhill over the
last year" at this South Kensington bistro, where service is
"chaotic"; the "cramped", "fun" and "buzzy" atmosphere still
pleases.* / 11 pm; no Amex & no Switch; set weekday L & early eve £18(FP).

Le Bouchon Bordelais SW11   £26   ④④❷

9 Battersea Rs   738 0307   10–2C
*"Very French" Battersea bistro which, in spite of rather
"run-of-the-mill" fare, remains a popular (sometimes
"smoky") local; kids are well catered for at the weekend.*
/ 11.30 pm; set weekday L £16(FP).

Boudin Blanc W1   £ 27   ❸❸❷

5 Trebeck St   499 3292   3–4B
*Very "charming" and "cosy" central rendezvous (with a pretty
Shepherd Market location) whose "reliable", "simple but
good" Gallic fare comes at a "reasonable price" – "the
pre-8pm menu", in particular, "is a great deal". / 11 pm;
set pre-th. £17(FP).*

La Bouffe SW11   £ 28   ❸❸❷

13 Battersea Rs   228 3384   10–2C
*"Solid" Gallic fare (and "excellent cheap lunches") make
this Clapham bistro a local favourite; the cooking can seem
"over-elaborate". / 11 pm.*

Boulevard WC2   £ 25   ❸❸❸

40 Wellington St   240 2992   4–3D
*"Consistent", "tasty French farmhouse-style dishes" make this
"competitively priced" Covent Garden brasserie a "reliable"
pre-theatre standby; service is "fast when needed". / Midnight.*

The Bow Wine Vaults EC4   £ 25   ❸❸❸

10 Bow Church Yd   248 1121   9–2C
*Unpretentious spot, "nicely located by St Mary-le-Bow",
that's "good for an informal City lunch". / L only; closed Sun.*

Boyd's W8   £ 38   ❷❷④

135 Kensington Ch St   727 5452   5–1A
*Mr Boyd may no longer be chef/patron but, if anything, the
modern British cooking has improved at this "dependable" –
if always slightly characterless – Kensington "standby". / 11 pm;
closed Sun.*

The Brackenbury W6   £ 27   ❷❸❸

129-131 Brackenbury Rd   0181-748 0107   7–1C
*Most feel that this Shepherd's Bush modern British favourite –
whose fame belies its size and obscure location – is
"as wonderful as ever under new management"; however,
the cooking is not entirely consistent, "half the menu is often
unavailable", and supercilious or "very, very slow" service can
let the side down. / 10.45 pm; closed Sat L & Sun D.*

Bradley's NW3   £ 34   ❸❷❷

25 Winchester Rd   722 3457   8–2A
*The "best kept secret" in Swiss Cottage, this "elegant and
unpretentious" modern British restaurant, offers many
interesting fish dishes; it's a "good all-rounder" and deserves
a wider following. / 11 pm; closed Sat L*

Brady's SW18   £ 17   ❷❸④

513 Old York Rd   0181-877 9599   10–2B

*"Exceptional consistency and high quality" win praise
from the people of Wandsworth for Mr Brady's superior but
"reasonably priced" chippy; the Fulham branch is sadly no
more.* / 10.45 pm; Apr-Sep closed Sun D; no credit cards; no booking.

Brass. du Marché aux Puces W10   £ 29   ❷❶❷

349 Portobello Rd   0181-968 5828   6–1A

*"Very French", "lots of fun" and with a "real bistro feel", this
"ideal neighbourhood joint", on a North Kensington corner,
goes from strength to strength.* / 11.30 pm; closed Sun D; no Amex.

La Brasserie SW3   £ 29   ④④❷

272 Brompton Rd   584 1668   5–2C

*"True French arrogance" is just part of the authentic
approach of this long-standing, "always buzzy" Brompton
Cross fixture – particularly known as a "fun" weekend
breakfast venue; it's a "bit pricey" for what it is.* / Midnight.

Brasserie Rocque EC2   £ 35   ④④❸

37 Broadgate Circle   638 7919   9–2D

*With its "good location", by the City's Broadgate ice-rink, and
its great outside tables in summer, it's hardly surprising if this
modern British brasserie/restaurant is a touch "pricey"; the
cooking, though, is at least "consistent".* / brasserie 8.30 pm;
closed Sat & Sun; book only in restaurant.

Brasserie St Quentin SW3   £ 35   ❸❷❷

243 Brompton Rd   589 8005   5–2C

*This "smart" Knightsbridge brasserie – a "real bit of France
in London" – has "lost its edge" under the ownership of
Groupe Chez Gérard; it's now just "a good place for a
standard, unsurprising dinner".* / 11 pm.

Brick Lane Beigel Bake E1   £ 3   ❷❶④

159 Brick Ln   729 0616   1–2D

*"Lovely fresh bagels, apple tarts, cheesecakes" and salt-beef
sandwiches, "mucho cheap", keep this "wonderful" East End
institution "buzzing" round the clock.* / 24 hr; no credit cards.

Brinkley's SW10   £ 28   ④❸❷

47 Hollywood Rd   351 1683   5–3B

*It's "nice to dine in the garden in summer" at this long-
established Chelsea bar/restaurant; the modern British fodder,
though, is "predictable" at best – "go to people-watch, and
maybe eat".* / 11 pm; D only; closed Sun.

Brook W6　　　　　　　**£ 26**　　③④③

320 Goldhawk Rd　0181-741 1994　7–1B

Much-revamped boozer (formerly the Stamford), by Queen
Charlotte's Hospital, hailed by some for "whizz" cooking –
"well above average for a gastropub"; we agree with those
who find the food "good, but expensive", the atmosphere a
bit "strange" and service "in slow motion". / 10 pm.

Brown's Hotel W1　　　　**£ 40**　　③③②

Albemarle St　493 6020　3–3C

Breakfast – "best for business" – and afternoon tea are the
special strengths of this charmingly creaky Mayfair hotel.
/ 10.15 pm (tea daily 3 pm-5 pm); no booking.

Browns　　　　　　　　**£ 29**　　④③③

47 Maddox St, W1　491 4565　3–2C
82-84 St Martin's Ln, WC2　497 5050　4–4B
114 Draycott Av, SW3　584 5359　5–2C

Though they are not without their fans (who speak of an
"ideal pre/post theatre" choice), many feel that "these
reliable university-town favourites seem to have flopped in
London"; yes, the branches are "friendly" and "informal",
but in the Smoke the formula of "a pleasant burger/salad
menu at inflated prices" just seems passé and provincial.
/ 11.30 pm.

Bu San N7　　　　　　　**£ 20**　　②③⑤

43 Holloway Rd　607 8264　8–2D

"Good value", interesting Korean food attracts a loyal
following to this simple local, around the corner from
Highbury and Islington tube; the décor could use a make-over.
/ 11 pm; closed Sat L & Sun L; no Amex; set weekday L £12(FP).

Bubb's EC1　　　　　　　**£ 39**　　③④④

329 Cent Mkts, Farringdon St　236 2435　9–2A

"For an old fashioned City lunch" ("when you have time")
some tip this "small", cramped Smithfield corner, that's
"as French as you can get this side of the Channel"; the
fare is "solid" and "heavily sauced". / L only; closed Sat & Sun.

Bucci SW3　　　　　　　**£ 27**　　③②③

386 King's Rd　351 9997　5–3B

"Very friendly and family-orientated" Italian, reasonably priced
by Chelsea standards, and attracting a growing following.
/ 11.30 pm.

Buchan's SW11   **£30**   ④❸④

62-64 Battersea Br Rd   228 0888   5–4C
*This popular local wine bar/restaurant, just south of
Battersea Bridge, serves "erratic, sometimes good" modern
Caledonian food. / 10.45 pm.*

Buona Sera SW11   **£21**   ❷❸❷

22 Northcote Rd   228 9925   10–2C
*"Great", "noisy", "fast" and "frantic", this pizza and pasta
joint near Clapham Junction is one of the most consistently
successful places in south London. / Midnight; no Amex.*

Busabong Too SW10   **£28**   ❷❸④

1a Langton St   352 7414   5–3B
*"Tastes like Thailand" win strong local support for this
consistently popular, if not hugely atmospheric, World's End
outfit. / 11.15 pm; D only.*

Busabong Tree SW10   **£30**   ❷❸❸

112 Cheyne Walk   352 7534   5–4B
*"Can't understand why it's not more popular", say fans of this
consistent Chelsea Thai; perhaps it's something to do with its
'road to nowhere' Embankment-side location. / 11.15 pm;
smart casual; set weekday L £16(FP).*

The Butlers Wharf Chop-house SE1 £42   ❸❸❸

36e Shad Thames   403 3403   9–4D
*This light and understated Conran river-sider, overlooking
Tower Bridge, is winning a more consistent following for its
"reliable, though never brilliant" English fare; eating at the bar
offers better value than the restaurant, and brunch comes
recommended. / 11 pm; closed Sat L & Sun D.*

Byron's NW3   **£26**   ④④❸

3a Downshire Hl   435 3544   8–2A
*Some feel new ownership has given the modern British
cooking the "kick it needed" at this "nice but too quiet"
Hampstead side street townhouse; to us it appeared relatively
little changed – "solid" but "a bit dull". / 11 pm; no smoking area.*

Cactus Blue SW3   **£29**   ④④❷

86 Fulham Rd   823 7858   5–2C
*Cool, if rather cavernous, younger Chelsea hang-out (opposite
the Royal Marsden Hospital), with "spectacular" décor and a
"nice bar"; the "interesting and different" Latin American-
inspired food "has potential", but can be "bland". / 11.45 pm;
smart casual; no smoking area.*

Café 206 W11 £ 29
206 Westbourne Grove   221 1535   6–1B
*This new "good lunch spot" – which offered an ideal break
from Portobello browsing – has been so successful that a
relaunch as a fully-blown modern Italian restaurant is pending
as we go to press.* / 11 pm; no Amex.

Café 209 SW6 £ 14   ④❷❸
209 Munster Rd   385 3625   10–1B
*Joy (the proprietress) "is an inspiration" at this "laid back",
younger scene Fulham Thai – "not great food, but cheap and
very cheerful"; BYO.* / 10.45 pm; D only; closed Sun; no credit cards.

Café Bohème W1 £ 28   ❸❸❶
13 Old Compton St   734 0623   4–2A
*"Casual but moody", this large and "lively" ("sweaty") Soho
corner bar-café-brasserie packs 'em in at all hours of the day
and night; the food's "nothing to shout about", of course, but
"surprisingly good for the type of place".* / 2.45 am, Thu-Sat open
24 hours, Sun 11.30 pm.

Café de la Place SW11 £ 20   ❸④❸
11/12 Battersea Sq   978 5374   5–4C
*Unpretentious Battersea standby, recommended for breakfast
and for its "good French set dinner menu".* / 11 pm; closed Sun D;
no Amex; set weekday L £13(FP).

Café de Paris W1 £ 45   ⑤⑤④
3 Coventry St   734 7700   4–4A
*This relaunched Art Deco "nightclub/bar/restaurant" may
currently benefit from 'It' status, but – at least as a place to
eat – is surely "destined for empty-dom", thanks to its
"high cost, unimaginative" fare and "lousy" service.* / 11.30 pm
(bar 3 am); D only, closed Sun; smart casual.

Café Delancey NW1 £ 25   ④④❷
3 Delancey St   387 1985   8–3B
*Large, "relaxing", all-day Camden institution, which is much
recommended, "but only for breakfast" or brunch – other
fare is "pedestrian".* / 11.30 pm; no Amex.

Café des Amis du Vin WC2 £ 12   ❷❸④
11-14 Hanover Pl   379 3444   4–2D
*Ignore the dated brasserie and the restaurant of this tired
Covent Garden fixture – and head straight for the crush of
the convivial basement 'Bar des Amis' – rated here – for the
"great value" of the "superb" cheese board.* / 11.30 pm;
closed Sun.

Café des Arts NW3 £ 30 ④❸❷

82 Hampstead High St 435 3608 8–2A

*"Warm and cosy" bistro, characterfully located in a series of
rooms, some panelled, in the centre of Hampstead; it offers
"good", but "inconsistent" modern British fare.* / 11.30 pm;
no smoking area; set weekday L & pre-th. £15(FP).

Café du Jardin WC2 £ 33 ❸④❸

28 Wellington St 836 8769 4–3D

*Some feel that – "improved by renovation" – this now quite
striking modern British restaurant in Covent Garden is
"really underrated"; the consensus remains, however, that its
prime virtues are the "reasonable fixed-price lunch" and the
"excellent pre-theatre value".* / Midnight; set weekday L & pre-th.
£21(FP).

Café du Marché EC1 £ 30 ❷❸❶

22 Charterhouse Sq 608 1609 9–1B

*"A beautiful French country restaurant" with a "very pleasant,
non-frantic ambience" makes a "surprising find" on the fringe
of Smithfield; most remain full of praise for the "excellent"
Gallic dishes, too, but standards are not quite as lofty as they
were.* / 10 pm; closed Sat L & Sun; no Amex.

Café Emm W1 £ 20 ❸④❸

17 Frith St 437 0723 4–2A

*"Very reasonable prices" for "acceptable" grub in "huge
portions" make this "friendly" and "relaxed" Soho bistro
"always great value" – "expect long queues at night";
fogies find "the intimate atmosphere spoilt by the loud
music".* / 10.30 pm, Fri & Sat 12.30 am; closed Sat L & Sun L;
no smoking area; book L only.

Café Fish SW1 £ 32 ❸④④

39 Panton St 930 3999 4–4A

*This "lively" central institution has always left us a little cold
and we sympathise with those who say it offers "ordinary
food for Theatreland tourists" in "overcrowded" conditions;
that is not to deny, however, that many laud its "excellent
range of fish and seafood".* / 11.30 pm; closed Sat L & Sun;
no smoking area.

Café Flo   **£ 25**   ④④❸

11 Haymarket, SW1   976 1313   4–4A
13 Thayer St, W1   935 5023   2–1A
51 St Martin's Ln, WC2   836 8289   4–4C
676 Fulham Rd, SW6   371 9673   10–1B
127 Kensington Ch St, W8   727 8142   6–2B
334 Upper St, N1   226 7916   8–3D
205 Haverstock Hl, NW3   435 6744   8–2A
38-40 Ludgate Hill, EC4   329 3900   9–2A
The bright and breezy new look of some of this French-owned
chain's branches confirms its position as the best of the
budget Gallic bistro chains; they provide "good value"
standbys (especially if you stick to the two-course prix-fixe
menu, l'Idée Flo). / 11.30 pm, Sun 11 pm.

Café Grove W11   **£ 18**   ④④❷

253a Portobello Rd   243 1094   6–1A
It's the "excellent" terrace – the ideal vantage point for
Portobello Market people-watching – which makes this
Bohemian breakfasts, salads and cakes spot a good brunch
choice. / winter 5 pm, summer 10.30 pm; winter L only – summer,
closed Sat D & Sun D; no credit cards; no booking.

Café Indiya E1   **£ 23**   ❸❷❸

30 Alie St   481 8288   9–3D
"Not Namaste, but not bad", say fans of this new east-City
Indian (occupying the site vacated by its illustrious rival); it
serves some "serious" food (including Goan specialities) and
the "warm atmosphere" helps compensate for the bleak
location. / 11 pm; closed Sat & Sun; no smoking area.

Café Japan NW11   **£ 22**   ❷❷④

626 Finchley Rd   0181-455 6854   1–1B
"Succulent and delicious sushi" is the prime attraction on
the "limited menu" at this "unusually cheap" and "friendly"
Nipponese, near Golder's Green tube. / 10.30 pm; D only, closed
Sun; no Amex.

Café Jeune SW9   **£ 21**   ❸④❸

24 Clapham Rd   793 0770   10–1D
"Dependable bistro", near Oval tube, which offers a good
degree of charm in a soulless area; in summer, it benefits
from outside tables front and back. / 11 pm.

Café Latino W1   **£ 23**   ❸❷❷

25 Frith St   287 5676   4–2A
"Groovy", loud, but welcoming, new Soho bar-café whose
good Latin American snack food and charming service
generate "a high feel-good factor". / 11 pm, Thu-Sat 1 am.

Café Lazeez SW7 £30 ④❸❸
93-95 Old Brompton Rd 581 9993 5–2C
*Since its promising '92 debut, this stylish, "un-Indian" South
Kensington café-restaurant has become ever more "mean"
with its portions and "overpriced" – a shame as some of the
light 'evolved' cooking is "delicious". / 12.30 am, Sun 10.30 pm;
smart casual; no smoking area; set weekday L £17(FP).*

Café Med £28 ④❸❷
2 Hollywood Rd, SW10 823 3355 5–3B
184a Kensington Pk Rd, W11 221 1150 6–1A
*They may be "fun", "cosy" and "atmospheric", but these
trendy bistros charge "just too much" for their "limited menu"
of "dull" dishes. / 11.30 pm.*

Café Montpeliano SW3 £24 ❸❸❷
144 Brompton Rd 225 2926 5–1C
*"For a quick pasta or salad" or an "excellent Italian coffee",
this "buzzy" and "crowded" place – just across the road from
Harrods – is "fast and reliable". / 11 pm; closed Sun D; no Switch.*

Café O SW3 £27 ❸❶④
163 Draycott Ave 584 5950 5–2C
*"Different", "upmarket" Greek, near Brompton Cross,
applauded by some for its interesting approach to Hellenic
cuisine ("with enough old favourites to please traditionalists")
and its attentive service. / 11.30 pm; closed Sun L*

Café Pacifico WC2 £26 ❸④❷
5 Langley St 379 7728 4–2C
*"The best Mexican food in London" – though that's not saying
much – continues to make this "loud and raucous" Covent
Garden cantina "very popular"; "slow" service can show the
strain. / 11.45 pm; no smoking area; book pre 6.30 pm only.*

Café Pasta £21 ④❷❸
184 Shaftesbury Ave, WC2 379 0198 4–2B
2-4 Garrick St, WC2 497 2779 4–3C
270 Chiswick High Rd, W4 0181-995 2903 7–2A
229-231 Kensington High St, W8 937 6314 5–1A
8 Theberton St, N1 704 9089 8–3D
200 Haverstock Hl, NW3 431 8531 8–2A
*"Reliable and speedy" pasta-stops – "just the place for a
quick, pleasant meal for 'non-event' occasions". / 11.30 pm;
no Amex; some have no smoking area; book L and early eve only.*

Café Portugal SW8   **£ 25**   ❶❸④

5a & 6a Victoria Hs, S Lambeth Rd   587 1962   10–1D
Engaging Vauxhall café/tapas bar (by day) and Portuguese
restaurant (by night), where the Branco family dishes up some
extremely satisfying fare at very reasonable prices. / 11 pm;
closed Sun; no Amex.

Café Rouge   **£ 23**   ⑤⑤④

15 Frith St, W1   437 4307   4–2A
46-48 James St, W1   487 4847   3–1A
34 Wellington St, WC2   836 0998   4–3D
27-31 Basil St, SW3   584 2345   5–1D
390 King's Rd, SW3   352 2226   5–3B
855 Fulham Rd, SW6   371 7600   10–1B
102 Old Brompton Rd, SW7   373 2403   5–2B
31 Kensington Pk Rd, W11   221 4449   6–1A
Whiteleys, W2   221 1509   6–1C
227-229 Chiswick High Rd, W4   0181-742 7447   7–2A
158 Fulham Palace Rd, W6   0181-741 5037   7–2C
98-100 Shepherd's Bush Rd, W6   602 7732   7–1C
2 Lancer Sq, Kensington Ch St, W8   938 4200   5–1A
30 Clifton Rd, W9   286 2266   8–4A
6 South Grove, N6   0181-342 9797   8–1B
18 Chalk Farm Rd, NW1   428 0998   8–2B
38-39 High St, NW3   435 4240   8–1A
120 St John's Wood High St, NW8   722 8366   8–3A
Hay's Galleria, Tooley St, SE1   378 0097   9–4D
147 St John's Hill, SW11   924 2112   10–2C
39-49 Parkgate Rd, SW11   924 3565   5–4C
248 Upper R'mond Rd, SW14   0181-878 8897   10–2A
200 Putney Br Rd, SW15   0181-788 4257   10–2B
40 Abbeville Rd, SW4   0181-673 3399   10–2D
140 Fetter Ln, EC4   242 3469   9–2A
Hillgate Hs, Limeburner Ln, EC4   329 1234   9–2A
Though this "continually disappointing" faux-French chain
has its supporters, we're 100% behind those who find it
"quite simply dreadful in every way". / 11 pm, City & W2 earlier;
City & W2 closed some or all Sat & Sun.

Café Royal Grill Room W1   **£ 60**

68 Regent St   437 9090   3–3D
In mid-'97, Herbert Berger was pitched out from this
magnificent, but under-appreciated rococo dining room to
make way for… yet another Marco Pierre White clone; the
aim, apparently, is a traditional grand Gallic style, rather than
wholesale imposition of the 'MPW cookbook'. / 10.30 pm;
closed Sat L & Sun; jacket & tie; set weekday L & pre-th. £35(FP).

Café Sofra　　　　　£ 13　　**❸❸**④

10 Shepherd Mkt, W1　495 3434　3–4B
33 Old Compton St, W1　494 0222　4–2A
63 Wigmore St, W1　486 7788　3–1A
1-3 New Oxford St, WC1　430 0430　2–1D
15 Catherine St, WC2　240 9991　4–3D
5 Garrick St, WC2　240 6688　4–3C
101 Fleet St, EC4　583 6669　9–2A
"Very fresh", "tasty" and "healthy" Turkish food makes this "reliable" café/bistro chain worth remembering; "they're not great places for lingering", though. / Midnight, Old Compton St 2 am, EC4 9 pm; no credit cards; no smoking area; no booking.

Café Sogo SW1　　　　　£ 24　　**❸❸**④

39-45 Haymarket　333 9036　4–4A
One of the few civilised fast food joints near Piccadilly Circus; you get "good Japanese food" – primarily sushi – "without frills". / 9.30 pm; closed Sun L.

Café Spice Namaste　　　　£ 27　　**❶❷❷**

247 Lavender Hill, SW11　738 1717　10–2C
16 Prescot St, E1　488 9242　1–2D
It may be "the devil to get to", but pilgrims to this "'70's psychedelia"-style east-City yearling usual find that Cyrus Todiwala's "innovative and unusual" Indian cooking justifies the trip; an offshoot, near Clapham Junction, is scheduled to open shortly after we go to press. / 10.30 pm; closed Sat L & Sun.

Caffe Graffiti NW3　　　　£ 28　　**❸❸❸**

71 High St　431 7579　8–2A
Brightly decorated, tightly packed brasserie which makes a useful standby in central Hampstead. / 11 pm.

Caffè Uno　　　　　£ 23　　④**❸**④

28 Binney St, W1　499 9312　3–2A
5 Argyll St, W1　437 2503　3–1C
64 Tottenham Court Rd, W1　636 3587　2–1C
24 Charing Cross Rd, WC2　240 2524　4–3B
37 St Martin's Ln, WC2　836 5837　4–4C
805 Fulham Rd, SW6　731 0990　10–1B
106 Queensway, W2　229 8470　6–1C
11 Edgware Rd, W2　723 4898　6–1D
163-165 Chiswick High Rd, W4　0181-742 1942　7–2A
continued on next page

Caffè Uno (continued)
9 Kensington High St, W8   937 8961   5–1A
62 Upper St, N1   226 7988   8–3D
4 South Grove, N6   0181-342 8662   8–1B
40-42 Parkway, NW1   428 9124   8–3B
122 St John's Wood High St, NW8   722 0400   8–3A
375 Lonsdale Rd, SW13   0181-876 3414   10–1A
"Cheerful", if rather "spartan", pasta and pizza stops,
which are praised by many for "efficient" service and
"reliable", "value for money" fare; the "too plastic" design,
however, does them no favours. / Midnight; some branches have no
smoking areas.

La Cage Imaginaire NW3   £ 27   ④❸❸
16 Flask Wk   794 6674   8–1A
Sweetly pretentious Gallic establishment, located in a cute
Hampstead backwater; the set menus at lunch and dinner
are thought "good value" by some – others say the place is
"convenient and charming, but that's it". / 11 pm, Sat 11.30 pm;
closed Mon L; set weekday L £17(FP).

Calabash WC2   £ 20   ❸④⑤
38 King St   836 1976   4–3C
"Well cooked, unusual food" makes a safari to the
restaurant of Covent Garden's Africa Centre an interesting
trip; the basement setting is "authentically clean, but shabby".
/ 10.30 pm; closed Sat L & Sun; no Switch.

Caldesi W1   £ 27   ❸❷④
15-17 Marylebone Ln   935 9226   3–1A
"Classic", small Italian, which "tries hard" and is of particular
use pre/post a visit to the Wigmore Hall. / 11 pm; closed Sat L
& Sun; smart casual; no smoking area.

Calzone   £ 19   ❸❸❸
335 Fulham Rd, SW10   352 9797   5–3B
2a Kensington Pk Rd, W11   243 2003   6–2B
35 Upper St, N1   359 9191   8–3D
66 Heath St, NW3   794 6775   8–1A
"If you like thin, crispy" pizza, many would still recommend
this stylish small chain; an increasing minority, though,
think it's "nothing special". / Midnight, SW10 Fri & Sat 12.45 am;
no Amex.

Cambio de Tercio SW5   £ 28   ④❸❸
163 Old Brompton Rd   244 8970   5–2B
Small "fun" and "stylish" South Kensington Spaniard where
some "excellent tapas" (and more substantial dishes) come
at prices which seem just a touch too much. / 11 pm.

Camden Brasserie NW1   **£ 28**   ❸❷❸

216 Camden High St   482 2114   8–2B

"Sound consistency" of the Mediterranean and grills menu is just one of the assets of this self-descriptive establishment – its "jolly atmosphere" and "friendly staff" make it "a great place for chilling out". / 11.30 pm; no Amex.

The Canteen SW10   **£ 40**   ❷❸❷

Chelsea Harbour   351 7330   5–4B

"Wonderful" modern British food and a "glamorous" atmosphere justify the trek to this "consistently professional" Chelsea Harbour establishment – especially "if you can get a table with a view"; a few wonder whether it "has lost some of its previous sparkle". / 11 pm, Fri & Sat midnight; closed Sat L & Sun D.

Canteloupe EC2   **£ 26**   ❸❷❷

35-42 Charlotte Rd   613 4411   9–1D

A "very cutting-edge arty crowd" is attracted to this "trendy" bar/restaurant, whose shabby-chic north-City side street location evokes the spirit of New York's SoHo; the "shortish menu of hearty rustic stuff is generally well executed", and there are "good bar snacks", too. / Midnight; closed Sat L & Sun; no smoking area.

Cantina del Ponte SE1   **£ 35**   ⑤⑤④

36c Shad Thames   403 5403   9–4D

Some "have never understood" our perennial criticisms of this Tower Bridge-side Italian; continuing reports, however –"probably the worst food of the year", "slow" and "inattentive" service "with attitude", "a terrible waste of a perfect location" – make us conclude that the real mystery is why Conran Restaurants doesn't sort this place out. / 10.45 pm.

La Capannina W1   **£ 30**   ❸❷④

24 Romilly St   437 2473   4–3A

"Hilarious waiters and good food" make this long-standing, very well worn-in Soho trattoria a central standby worth knowing about. / 11.15 pm; closed Sat L & Sun.

Capital Hotel SW3   **£ 63**   ❷❸④

22-24 Basil St   589 5171   5–1D

"Stylish", but unatmospheric Knightsbridge hotel dining room, whose fans praise the "amazing technical refinement" of Philip Britten's modern French cooking; "why is it so over-priced?" is not an uncommon reaction however, though no one doubts the value of the "wonderful" set lunch. / 11.15 pm; dinner, jacket & tie; set weekday L £37(FP).

Capital Radio Restaurant WC2   £ 27   ④❷❸
29-30 Leicester Sq   484 8888   4–4B
*As themed places go, you could do much worse than this
"busy", "friendly" central venue with "lots going on"; the
American-inspired food is, of course, "bland and expensive" –
but less so if you know that many dishes are big enough to
share.* / Midnight; no smoking area.

LE CAPRICE SW1   £ 40   ❷❶❶
Arlington Hs, Arlington St   629 2239   3–4C
*"Impeccable" standards in every respect make this ultra-
discreet modern British St James's brasserie a model of
"all round consistency"; it's "great for star-gazing", too –
if you're not part of this charmed circle, book well ahead.*
/ Midnight.

Caraffini SW1   £ 31   ❸❷❸
61-63 Lower Sloane St   259 0235   5–2D
*"Full of life and enthusiasm", this "very jolly" Italian near
Sloane Square offers "good", "reasonably priced" cooking and
"very welcoming" staff; it's "terribly noisy", though.* / 11.30 pm;
closed Sun.

Caravaggio EC3   £ 45   ④④❸
107-112 Leadenhall St   626 6206   9–2D
*"Bright in style and bubbly in atmosphere", this large Italian
newcomer, near Lloyd's, is "a welcome addition to the Square
Mile"; prices are reasonable only by local standards, but male
customers are consoled by "some of the prettiest waitresses
in London".* / 10 pm; closed Sat & Sun.

Caravan Serai W1   £ 29   ❸❸❷
50 Paddington St   935 1208   2–1A
*"Carpets virtually everywhere" set the tone at this welcoming
Marylebone Afghan whose interesting menu (India meets
Persia) is conscientiously realised.* / 11 pm, Fri & Sat 11.30 pm;
no smoking area; set weekday L £16(FP).

Carnevale EC1   £ 22   ❷❷❸
135 Whitecross St   250 3452   9–1B
*This "small" and "cramped" Barbican-side veggie enjoys a
disproportionate following thanks to "imaginative" cooking,
"super-efficient" staff and "excellent wines by the glass".*
/ 10.30 pm; closed Sun; no Amex.

Casale Franco N1 £ 32 ❸⑤❸
134-137 Upper St   226 8994   8–3D
*Queues attest to the quality of the "wonderful Italian fare
and pizzas" of this "Islington favourite", characterfully tucked
away down an alley; it's no bargain, though, and a shame
about the too often "lousy" or "arrogant" service. / 11.30 pm;
closed Mon, D only Tue-Thu; no Amex; no smoking area; book L only.*

Cave W1 £ 40 ❷❷❸
161 Piccadilly   409 0445   3–3C
*The Caviar House's now rather wacky restaurant (entered
through the shop) is "much improved" by its "smart new
style"; "great seafood", "very good" service and an "excellent
lunchtime menu" are among the attractions. / 10 pm, Thu–Sat
10.30 pm; closed Sun.*

Cecconi's W1 £ 58 ⑤④④
5a Burlington Gdns   434 1509   3–3C
*"Faded", but "staggeringly expensive" Mayfair Italian, which
offers "nothing special except the price". / 11.30 pm; closed Sat L
& Sun; jacket.*

Chaba SW10 £ 21 ❸❸④
206 Fulham Rd   352 8664   5–3B
*"Friendly", "basic" Chelsea cellar, "worth a try" for its
"authentic Thai flavours". / 11.15 pm; closed Sat L & Sun L.*

Chada SW11 £ 28 ❸❸④
208-210 Battersea Pk Rd   622 2209   10–1C
*This Battersea Thai offers "guaranteed good food at a
reasonable price"; "a shame it's not better patronised".
/ 11 pm, Fri & Sat 11.30 pm; closed Sat L; smart casual.*

Le Champenois EC2 £ 40 ④❸④
10 Devonshire Sq   283 7888   9–2D
*"Serene and spacious" ("dull") basement near Liverpool
Street which is "effective for business" – it has "quick service"
and the "expensive" French cooking could be worse. / L only;
closed Sat & Sun; smart casual.*

The Chapel NW1 £ 23 ❸④❸
48 Chapel St   402 9220   6–1D
*"Come-as-you-are gastropub", in the wasteland by Edgware
Road tube, that provides "good" cooking at "reasonable
prices" in a sometimes "smoky" and "noisy" setting. / 9.50 pm.*

Charco's SW3 £32 ❸④④
1 Bray Pl 584 0765 5–2D
*This long-established Chelsea wine bar's "bland" basement
offers modern British fare "much better than the surroundings
or menu would lead you to expect".* / 10.30 pm; closed Sun.

Chavot SW3 £52
257-259 Fulham Rd 351 7823 5–2C
*Eric Crouillière-Chavot's new restaurant opens on the site of
the former Fulham Road (RIP) in November '97; during a
brief interlude in Fitzrovia, he made quite a name for the type
of dependable cuisine that so commends itself to the Michelin
men.* / 11 pm; closed Sat L & Sun; set weekday L £28(FP).

Chelsea Bun Diner SW10 £16 ❸❸❸
9a Lamont Rd 352 3635 5–3B
*This World's End institution ("NY diner meets transport
caff meets Chelsea toff clientèle") gets high praise for its
"excellent selection of all-day breakfasts"; it "caters well for
vegetarians", too, and you can BYO; (the other branches,
not listed, are much less interesting).* / 11 pm.

Chelsea Kitchen SW3 £11 ④❷④
98 King's Rd 589 1330 5–2D
*"An amazing survivor in such a location", this Chelsea
institution can "always be relied on" for "canteen food at
canteen prices" and "instant, cheerful service".* / 11.30 pm;
no credit cards; no smoking area.

Chelsea Ram SW10 £25 ❶❸❷
32 Burnaby St 351 4008 5–4B
*"Excellent modern British cooking" has made this "relaxed,
fun, young pub", implausibly located near Chelsea's Lots Road
power station, a "brilliant" success; it's "always absolutely
packed", and can be "deathly smoky".* / 10 pm, Sun 9 pm;
no Amex; no booking.

The Chelsea Restaurant SW1 £34 ❷❸④
17 Sloane St 235 4377 2–4A
*Celeb-chef, Bruno Loubet's odd new venture is as consultant
chef to the restaurant overlooking the shiny foyer of the
Chelsea Hotel; it has received little attention, but the few who
ventured in found, as we did, "adventurous cooking, mostly
with good results" served by "young, eager staff".* / 10.45 pm;
closed Sun D.

Chelsea Square SW3 £ 25 ④❸❸
145 Dovehouse St   351 1155   5–2C
The "nice terrace in the summer" endears this backwater site
(formerly the Princess of Wales) to Chelsea's Dolce Vita set;
the brasserie fare is not entirely consistent, however, and the
cacophony of "metallic chairs on flagstones" is hardly
soothing. / 11 pm; closed Sun D; no Amex.

Cheng Du NW1 £ 30 ❸❷❸
9 Parkway   485 8058   8–3B
Though a minority think it "expensively ordinary", most praise
this "trustworthy" Camden Town Chinese for quality cooking
and "unobtrusive" service. / 11.30 pm.

CHEZ BRUCE SW17 £ 37 ❶❶❷
2 Bellevue Rd   0181-672 0114   10–2C
Bruce Poole's "superb" modern British cooking offers
"top value" – "it would cost twice as much in the West End";
the "relaxed and unpretentious" approach of this excellent
Wandsworth Common destination is also loudly applauded,
drowning out any quibbles that it is a mite "slow" or
"cramped". / 10.15 pm; closed Sun D.

Chez Gérard £ 27 ④❸❸
31 Dover St, W1   499 8171   3–3C
8 Charlotte St, W1   636 4975   2–1C
119 Chancery Ln, WC2   405 0290   2–2D
45 East Ter, Covent Gdn, WC2   379 0666   4–3D
This generally "reliable", but "unexciting" chain is famed for
its steaks and "the best frites in town" – it makes a useful
business standby; there were more complaints of "careless"
meals this year, though. / 10 pm-11.15 pm; Charlotte St
closed Sat L, Dover St closed Sun L, Chancery Ln & EC2 closed Sat & Sun;
no smoking area.

Chez Liline N4 £ 29 ❶❸⑤
101 Stroud Green Rd   263 6550   8–1D
"Excellent", "very unusual", "spicy" Mauritian fish dishes
at "good prices" justify the schlep to this Finsbury Park
institution, though it has a "dour" setting, and service can be
"slow". / 10.30 pm; closed Sun.

Chez Moi W11 £ 37 ❸❷❸
1 Addison Ave   603 8267   6–2A
"Reliable for over 30+ years", this "slightly camp but
comforting" Holland Park restaurant injects the odd "exotic"
twist into its Gallic menu, and keeps its loyal regulars amused.
/ 11 pm; closed Sat L & Sun; smart casual.

CHEZ NICO AT NINETY
GROSVENOR HOUSE HOTEL W1 £87   ❷❸④

90 Park Ln   409 1290   3–3A

"A terrific gourmet paradise" – to its devotees, Nico Ladenis's
Mayfair shrine to haute cuisine provides "unbeatable" cooking
that justifies the "massive" cost; to others, though, the "cold"
and "clinical" ethos of the place seems a surreal parody of
'textbook' Michelin grand style. / 11 pm; closed Sat L & Sun;
no Switch; jacket & tie; set weekday L £53(FP).

Chezmax SW10   £33   ❶❶❸

168 Ifield Rd   835 0874   5–3A

"Superb", meaty French cooking distinguishes this slightly
"kinkily" decorated Chelsea-fringe basement; the "maitre d'
deserves an Oscar" – "his menu run-down is better than
some West End plays". / Midnight; closed Mon & Sun; set weekday L &
early eve £17(FP).

Chiang Mai W1   £27   ❷⑤④

48 Frith St   437 7444   4–2A

Though it's not that well known, some Thai connoisseurs
argue that this Soho spot, which offers "lots of regional
dishes" (and plenty for veggies), is the "best in town";
"service gives Fawlty Towers a run for its money".
/ 11 pm; closed Sun L; no Switch.

Chicago Pizza Pie Factory W1   £22   ④❸④

17 Hanover Sq   629 2669   3–1C

This long-established Mayfair basement can seem a bit
"tired" nowadays, but it's a good place with kids and makes
a useful refuge from Oxford Street. / 11.30 pm; no smoking area.

Chicago Rib Shack SW7   £25   ④❸④

1 Raphael St   581 5595   5–1C

"Still the best ribs", say fans of this cavernous Knightsbridge
joint – "shame it's rather dated". / 11.45 pm; no smoking area;
no booking Sat.

China Blues NW1   £38   ④④❸

29-31 Parkway   482 3940   8–3B

Perhaps melancholic owners explain the name-change
(from China Jazz) of this Camden Town Chinese – aimed at
those on a Big Night Out; fans say that "great live" music and
"good" food make "quite a combination", but others leave
"disappointed". / Midnight; closed Sat L; smart casual; no smoking area.

China City WC2 £24 ❸④④
25a Lisle St 734 3388 4–3A
An unusual location – in its own "lovely courtyard" (complete with naff fountain) – sets the tone for this "roomy" Chinatown outfit; "superior quality" for the area, but still "cheap".
/ 11.45 pm; no smoking area; Sun, no booking.

Chinon W14 £36 ❶④④
23 Richmond Way 602 4082 7–1C
"Highly, highly recommended" for its "beautiful", "exceptional value" modern French fare, this "idiosyncratic" restaurant has only two real drawbacks – "bizarre and haphazard" service, and a location obscure even by Shepherd's Bush standards.
/ 10.30 pm; D only, closed Sun.

Chiswick Restaurant W4 £29 ❷❷④
131-133 Chiswick High Rd 0181-994 6887 7–2B
"Quality" modern British cooking at "amazing value" prices ensures this Chiswick foodie hotspot is "always buzzing"; some find the simple setting somewhat "soulless". / 11.30 pm; closed Sat L & Sun D.

Chor Bizarre W1 £33 ❸④❸
16 Albemarle St 629 9802 3–3C
Eclectically decorated Mayfair newcomer (formerly a Gaylord, RIP) whose 'thieves' bazaar' décor does not, to our mind, quite come off; initially at least, the same might be said of the "pricey" nouvelle Indian cooking and the haphazard service.
/ 11.30 pm; closed Sun; no smoking area.

Christopher's WC2 £43 ❸④❷
18 Wellington St 240 4222 4–3D
They've rebuilt the kitchen (literally) at this glamorous Covent Garden American, where an early revisit found the steaks and seafood menu improved on its previous perennially "ordinary" form; the "moody", "beautiful and vacant" service of which many have complained was not in evidence on our visit.
/ 11.45 pm; closed Sun D; smart casual; set pre- & post-th. £26(FP).

Chuen Cheng Ku W1 £23 ④④④
17 Wardour St 437 1398 4–3A
This huge Chinatown landmark is a regular contender for "best dim sum in town" – all the kerfuffle with the trollies certainly makes it entertaining; at other times it's less notable.
/ 11.45 pm; no smoking area.

Churchill W8 £13 ❷④❸
119 Kensington Ch St 792 1246 6–2B
"Great Thai food at amazingly cheap prices" wins a huge following for this Kensington pub-annex – "arrive early or book". / 9.30 pm; closed Sun L; no Amex.

Chutney Mary SW10   £35   ❸❸❸
535 King's Rd   351 3113   5–4B
*Though this very well-known Chelsea Anglo-Indian can still
provide "beautifully planned meals" that are "big on flavour",
"standards are slipping" somewhat; some find the styling
"pretentious" and "OTT" – try to sit in the conservatory.*
/ 11.30 pm; smart casual; no smoking area.

Chutneys NW1   £15   ❸④❸
124 Drummond St   388 0604   8–4C
*"You could charge double the price", say fans of the "superb"
bargain buffet (served lunchtime and all day Sunday) at this
simple 'Little India' veggie café.* / 11 pm; no Amex & no Switch.

Ciabatta SW3   £24   ❸④❸
356 King's Rd   352 0595   5–3C
*"Relaxed, real pizza joint", with a wood-burning oven, whose
"well-produced" fare makes it a useful, younger crowd
Chelsea standby.* / 11 pm, Fri & Sat midnight; no credit cards; no booking.

Cibo W14   £40   ❷❸④
3 Russell Gdns   371 6271   7–1D
*"Some of the most innovative and delicious Italian cooking
in town" has created a strong reputation for this "oddly
decorated" foodie hotspot, unpromisingly located near the
Olympia railway tracks.* / 11 pm; closed Sat L & Sun D; smart casual.

La Ciboulette SW3   £32   ❷❷④
138a King's Rd   823 7444   5–2C
*"An unexpected corner of France on a culinarily barren
stretch of the King's Road" – this excellent Chelsea basement
newcomer offers "sophisticated, well prepared" cooking and
it's relatively "inexpensive", too; "if only the ceilings were
higher, it would be paradise".* / 10.45 pm; closed Sun D; no Amex.

Circus W1   £35
1 Upper James St   534 4000   3–2D
*The team from the Avenue is set to launch a new Soho-fringe
venture around our publication date; an eminent architect
has been employed, and 'something completely different' is
promised – at prices lower than in St James's.* / Midnight, Fri
& Sat 12.30 am; closed Sun D.

City Brasserie EC3   £45   ④④❸
Plantation Hs, Mincing Ln   220 7094   9–3D
*It's "vastly overpriced, even for the City", but "no one cares
and the food is very good" at this popular basement which,
for its business following, "always delivers"; in Easter '98,
it's to relocate to 55 Mark Lane, nearby.* / L only, ex bar 9 pm;
closed Sat & Sun; smart casual; no booking in bar.

City Miyama EC4 £ 53 ❷❷④

17 Godliman St 489 1937 9–3B

"Expensive", but "very high quality", City oriental with a "typically Japanese sterile atmosphere". / 10 pm; closed Sat D & Sun.

CITY RHODES EC4 £ 46 ❶❷❸

New Street Sq 583 1313 9–2A

Gary the Lad is back with a bang, once again delivering his special brand of "innovative", "rugged" British food – Jaffa Cake pudding, in particular, gets rave reviews – and at "reasonable prices", too; the surprisingly attractive office-block premises, just off Fleet Street, and the "crisp" service have already made the place a top business venue. / 9 pm; closed Sat & Sun.

Claridges Restaurant W1 £ 55 ❸❷❷

Brook St 629 8860 3–2B

Is nothing sacred? – the Anglo/French cooking in the dining room of Society's favourite hotel has actually been described as "interesting"; given the "very nice service" – "three waiters at a time" – and the "formal" charms of this Art Deco gem, the whole place risks becoming thoroughly recommendable! / 11.15 pm; jacket & tie.

CLARKE'S W8 £ 42 ❶❶❸

124 Kensington Ch St 221 9225 6–2B

It "never fails", say fans of Sally Clarke's "serious" modern British restaurant near Notting Hill Gate whose "professional approach to food" and "attentive not intrusive" service make for "a very enjoyable eating experience" (in spite of, at dinner, a no-choice menu); the basement, in particular, is "cramped", and the "intimate" atmosphere is "best upstairs". / 10 pm; closed Sat & Sun; no smoking area; set weekday L £27(FP).

The Clerkenwell EC1 £ 29 ❸❸④

73 Clerkenwell Rd 831 7595 9–1A

This rather isolated east-City spot can still produce some "reliable", "powerfully flavoured", "Italianate" cooking; it's "fallen back" a little from its "promising start", though, and the "cheery" service can be "frustratingly slow at lunchtimes". / 10.45 pm; closed Sat & Sun; smart casual.

Coast W1 £ 42 ❸④④

26b Albemarle St 495 5999 3–3C

Large, "spartan" trendy Mayfair scene, which some find "too, too pretentious", "hideously over-designed", "uncomfortable" and with "terrible acoustics" ("a table downstairs is not advisable"); the "unbelievably innovative and tasty" modern British cuisine wins wider praise, but its realisation is "hit and miss". / Midnight.

Coins W11   **£ 10**   ③④③
105-107 Talbot Rd   221 8099   6–1B
*Airy and artified Notting Hill café which does good coffee and
cooked breakfasts at prices which betray its Trustafarian
following; quiet outside tables. / L only.*

The Collection SW3   **£ 40**   ④④③
264 Brompton Rd   225 1212   5–2C
*"It was fun at first, now it's overpriced and horrible" is a fairly
typical reaction to this "happening" ("posy") Brompton Cross
bar/restaurant – the haunt of "a sometimes grim collection
of Eurotrash wannabees"; the Asian-inspired cooking is beside
the point and the service "aloof, until they see a gold card".
/ 11.30 pm.*

Como Lario SW1   **£ 34**   ④③③
22 Holbein Pl   730 2954   5–2D
*"Still going strong", this "friendly", tightly-packed trattoria
near Sloane Square may be a touch "complacent", but is
many people's idea of a "safe bet". / 11.30 pm; closed Sun;
smart casual.*

CONNAUGHT W1   **£ 77**   ③①②
Carlos Pl   491 0668   3–3B
*"Like the House of Lords, and with prices to match",
this "truly grand" Mayfair hotel's dining room (and grill),
with its "stiff-collared but friendly staff", is "outstanding",
for traditionalists; as ever, Michel Bourdin's immutable
Anglo-French cooking is thought "magnificent" by most –
"bland and expensive" by some. / 10.45 pm; no Switch; jacket & tie;
appreciated if guests try to refrain from smoking; set weekday L £43(FP), Sun L
£48(FP).*

Conrad Hotel SW10   **£ 36**   ②②③
Chelsea Harbour   823 3000   5–4B
*"The best buffet brunch it town" (complete with half a bottle
of fizz) is to be had at this "soulless" hotel, lost in the midst
of the "brass and glass Chelsea Harbour carbuncle";
"impressive views". / 10.30 pm; no Switch; smart casual.*

The Cook House SW15   **£ 30**   ③②④
56 Lower Richmond Rd   0181-785 2300   10–1A
*"Very small" modern British Putney "neighbourhood place"
which, though a touch "under-atmosphered", is "trying very
hard and succeeding" with its short "adventurous" menu; it's
"not that cheap", but the BYO policy helps. / 11 pm; D only, closed
Sun & Mon; no Amex.*

Coopers Arms SW3   £ 18   ❸❷❷
87 Flood St   376 3120   5–3C
*A "good variety" of "genuine, home-prepared" food is
served – now in the evenings, too – in the "comfortable",
understated surroundings of this congenial Chelsea pub.*
/ 10 pm; book Sun L only.

Le Coq d'Argent EC3
1 Poultry   tel n/a   9–2C
*Conran's forces – long waylaid at Tower Bridge – are now
massing to storm the City itself; a rooftop restaurant, by Bank,
with outside dining in summer, is scheduled to open in the
spring of '98.* /

Cork & Bottle WC2   £ 23   ❸❸❷
44-46 Cranbourn St   734 7807   4–3B
*This "tight, cosy" cellar, next to a Leicester Square sex shop,
remains a hugely popular central rendezvous thanks to its
"lively", "fun" atmosphere, its "reliable", if "pricey, fare and
its "wonderful wine selection".* / 11.30 pm; no booking after 6 pm.

Cosmo NW3   £ 24   ❸❷④
4 Northways Pde, Finchley Rd   722 1398   8–2A
*A new chef is shaking up this South Hampstead stalwart,
modernising the dated mittel-European menu with some
"interesting" dishes; "homely, attentive" service survives
unchanged, as does the "dodgy", but characterful décor.*
/ 11 pm.

Costa's Fish Restaurant W8   £ 13   ❷❷④
18 Hillgate St   727 4310   6–2B
*Cognoscenti tip this "quick and friendly" chippy, just off
Notting Hill Gate as "overall, much better value than its
famous neighbour, Geale's".* / 10 pm; closed Mon & Sun;
no credit cards.

Costa's Grill W8   £ 13   ❷❶❷
12-14 Hillgate St   229 3794   6–2B
*"Excellent cheap and cheerful" and "charming" taverna,
just off Notting Hill Gate, long known for brilliant value –
given the prices, "one wonders how they survive".* / 10 pm;
closed Sun; no credit cards.

Côte à Côte SW11   £ 16   ⑤④❸
74-75 Battersea Br Rd   738 0198   5–4C
*"Extremely cheap, simple food" makes this "dark and cosy"
Battersea dive "a fun place for a party if you bag one of
the boats"; "prices are bargain basement, so expectations
are low" – rightly so.* / 11 pm; no Amex.

Cottons NW1 £ 26 ④④❷
55 Chalk Farm Rd   482 1096   8–2B
*No one doubts the groovy atmosphere and "great cocktails"
at this fun Camden Town Caribbean; but while its loyal local
fans applaud the "excellent West Indian food", we're with
those who feel it's all "kind of expensive". / 11 pm, Fri & Sat
11.30 pm; closed Mon L; no smoking area.*

The Cow W11 £ 28 ❷❷❷
89 Westbourne Park Rd   221 0021   6–1B
*The new régime is, at last, realising the potential of the
"warm", "cosy" and "cramped" first floor room over this
trendy Notting Hill pub – "super", "simple", "dinner-party"
cooking is "charmingly" served; downstairs there is some
"excellent seafood" at the bar. / 11.30 pm; restaurant Mon-Sat
D only, Sun L only.*

Cranks £ 16 ④④④
23 Barrett St, W1   495 1340   3–1B
8 Marshall St, W1   437 9431   3–2D
9-11 Tottenham St, W1   631 3912   2–1B
1 The Market, WC2   379 6508   4–3D
17-19 Great Newport St, WC2   836 5226   4–3B
Unit 11, 8 Adelaide St, WC2   836 0660   4–4C
*Few seem to care that the food is all organic or to appreciate
the smart face this venerable veggie chain now presents to
the world – it's "just too pricey to be worth it". / 7 pm - 11 pm;
no smoking; no booking.*

The Crescent SW3 £ 24 ④❸④
99 Fulham Rd   225 2244   5–2C
*"The food doesn't match up", but "the wine list is
extraordinary" at this "tiny" wine bar-diner, fashionably
located near Brompton Cross – 200 choices, including over
20 by the glass. / 11 pm; no booking.*

THE CRITERION W1 £ 42 ❸④❶
Piccadilly Circus   930 0488   3–3D
*"The most beautiful room in London" – in extraordinary
neo-Byzantine style – provides the setting for what is by far
the most satisfactory of the Marco Pierre White restaurants;
even here, though, the service – "terrible", "condescending",
"rude" – has ruined more than one evening. / Midnight, Sun
10.30 pm; set weekday L £27(FP).*

The Cross Keys SW3 £ 29 ④❸❷
1 Lawrence St   349 9111   5–3C
*A "great, stylish" Chelsea pub-conversion with a "beautiful"
conservatory; the modern British fare is "patchy", though.
/ 11 pm.*

Crown & Goose NW1   £21   ❸④❸
100 Arlington Rd   485 8008   8–3B
"Good pub food" ("hamburgers to die for") is one of the
reasons why this vaguely trendy Camden Town boozer is
"always too busy". / 10 pm; no credit cards.

Cuba Libre N1   £29   ④❸❸
72 Upper St   354 9998   8–3D
*Vibrant Islington Latin American which groans at the
seams on popular nights (when it can be "smoky" and
"unbearable"); the grub "looks promising but lacks flavour".*
/ 11.30 pm, Fri & Sat 12.30 am; no Amex.

Cucina NW3   £28   ❸❷❸
45a South End Rd   435 7814   8–2A
*"Inventive, fresh, well cooked food" and efficient staff make
this "busy", "trendy" modern Briton "the best of Hampstead
eateries"; some "cannot understand the hype", but, given the
dearth of local alternatives, it's small wonder people leave
impressed.* / 10.30 pm, Fri & Sat 11 pm; closed Sun D; smart casual.

Czech Club NW6   £19   ❸④④
74 West End Ln   372 5251   1–1B
*"Czech beer heaven", the "best goulash" and "a fun
atmosphere on a busy night" are the attractions at this quirky
émigrés' club in West Hampstead; some dishes are "so-so".*
/ 9.30 pm; closed Mon (ex bank hols) Sat D & Sun D; no credit cards.

Da Mario SW7   £24   ❸④④
15 Gloucester Rd   584 9078   5–1B
*Long-established South Kensington pizzeria (a disguised
PizzaExpress) "popular with local Moms and Pops" and
convenient for the Albert Hall; if you want a budget party,
the "tacky disco" in the basement is worth knowing about.*
/ 11.30 pm; no Switch; book for disco.

Da Pierino SW7   £20   ❸❸④
37 Thurloe Pl   581 3770   5–2C
*"Unpretentious", "very Italian" family-run diner, by South
Kensington tube, serving "consistently good", "cheap food",
including "great pizza".* / 11.15 pm; closed Mon; no Amex & no Switch.

Dan's SW3   £35   ④❷❶
119 Sydney St   352 2718   5–3C
*Romantics coo over the "intimate" ambience and lovely
"garden atmosphere" of this "well established" English
restaurant in Chelsea; fans claim "food better than is often
reported", but there are those who think it "sad".* / 10.30 pm;
closed Sun D.

FSA

Daphne NW1   £20   ❸❷❸
83 Bayham St   267 7322   8–3C
*"OK" food (but "excellent meze") make this Camden Town
Greek a popular standby; in summer, you can dine on the
roof. / 11.30 pm; closed Sun; no Amex.*

Daphne's SW3   £40   ❸④❷
110-112 Draycott Ave   589 4257   5–2C
*This pretty "ladies-who-lunch place", right by Brompton Cross,
"may not be as 'in' as it was", but that's helping the staff to
rein in their still sometimes "breathtakingly rude" attitude to
"non-celebs"; the Mediterranean cooking is improving.
/ 11.30 pm.*

Daquise SW7   £16   ④❸❸
20 Thurloe St   589 6117   5–2C
*"A delightful time-warp frequented by East European exiles",
say fans of this aged South Kensington institution; in a harsher
light, the "cheap food in primitive surroundings" can be found
"as depressing as a real Polish restaurant". / 1.30 am; no Amex;
no smoking area.*

De Cecco SW6   £29   ❷❸❷
189 New King's Rd   736 1145   10–1B
*"Great food at reasonable prices" continues to please at
this "fun", "cheerful" and extremely popular Parson's Green
Italian – fish dishes, in particular, are praised; the "tacky, '70s
premises" are scheduled for expansion. / 11 pm; closed Sun.*

Deals   £28   ④④④
14-16 Foubert's Pl, W1   287 1001   3–2C
Chelsea Harbour, SW10   795 1001   5–4B
Broadway Centre, W6   0181-563 1001   7–2C
*Some praise these aristo-owned diners for their "decent"
burgers, or say they are "great for a quick lunch"; on the
whole, however, enthusiasm is notably lacking. / 11 pm, W1 &
W6 – Sat & Sun 11.30 pm; W1 closed Sun.*

Del Buongustaio SW15   £31   ❶❷❷
283 Putney Br Rd   0181-780 9361   10–2B
*In a plain Putney street, an "unprepossessing" frontage
"masks a great restaurant" – "like stepping into Italy" –
with "wonderful", "rustic cooking at its best" and a
"crowded", "unpretentious" atmosphere. / 11.30 pm;
closed Sat L, Jun-Aug closed Sun L; no Switch.*

66

La Delizia £20 ❷④❸
63-65 Chelsea Manor St, SW3   376 4111   5–3C
Farmers Mkt, Sydney St, SW3   351 6701   5–3C
246 Old Brompton Rd, SW5   373 6085   5–2A
Small Chelsea chain praised for "very good" pizza and "great" pasta, even if the "authentic macho service" can grate; on a sunny day, the largely outdoor, BYO Farmers Market branch detaches itself completely from London and becomes Eurotrash Central. / Midnight; no credit cards; no booking.

dell'Ugo W1 £35 ④⑤❸
56 Frith St   734 8300   4–2A
The "buzz" is the best feature of this three-floor Soho landmark; some may applaud "great" Mediterranean-inspired dishes and "helpful and hilarious" staff, but too many come away bewailing "service so dreadful it almost makes you forget how poor the food is". / Midnight; closed Sun.

The Depot SW14 £27 ④❸❷
Mortlake High St   0181-878 9462   10–1A
With its "great riverside location", this "relaxed" Barnes brasserie has many admirers; the modern British menu is "reasonably priced" but, although it's now more "varied" and ambitious than it was, it still "does not thrill". / 11 pm; no smoking area.

Diverso W1 £41 ❸❷④
85 Piccadilly   491 2222   3–4C
This pretty, well spaced Mayfair Italian yearling has secured a rather limited following; its fans do commend "excellent food and service", but prices are high. / 11.30 pm; closed Sun L.

Diwana Bhel-Poori House NW1 £14 ❷❸④
121 Drummond St   387 5556   8–4C
"Still the best of the Drummond Street vegetarian restaurants", this 'Little Indian', near Euston, "has been the same for the past 25 years"– it offers "tasty, cheap food" and "excellent value" (especially from the lunchtime buffet); BYO. / 11.30 pm; no Switch; no smoking; Fri–Sun no booking.

Dixie's Bar & Grill SW11 £19 ⑤④❷
25 Battersea Rs   228 7984   10–2C
Very buzzy Battersea Tex/Mex best liked for its "good hangover comfort food"; a regular opines the grub's "got better recently", but that still leaves plenty of scope for further improvement. / 11.30 pm.

Dôme **£ 20** ④④❸

57-59 Old Compton St, W1   287 0770   4–3A
32 Long Acre, WC2   379 8650   4–2C
8 Charing Cross Rd, WC2   240 5556   4–4B
354 King's Rd, SW3   352 2828   5–3B
194-196 Earl's Court Rd, SW5   835 2200   5–2A
Kensington Ct, W8   937 6655   5–1A
341 Upper St, N1   226 3414   8–3D
58-62 Heath St, NW3   431 0399   8–1A
57-59 Charterhouse St, EC1   336 6484   9–1A
4 St Paul's Churchyard, EC4   489 0767   9–2B
*Attractive chain, whose faux-Belle Epoque interiors – in
defiance of all logic and taste – work; the "surprisingly good"
breakfasts are their best point, and the £5 set meals are
"good value" too.* / 10.30 pm-11 pm; EC1 closed Sat & Sun; some
no Amex; set always available £12(FP).

Don Pepe NW8 **£ 20** ❸❷❸

99 Frampton St   262 3834   8–4A
*London's oldest tapas bar – just around the corner from Lords
– offers "cheap and good food, often with live music".*
/ Midnight; closed Sun.

Dorchester Grill
Dorchester Hotel W1 **£ 54** ❷❶❷

53 Park Ln   317 6336   3–3A
*"Consistent" English cooking – at reasonable prices by grand
hotel standards (especially if you stick to the "excellent value"
set menu) – combines with "unimaginably good" service and
"well spaced tables" to make this Spanish Baronial-style
Mayfair dining room very popular.* / 11 pm; smart casual.

Dorchester, Oriental
Dorchester Hotel W1 **£ 64** ❷❸④

53 Park Ln   317 6328   3–3A
*"Terribly expensive, but well worth it", this "excellent
Chinese" – the capital's grandest oriental – is universally
acclaimed for its "perfect" food; "shame about the
atmosphere", though, which tends to the "clinical".* / 10.45 pm;
closed Sat L & Sun; smart casual; set weekday L £40(FP).

La Dordogne W4 **£ 35** ❷❶❷

5 Devonshire Rd   0181-747 1836   7–2A
*"Turn up in a 2CV" for the full effect at this Chiswick fixture –
it's "like dining in a small town somewhere in France";
"attentive" service and "classic" cooking complete an
"excellent" all-round package.* / 11 pm; closed Sat L & Sun L.

Dove W6 £ 17 ❸❸❷

19 Upper Mall   0181-748 5405   7–2B
*"Arrive early for Sunday lunch" at this famous riverside
Hammersmith pub; at other times tolerable Thai cooking is
served, as well as more standard fare.* / 10 pm; no booking.

Dover St Wine Bar W1 £ 39 ⑤⑤❸

8-9 Dover St   629 9813   3–3C
*Who cares if it's "a rip-off", when this Mayfair cellar remains
(astonishingly) one of the only central venues where you can
dine-and-boogie? – not the punters, it seems, as expansion is
planned.* / 2 am; closed Sat L & Sun; no jeans.

Down Mexico Way W1 £ 24 ⑤❸❷

25 Swallow St   437 9895   3–3D
*Remember that "the food is beside the point", and you may
enjoy this "fun" Mayfair Mexican (whose impressively tiled
bar is particularly atmospheric); it's "excellent for parties".*
/ 11.45 pm, Sun 10.30 pm.

Drones SW1 £ 37 ④❸❷

1 Pont St   259 6166   2–4A
*"The place is pretty to look at, but the food's really not great"
at this "smart" modern British Belgravian.* / 10.15 pm; set
weekday L £23(FP).

The Eagle EC1 £ 21 ❷④❸

159 Farringdon Rd   837 1353   9–1A
*"Getting a table can be a nightmare" at this "busy", "noisy",
and "smoky" City-fringe super-pub, famed for its "creative",
"robust" and "unpretentious" Mediterranean fare.* / 10.30 pm;
closed Sun; no credit cards; no booking.

East One EC1 £ 25 ❸❸❸

175-179 St John St   566 0088   9–1A
*We don't go a bundle on these "take your own ingredients
to be wokked" orientals, but most seem to like this "brash",
"shiny" "fun" outfit, north of Smithfield; it certainly wins credit
for its "excellent variety of fresh ingredients".* / 11 pm; closed Sat L
& Sun D.

Ebla W6 £ 22 ❸❷④

262-264 King St   0181-741 1177   7–2B
*Hammersmith Turk yearling offering carefully prepared grub;
service tries hard to please.* / 11.30 pm.

Ebury Street Wine Bar SW1 £33 ❸④❸
139 Ebury St   730 5447   2–4A
*Modern British fare "without pretension or great
sophistication" makes this "busy but small and attractive"
Belgravia fixture a "reliable" standby – "from entertaining
granny to a first date". / 10.30 pm.*

Eco SW4 £21 ❶④❸
162 Clapham High St   978 1108   10–2D
*"Quite simply the greatest pizza in town" makes for
"long queues" at this "trendy" and "very noisy" Clapham
phenomenon. / 11 pm, Sat & Sun 11.30 pm; Mon-Fri only,
no smoking area.*

Ed's Easy Diner £21 ❷❷❷
12 Moor St, W1   439 1955   4–2A
Trocadero, W1   287 1951   3–3D
362 King's Rd, SW3   352 1956   5–3C
16 Hampstead High St, NW3   431 1958   8–1A
*"All round the best place for a burger in London" is
the verdict on this "simple, fast and smiling" '50s-fantasy
diner-chain; the stools are not designed to encourage
lingering. / Midnight, Fri & Sat 1 am, W1 Sun 11 pm; no booking.*

Efes Kebab House £20 ❸❷❸
1) 80 Great Titchfield St, W1   636 1953   2–1B
2) 175-177 Gt Portland St, W1   436 0600   2–1B
*"Excellent kebabs and so on combined with friendly, slightly
mad service" maintain the wide-ranging appeal of these
"reliable" and "good value" Fitzrovia Turks; Efes II offers
belly dancing nightly. / 11.30 pm, Fri & Sat 3 am; I closed Sun.*

Elena's L'Etoile W1 £38 ❷❷❷
30 Charlotte St   636 7189   2–1C
*"Personal" and "professional" service (presided over by the
indomitable Elena) contributes to the "warm, relaxed and
happy atmosphere" at this Fitrovia classic – a Gallic outpost
since 1904 – which now offers "good, straightforward
cooking". / 11 pm; closed Sat L & Sun; smart casual.*

Elistano SW3 £25 ❷❷❸
25-27 Elystan St   584 5248   5–2C
*"Great pasta", "flirtatious waiters" and "beautiful people"
make for a heady brew at this "good local Italian" near
Chelsea Green; "it can be hard to book". / 11 pm; closed Sat L
& Sun.*

FSA

Emile's £ 23 ❸⓿❸
144 Wandsworth Br Rd, SW6 736 2418 10–1B
96-98 Felsham Rd, SW15 0181-789 3323 10–2B
*These "cosy and nice" ("suburban") Putney and Fulham locals
win strong support for their "well cooked and served"
fixed-price formula; "the best Beef Wellington in London"
is rightly celebrated. / 11 pm; D only; closed Sun; no Amex.*

Enak Enak SW11 £ 29 ❸④❸
56 Lavender Hill 924 3148 10–2C
*Fans of TV chef Nancy Lam vaunt the "wonderful" Indonesian
home cooking at her tiny – you must book ahead – no-frills
Battersea HQ; the style is not, shall we say, rushed, and we
found Ms Lam's trademark banter spicier than her cooking.
/ 9 pm; D only, closed Sun-Tue; no smoking; booking required.*

The Engineer NW1 £ 28 ❸④❷
65 Gloucester Ave 722 0950 8–3B
*"Still the place to be" for "trendy" Primrose Hill-types, this
pub-conversion (with its "beautiful garden") offers "fresh
and light" modern British grub; when busy – which is often –
"chaos reigns". / 11 pm; no Amex.*

English Garden SW3 £ 43 ❸❷❷
10 Lincoln St 584 7272 5–2D
*"Gracious" service and excellent atmosphere win consistent
praise for this Chelsea establishment, whose assets include
an agreeable conservatory and pleasant private rooms; the
"pricey" modernish British cooking gets a more mixed press.
/ 11.15 pm; set weekday L £23(FP), Sun L £27(FP).*

English House SW3 £ 43 ❸❷❷
3 Milner St 584 3002 5–2D
*"Twee", "Laura Ashley" Chelsea townhouse which provides
"cosy surroundings", "attentive" service and pricey, rather
"variable" modern British fare; the "private rooms are very
good for business". / 11.15 pm; set weekday L £24(FP).*

Enoteca Turi SW15 £ 32 ❷❷❸
28 Putney High St 0181-785 4449 10–2B
*Putney Italian whose "variety of well presented, unusual
dishes", "excellent" wine list and "friendly" service win it
a strong, if still mainly local, fan club; avoid the "dingy"
basement. / 11 pm; closed Sat L & Sun; smart casual.*

The Enterprise SW3   **£30**   ❸❸❷

Walton St   584 3148   5–2C

*"For a casual dinner", this "buzzy" Chelsea pub-conversion
reliably offers "good, standard food" – "better than you
expect in such a fashionable address"; the "fascinating local
clientèle" is an added attraction.* / 11 pm; smart casual; book Mon-Fri
L only.

Entrecote SW1   **£32**   ④❸④

116 Knightsbridge   584 4575   5–1D

*The eponymous special (with Café de Paris sauce and good
frites) is done well at this elegant Knightsbridge yearling; a
shame, then, that toppish prices (plus dotty wine list) put off
too many punters.* / 11 pm; closed Sun.

Esarn Kheaw W12   **£22**   ❶④④

314 Uxbridge Rd   0181-743 8930   7–1B

*"A great find"; "real Thai food the Thais eat" draws fans from
all over town to this decoratively uninspired Shepherd's Bush
ethnic.* / 11 pm; closed Sat L & Sun L; no Switch.

L'Escargot W1   **£36**   ❷❷❸

48 Greek St   437 2679   4–2A

*"Much busier now the food has improved", this once-famous
Soho brasserie-restaurant is finally getting its act together;
the modern French cooking can be "superb", and age seems
to be improving the smart, but soulless new look acquired a
couple of years ago.* / 11.30 pm; closed Sat L & Sun.

L'Escargot Doré W8   **£33**   ❸❷④

2 Thackeray St   937 8508   5–1A

*Little known Gallic basement, off High Street Kensington,
offering quality cooking and "attentive service"; to say it's
"never too crowded" is rather two-edged – "eat later for more
atmosphere" sounds like a good tip.* / 11.30 pm; closed Sat L & Sun;
smart casual.

L'Estaminet WC2   **£34**   ❸❶④

14 Garrick St   379 1432   4–3C

*"Very good value pre-theatre" and an "excellent cheese
board" are the particular strengths of this implausibly
suburban French restaurant, in the heart of Covent Garden;
we've frankly never liked it, but many do, and "quietly
efficient" service is an undoubted plus.* / 11 pm; closed Sun; set pre-
th. £18(FP).

Euphorium N1   £ 33
203 Upper St   704 6909   8–2D
*The last quarter of '97 will see major upheavals at this
"pseudy" modern British Islingtonian two-year-old, which has
been through a roller-coaster of acclaim and disappointments
– an all-day brasserie will take over the current site, and the
restaurant will move to a new conservatory at the rear.*
/ 10.30 pm; closed Sun D; no smoking area.

Fables SW6   £ 39   ④⑤⑤
839 Fulham Rd   371 5445   10–1B
*This Fulham yearling has failed to live up to its initial promise
– "slow" and "amateurish" service now creates a "charmless"
environment for "just about OK" modern British cooking.*
/ 10.45 pm; closed Sun D.

Fakhreldine W1   £ 35   ❸④④
85 Piccadilly   493 3424   3–4C
*This glitzy, "excellent, but expensive Lebanese", overlooking
Green Park, can suffer from "over-attentive" service;
for authenticity, go late.* / Midnight; smart casual.

Il Falconiere SW7   £ 26   ❸❶❸
84 Old Brompton Rd   589 2401   5–2B
*"Good value set menus", "nice atmosphere" and particularly
pleasant service may not set the world alight, but they make
this traditional South Kensington trattoria a useful standby.*
/ 11.45 pm; closed Sun.

La Famiglia SW10   £ 35   ❸④❷
7 Langton St   351 0761   5–3B
*Thanks to its "happy", "snazzy" atmosphere and
"interesting clientèle", this "wonderful Italian" – a long-
running World's End success story – can ignore perennial
concerns that it's "too expensive"; visits are spoilt for some by
"surly" service.* / 11.45 pm.

Fashion Café W1   £ 30   ⑤⑤⑤
5-6 Coventry St   287 5888   4–4A
*"A waste of money", this "appalling" theme-restaurant,
"aimed at fickle female teenagers", charges "silly prices for
waif-like portions"; but there's worse – having "no redeeming
features", and being the worthy winner of the first ever
'Triple-5', the place is now set for a massive expansion!*
/ 11 pm; no smoking area; Fri-Sun, no booking.

Fat Boy's W4   **£ 24**   ❸❸❸
10a Edensor Rd   0181-994 8089   10–1A
*"Plush BYO Thai" (by day a Chiswick workmen's caff) which
charges "reasonable" prices for its "consistent" grub; if you
forget your booze, the place is licensed.* / 11 pm; D only;
no credit cards.

Fats W9   **£ 20**   ❸④④
178 Shirland Rd   289 3884   1–2B
*"Surprisingly excellent" Caribbean, Creole and Cajun
cooking is the reason to try this tiny Maida Vale café; it ain't
cheap, though.* / 11 pm; no credit cards; no smoking.

The Fence EC1   **£ 32**   ④❸❸
67-69 Cowcross St   250 3414   9–1A
*The "really excellent" wine list ("always something new to
try") and the garden ("a treat in the City") are the highlights
of this brash but popular Farringdon bar-restaurant; the food
very much plays third fiddle, but no one seems to mind.*
/ 10 pm; closed Sat & Sun.

Feng Shang NW1   **£ 32**   ❸❸❷
Opp 15 Prince Albert Rd   485 8137   8–3B
*This "Chinese boat in Regents Park canal" (near the zoo) is
thought, by some, an "exciting venue" for a night out.* / 11 pm;
no Switch.

Ffiona's W8   **£ 21**   ❸❷❷
51 Kensington Ch St   937 4152   5–1A
*"Ffiona is a real character", and her fan club just loves this
"small", "cosy" Kensington joint which offers "reasonably
priced" "home cooking".* / Midnight.

**The Fifth Floor at
Harvey Nichols SW1**   **£ 43**   ④❸❸
Knightsbridge   235 5250   5–1D
*"Very much a lunch place, not dinner" seems the best advice
about the "buzzy" restaurant atop Knightsbridge's AbFab
department store, where the modern British cooking is too
often "underinspired" and "overpriced"; the infamously
"sleazy" bar can be fun, though, if approached in the
right spirit.* / 11.30 pm; closed Sun D.

Fifth Floor at
Harvey Nichols (Café) SW1   £31   ③④❷
Knightsbridge   823 1839   5–1D
*"Much better value than the restaurant", the strikingly
styled all-day café at Harvey Nics is not only "great for a
mid shopping brunch" – with "top people-watching" –
but a good evening standby to boot.* / 10.30 pm; closed Sun D;
no smoking area; eve only.

Fileric   £9   ❷③④
57 Old Brompton Rd, SW7   584 2967   5–2C
12 Queenstown Rd, SW8   720 4844   10–1C
*"Excellent" South Kensington and Battersea pâtisseries –
so unpretentious they are easy to overlook – with an
authentically "French feeling".* / 8 pm; no booking.

Fina Estampa SE1   £26   ❷❷④
150 Tooley St   403 1342   9–4D
*"A real find", not far from Tower Bridge – a "husband and
wife team" dishes up "excellent Peruvian home cooking".*
/ 10.30 pm; closed Sun.

La Finca   £19   ③④❸
96-98 Pentonville Rd, N1   837 5387   8–3D
185 Kennington Ln, SE11   735 1061   10–1D
*These "fun, lively tapas bars" – both in thin areas – offer
a "hugely enjoyable", "noisy" environment with "lots of
character"; "good paella", too.* / 11.15 pm; Fri & Sat N1 1.30 am,
SE11 11.30 pm.

La Finezza SW1   £42   ❸❸④
62-64 Lower Sloane St   730 8639   5–2D
*Those of more mature years "still enjoy" this "steady and
reliable" grand trattoria near Sloane Square, which is
"comfortable, quiet and accommodating"; it's very pricey,
though.* / 11 pm; closed Sat L & Sun; no Switch.

First Floor W11   £39   ⑤④❷
186 Portobello Rd   243 0072   6–1B
*"Something's gone wrong in the last year" at this groovily
decorated Notting Hill scene; there are those who still
"love the room", but the food's gone right off the boil –
"pretentious", "overpriced", "tasted as if it came out of
the microwave".* / 11.30 pm; set weekday L £23(FP).

Fisk N1 £ 33 ④④④
265 Upper St   359 1022   8–2D
*This fishy Islington newcomer, in a comfortable but dull
basement, is "trying hard but missing" – service is so attentive
it's counter-productive, and the food, though good, is "pricey".*
/ 11 pm; D only; closed Mon & Sun.

Florians N8 £ 29 ❸❷❸
4 Topsfield Parade   0181-348 8348   1–1C
*"Very lively" Hornsey "local favourite"; the "busy" bar, with
its "above average" Italian dishes, is more fun than the
restaurant at the rear.* / 10.45 pm; no Amex.

La Fontana SW1 £ 40 ❸❸④
101 Pimlico Rd   730 6630   5–2D
*"Good", but "overpriced", this "friendly", small, "'70s"
trattoria, not far from Sloane Square, is best visited during
its annual trufflefest.* / 11 pm; no Switch.

Food for Thought WC2 £ 12 ❷❸④
31 Neal St   836 0239   4–2C
*"Tasty filling food, well worth the queue and the crush" is to
be had at this estimable Covent Garden basement veggie.*
/ 8.45 pm, Sun 3.45 pm; no credit cards; no smoking; no booking.

Football Football SW1 £ 24 ⑤❸④
57/60 Haymarket   930 9970   2–2C
*The "dire" food and "tacky" atmosphere are beside the point
at this "very expensive" "motorway café"-style theme place in
the heart of the West End; what is the point, exactly?* / 10 pm,
Fri & Sat 11 pm, Sun 9 pm; smart casual; no smoking area.

Footstool SW1 £ 31 ⑤④❸
St John's, Smith Sq   222 2779   2–4C
*An "attractive" setting is the saving grace at this Westminster
crypt; as one of the only options near Parliament (or before
a concert in the hall above), it gets away with an
"unimpressive" performance, "expensive for dinner-party
standards".* / L only but buffet concert eves; closed Sat & Sun except when
eve concerts; no smoking area.

Formula Veneta SW10 £ 31 ④❸❸
14 Hollywood Rd   352 7612   5–3B
*"Good, basic food" and "value for money", especially for
Chelsea, are often to be had at this fashionable side street
trattoria, which has a "great garden"; "it helps to be a
regular", though, and it can disappoint.* / 11.15 pm; closed Sun.

The Foundation SW1   **£34**   ④⑤⑤

Knightsbridge   201 8000   5–1D
*"Very disappointing, considering it's in Harvey Nics" –
curiously the modern British food is not that bad at this
Knightsbridge basement, and it is the "very cold" ambience
and "spaced-out" service which let the place down.* / 11 pm;
closed Sun D; no smoking area; no booking Sat L.

Four Regions SE1   **£27**   ❸❸❸

County Hall   928 0988   2–3D
*On a nice day, the stunning view of the Palace of Westminster
from the terrace of the former GLC building is the special
attraction of this competent Chinese newcomer; in the dining
room itself, however, a municipal function-suite atmosphere
prevails.* / 10.45 pm.

The Four Seasons W2   **£21**   ❸⑤⑤

84 Queensway   229 4320   6–2C
*Despite its "dreadful" décor and sometimes "obnoxious"
service, this Bayswater Chinese is still thought worth braving
by die-hard oriental fans.* / 11.30 pm.

**Four Seasons
Four Seasons Hotel W1**   **£56**   ❷❷❸

Park Ln   499 0888   3–4A
*Very competent modern French fare – at bargain basement
prices, by grand hotel standards – and "superb" service make
this one of the best value deals in town (especially if you stick
to the set menus); shame about the embarrassing décor of
the room, though, even if some do find its setting, overlooking
the park, "romantic".* / 10.30 pm; no Switch; eve, jacket; set weekday L
£34(FP).

Fox & Anchor EC1   **£20**   ❷❸❷

115 Charterhouse St   253 4838   9–1B
*"Awesome mixed grills, good beer and friendly service of the
bang-down-the-plate-and-cutlery variety" make this famous
Smithfield pub, licensed from 7am, one of the best breakfast
bets in town; book.* / Bkfast & L only; closed Sat L (but open Sat bkfast)
& Sun.

The Fox Reformed N16   **£22**   ❸❸❷

176 Stoke Newington Ch St   254 5975   1–1C
*"Cosily cramped" and "friendly", this Stoke Newington
wine bar" offers "an eclectic choice of above-par food";
it's "great for chess and the nice garden", and has good
wines, too.* / 10.30 pm.

Foxtrot Oscar   £ 27   ④❸❸

79 Royal Hospital Rd, SW3   352 7179   5–3D
16 Byward St, EC3   481 2700   9–3D
*"A friendly joint with Royal Ascot atmosphere" – the original
Chelsea branch of this wine bar-diner chain is "always
popular", even though the scoff (burgers excepted) tends
to the humdrum; the recent City opening suggests that the
formula doesn't really work outside Nobsville. / SW3 11.30 pm,
EC3 L only; EC3 closed Sat & Sun.*

Francofill SW7   £ 21   ❷❷④

1 Old Brompton Rd   584 0087   5–2C
*"Very good value" fare and "friendly staff" make this Gallic
eatery by South Kensington tube – offering "French burgers",
"great salads" and a selection of bistro dishes – "good for a
quick bite". / 11 pm; no smoking area.*

Frederick's N1   £ 35   ❸❷❷

106 Camden Pas   359 2888   8–3D
*The "beautiful setting" – "not too stuffy, but classy" –
is at the heart of the continuing success of this impressively
spacious Islington conservatory-restaurant; the modern British
cooking is "well prepared", if not exciting. / 11.30 pm; closed Sun;
smart casual; no smoking area; set Sat L £21(FP).*

French House W1   £ 31   ④④❸

49 Dean St   437 2477   4–3A
*The "interesting" boho upstairs dining room of this famous
Soho pub is much disimproved under new ownership; the
modern British food is now "limited and uninspired", and
there are odd reports of "nasty" run-ins with staff.
/ 11.15 pm; closed Sun.*

Frocks E9   £ 27   ❸❸❷

95 Lauriston Rd   0181-986 3161   1–2D
*This "relaxing" East End oasis (not far from Victoria Park) has
many supporters, but its "excellent weekend breakfasts" win
more praise than its standard English bistro fare; service is
"personal" and "friendly", but can be "very slow". / 11 pm;
closed Sun D.*

Front Page SW3   £ 21   ❷❸❷

35 Old Church St   352 2908   5–3C
*"Imaginative" food is just one of the attractions of this stylish
and "very friendly" Old Chelsea pub. / 10 pm; no Amex; no booking.*

Fryer's Delight WC1 £ 6 ❶❷❸
19 Theobald's Rd 405 4114 2–1D
*This "great local chippy" ("best in the world!"), behind Gray's
Inn, offers what is, for our money, the best value sustenance
available in central London. / 10 pm; no credit cards.*

Fuego EC3 £ 24 ❸④❷
1a Pudding Ln 929 3366 9–3C
*A "fun place" (if "a bit white sock-ish"), this lively Spaniard,
by the Monument, serves "authentic tapas" which can be
very good. / 9.30 pm; closed Sat & Sun; smart casual.*

Fung Shing WC2 £ 32 ❷④⑤
15 Lisle St 437 1539 4–3A
*"Consistently excellent food" – particularly the "wonderful
steamed fish" and seafood – means that fans of this
venerated Cantonese are unperturbed by its "Chinatown
school of charm service" and "scruffy" décor; as ever,
though, a few think it "good, but not that good". / 11.30 pm.*

Futures EC2 £ 23 ❸❸❸
2 Exchange Sq 638 6341 9–1D
*"Consistently good quality, simple, tasty food", "palatable
even to non-veggies", maintains the popularity of this smart,
if rather "bland", Broadgate bar/restaurant. / L only; closed Sat
& Sun; no smoking except bkfast.*

Futures EC3 £ 9 ❷❸ –
8 Botolph Alley 623 4529 9–3C
*"Everything veggie food should be"; this City take-away near
the Monument is, for our money, a much greater attraction
than its eat-in sibling. / L only; closed Sat & Sun; no credit cards;
no smoking; no booking.*

Gabriel W1 £ 32 ❸④④
9 Golden Sq 439 2424 3–2D
*Though its modern British cooking scores creditably, this
ambitious Soho newcomer "has not settled in"; the would-be
'with it' décor is, in fact, "strangely reminiscent of the lobby
of a firm of international accountants", and service,
if "friendly", is "amateurish". / 11.30 pm; closed Sat L & Sun.*

Galicia W10 £ 24 ❸④❸
323 Portobello Rd 0181-969 3539 6–1A
*"Service is brusque-to-rude", but that "is all part of the
atmosphere" at this long-established North Kensington tapas
bar/restaurant – "just like the real thing". / 11 pm; closed Mon;
smart casual; set weekday L £10(FP), Sun L £11(FP).*

Garden Café WC1   £ 12   ❸❸❸

32 Museum St   637 4309   2–1C
*"Civilised", if sometimes "tourist-ridden",
American/continental pâtisserie, near the British Museum,
whose "relaxing" top-lit rear room makes a pleasant place for
breakfast or a light lunch.* / L only; closed Sat & Sun; no smoking area;
no booking.

Garlic & Shots W1   £ 27   ④❸④

14 Frith St   734 9505   4–2A
*"Seriously weird in feel and clientèle", this Soho shooters'
bar/restaurant serves a "hearty, rich and very '70s" menu, all
laced with garlic, which – amazingly – not everyone finds
"revolting".* / 11.15 pm, Fri & Sat 12.15 am; D only; no Amex; no booking.

Gastro SW4   £ 21   ❷❸❷

67 Venn St   627 0222   10–2D
*"Hardly any English is spoken" at this "lively, friendly" and
"unpretentious" all-day Gallic café, opposite the Clapham
Picture House; the fare (including "excellent coffee and
pastries") is "wholesome" and "authentic".* / Midnight;
no credit cards; no smoking area.

The Gasworks SW6   £ 26   ⑤❸❷

87 Waterford Rd   736 3830   5–4A
*Real life, camp-horror Parson's Green experience, whose
weird, decadent style ("a great setting for a party") has
something of a cult following; we hope reports of impending
closure are just another twist in the plot.* / 11 pm; D only; closed
Mon & Sun; no credit cards.

The Gate W6   £ 24   ❶❷❸

51 Queen Caroline St   0181-748 6932   7–2C
*"Beautifully presented", "inventive", "tasty" and "imaginative"
fare makes this obscurely located Hammersmith destination
(off a churchyard) London's top veggie.* / 10.45 pm; closed Mon L,
Sat L & Sun.

El Gaucho SW3   £ 22   ❷④❸

Chelsea Farmers' Mkt, 125 Sydney St   376 8514   5–3C
*This "carnivorous BYO café" in Chelsea provides "possibly the
best place in London to eat steak al fresco"; "attitude has
come with success".* / 11 pm; no credit cards.

The Gaucho Grill W1   £31   ❷❸❷

19-25 Swallow St   734 4040   3–3D

*This "atmospheric" Mayfair basement, with its "amazing
décor" and "zebra upholstery", is now a pretty consistent
performer, providing "excellent Argentinean steak" and
"good New World wines"; a Hampstead branch is coming
soon.* / Midnight, Sun 10.30 pm.

LE GAVROCHE W1   £85   ❷❷❸

43 Upper Brook St   408 0881   3–2A

*Mayfair's "highly polished" haute cuisine warhorse is –
under Roux Jr – producing some "superb, but expensive"
cooking; praise for the "totally pampering" service remains
high, too, but the passé basement setting – to some,
a "flock nightmare" – is coming in for ever more flak.*
/ 11 pm; closed Sat & Sun; jacket & tie; set weekday L £40(FP).

Gay Hussar W1   £32   ❸❷❶

2 Greek St   437 0973   4–2A

*This famous "romantic" and "cosy" Soho trooper –
a "London Institution" – is a favourite for those "with old
fashioned values"; the "filling" Hungarian fare – though still
"not as good as it was" – is on the up.* / 10.45 pm; closed Sun;
smart casual.

Geale's W8   £20   ❷④⑤

2 Farmer St   727 7969   6–2B

*"Good old-fashioned fish and chips" have been sold since the
war at this large and well-known chippy, off Notting Hill Gate;
the ambience is "not cheerful", however, and service can be
"amateurish".* / 11 pm; closed Mon & Sun; no booking.

Gecko NW1   £23   ④❸❸

7-9 Pratt St   424 0203   8–3C

*Large, "love-it-or-hate-it" new Camden Town noodles and
more bar; it's "reasonably priced", but some say "the food
sounds better than it looks or tastes".* / 11 pm; closed Sun; no Amex.

Geeta NW6   £14   ❷❸⑤

59 Willesden Ln   624 1713   1–1B

*"Fine Indian café grub" – all vegetarian – is to be had at this
unlovely Kilburn fixture.* / 10.30 pm, Fri & Sat 11.30 pm; no Switch.

George & Vulture EC3   £27   ④❷❸

3 Castle Ct   626 9710   9–3C

*Traditional City types like this "unchanged" Dickensian
chop-house, but for its "fun" atmosphere and "sympathetic"
service rather than the "school dinners" fodder.* / L only;
closed Sat & Sun; no Switch; jacket & tie; limited booking.

F S A

Ghillies £ 27 ❸❸❸

271 New King's Rd, SW6   371 0434   10–1B
20 Bellevue Rd, SW17   0181-767 1858   10–2C
*Now a chain (what was Hoults in Wandsworth having been
added to the Parson's Green original), these "loud and busy",
"easy and relaxing" diners serve a "tasty" seafood menu.
/ 10.45 pm.*

Gilbert's SW7 £ 24 ⑤❸⑤

2 Exhibition Rd   589 8947   5–2C
*This well-established South Kensington treasure has
"completely lost its way" under new ownership – to keep the
old name when the formula is now so much inferior is just to
invite irritation and disappointment. / 10.30 pm; closed Mon
& Sun D; no Amex.*

Gladwins EC3 £ 49 ❸❷❸

Minster Ct, Mark Ln   444 0004   9–3D
*A superior City lunch venue on account of "better than
average" modern British fare and "good" service; the bright
basement setting is spacious, if a touch "bland". / L only;
closed Sat & Sun.*

Glaisters £ 25 ④⑤❸

4 Hollywood Rd, SW10   352 0352   5–3B
8-10 Northcote Rd, SW11   924 6699   10–2C
*"Inexpensive and romantic" though these Chelsea and
Clapham bistros may be, the food is "formulaic" and
"mediocre", and service can be "very slow and stroppy".
/ 11.30 pm.*

Golden Dragon W1 £ 21 ❶④④

28-29 Gerrard St   734 2763   4–3A
*This large Chinatown two-year-old is carving out quite a
reputation for its dim sum and for "the seasonal dishes
written only in Chinese". / 11.30 pm, Fri & Sat midnight.*

Good Earth SW3 £ 31 ❷❷❸

233 Brompton Rd   584 3658   5–2C
*"Not cheap, but dependable" Knightsbridge Chinese,
offering "fresh, clean tastes", "very good service" and a
pleasant atmosphere. / 11 pm.*

Goolies W8 £ 29 ❷❷❸

21 Abingdon Rd   938 1122   5–1A
*Locals swear by this bright, "fun", reasonably priced modern
British newcomer, just off Kensington High Street,
"which rarely disappoints". / 10.30 pm; closed Sat L & Sun.*

Gopal's of Soho W1   £ 25   ❶④❸

12 Bateman St   434 1621   4–2A

"Reliably excellent, classic dishes" are winning much improved
support for this *"smart"*, traditional Soho Indian; *"arrogant"*
service can let the side down. / 11.15 pm; smart casual;
no smoking area.

Gordon's Wine Bar WC2   £ 14   ④❷❶

47 Villiers St   930 1408   4–4D

"Decrepit" wine bar, near Embankment tube, adored for
its *"unforgettable atmosphere"*, reasonably priced wine and
simple but enjoyable food; for romance, *"the far corners of
the cellar are rewardingly dark and secluded"*. / 9.30 pm;
closed Sat L & Sun; no Amex; no booking.

Le Gothique SW18   £ 32   ❸❸❸

The Royal Victoria Patriotic Bldg, Fitzhugh Gr, Trinity Rd
0181-870 6567   10–2C

The *"perfect romantic setting"* of an extraordinary overblown
Victorian building in Wandsworth – *"particularly in the
cloister-garden during summer"* – ensures a devoted local
following for this Gallic spot. / 10.30 pm; closed Sat L & Sun.

Gourmet Pizza Company   £ 20   ❸④❸

7-8 Swallow St, W1   734 5182   3–3D
Gabriels Whf, Upper Ground, SE1   928 3188   9–3A
18 Mackenzie Walk, E14   345 9192   1–3D

*"They could beat PizzaExpress if they packaged themselves
better"*, says one of the many fans of this small chain's
"excellent pizzas and imaginative toppings"; *"for ambience,
Gabriel's Wharf is best"*, thanks to its *"great river views"*.
/ 10.45 pm; W1 & E14 no smoking area; need 8+ to book.

Gow's EC2   £ 37   ❸❸④

81/82 Old Broad St   920 9645   9–2C

This *"fine fish restaurant"* may be a *"City stalwart"*, but its
"crowded basement setting" limits its appeal. / L only; closed Sat
& Sun; smart casual.

Granita N1   £ 31   ❷❸④

127 Upper St   226 3222   8–2D

"Consistently imaginative" modern British cooking continues
to make this the *"perfect local"* for many Islingtonians;
it leaves some cold, though, thanks to *"small portions"*, the
"stark" setting and the *"sometimes slow or off-hand service"*.
/ 10.30 pm; closed Mon & Tue L; no Amex & no Switch.

Great Nepalese NW1 £ 23 ❷❸⑤
48 Eversholt St   388 6737   8–3C
*Though it's praised highly as "a genuine Indian restaurant
with unusual Nepali dishes", this inconspicuous ethnic by
Euston Station "will never win any awards for décor".
/ 11.30 pm.*

Greek Valley NW8 £ 20 ❸❸④
130 Boundary Rd   624 3217   8–3A
*"Prices are reasonable" at this "friendly" St John's Wood
taverna; it's "cramped", though, and "some times are better
than others". / Midnight; D only; closed Sun; no Amex.*

The Green Olive W9 £ 30 ❸❸❸
5 Warwick Pl   289 2469   8–4A
*A "great neighbourhood restaurant", say aficionados of this
modern Italian, just behind Little Venice's Clifton Nurseries,
who commend the "reliable" and "delicious" cooking; it's on
the pricey side, though. / 10.45 pm; D only Mon-Sat, Sun open L & D.*

Green's SW1 £ 45 ❸❷❸
36 Duke St   930 4566   3–3D
*"Traditional", "discreet", and "very British", this "club-like"
St James's bastion makes "a marvellous spot for lunch and a
glass of champers"; it's a bit "dull", though, and unsurprisingly
"expensive". / 11 pm; closed Sun D, but May-Sep closed Sun; smart casual.*

Greenhouse W1 £ 43 ❸❷❸
27a Hays Mews   499 3331   3–3B
*Many still approve the "dependable" modern British cooking
at this romantic Mayfair dining room; we, however, agree
with those who say that "it's a disaster since Rhodes left",
now offering "provincial 4-star hotel" fare in an irritatingly
overcrowded environment. / 11 pm; closed Sat L; smart casual.*

Grenadier SW1 £ 34 ⑤❸❶
18 Wilton Rw   235 3074   2–3A
*"A good place to take Americans", this mega-cute Belgravia
mews pub has an "overpriced" Brit-theme restaurant, but you
"can't beat their sausages at the bar", and the Bloody Marys
are also rightly celebrated. / 9.45 pm; no Switch.*

Gresslin's NW3 £ 31 ❷❸⑤
13 Heath St   794 8386   8–2A
*It's a shame that this central Hampstead yearling's "cold",
"stark" setting "lacks ambience", as it discourages the
following that the "creative", "very high standard" modern
British cooking – by far the best in the area – deserves.
/ 10.45 pm; closed Mon L & Sun D; no Amex; no smoking area;
set weekday L £19(FP).*

Grill St Quentin SW3 £31 ④④④
3 Yeoman's Rw   581 8377   5–2C
*Some still like this "authentic" Gallic brasserie in a large
and "noisy" Knightsbridge basement; sliding ratings for food
and service, however, show that new owners, Groupe Chez
Gérard, are working their special magic. / 11.30 pm; smart casual.*

Grissini SW1 £35 ❸❷❸
Hyatt Carlton Tower, Cadogan Place   858 7171   2–4A
*The Carlton Tower's new modern Italian restaurant boasts a
"graceful" setting (with views over Cadogan Gardens), notably
"warm and genuine" service and interesting cooking of a high
standard; bills can mount, though. / 10.15 pm; closed Sat L & Sun;
no smoking area.*

Grumbles SW1 £27 ④❸❸
35 Churton St   834 0149   2–4B
*"Very dated", candlelit English bistro in Pimlico which is
always packed, despite being very "pricey" for what it is.
/ 11.45 pm.*

The Guinea W1 £44 ❸❸④
30 Bruton Pl   499 1210   3–2B
*"Great steaks" and "excellent steak and kidney pies" win a
fair following for this cosily dated Mayfair pub dining room,
though some sneer that it's "expensive for an upmarket
Beefeater". / 11 pm; closed Sat L & Sun.*

Gung-Ho NW6 £25 ❷❷❷
330-332 West End Ln   794 1444   1–1B
*"Excellently prepared and unusual dishes", "very good
service" and attractive, "modern" décor make this
West Hampstead Chinese a good all-rounder, and very
popular locally. / 11.30 pm.*

Häagen-Dazs £ 6 ❸④④
14 Leicester Sq, WC2   287 9577   4–3B
Unit 6, Covent Gdn, WC2   240 0436   4–3D
83 Gloucester Rd, SW7   373 9988   5–2B
88 Queensway, W2   229 0668   6–1C
75 Hampstead High St, NW3   431 1430   8–2A
*"Nice ice cream but a bit pricey", say fans of these sinful
standbys; hard-nosed cynics deride "a very average chain,
turbo-charged by ferocious advertising". / 11.45 pm-12.45 am;
no credit cards at many branches; all but SW10 no smoking; no booking.*

Haandi NW1   £19   ❸❸④

161 Drummond St   383 4557   8–4C
*"Not the best atmosphere or service, but the food is great",
say fans of this 'Little India' establishment, where the buffet
lunch is the top attraction.* / 11.30 pm, Sat & Sun midnight;
closed Sat L; no Switch; set weekday L £10(FP).

Halcyon Hotel W11   £51   ❷❸❷

129 Holland Pk Ave   221 5411   6–2B
*Many swoon over this discreet Holland Park villa-hotel's
"wonderfully chic" and "romantic" air – especially the "nice
outdoor dining in summer" – and hail "great" modern British
cooking; we're with those who find "no warmth" in the
basement setting, and wonder if the package is not a little
"overpriced".* / 10.30 pm, Fri & Sat 11 pm; closed Sat L; smart casual.

Halepi W2   £26   ❸❷④

18 Leinster Ter   262 1070   6–2C
*Just north of Hyde Park, this "very friendly Greek restaurant –
with great seafood and good retsina" – is "cheerful", but
"crowded" and "expensive".* / 12.30 am; no Switch.

The Halkin SW1   £55   ❸❸❸

5 Halkin St   333 1234   2–3A
*"A jewel, sparkling and expensive", say fans of the "exquisite
Italian style" – culinary and decorative – of this Belgravia
hotel's "impressive" dining room; it's "so cool it's cold",
say detractors, who complain of "unbelievable money for
contrived food".* / 10.45 pm; closed Sat L & Sun L; smart casual; set
weekday L £34(FP).

Hamine W1   £16   ❸④④

84 Brewer St   439 0785   3–2D
*Cheap and cheerful "quality noodle joint" which makes a
useful Soho standby – particularly after midnight.* / 2.30 am, Sat
1.30 am, Sun midnight; no credit cards; no booking.

Hanover Square W1   £29   ❸❸④

25 Hanover Sq   408 0935   3–2C
*"It's not quite the Cork and Bottle" (its better-known sibling),
but this Mayfair basement wine bar offers "good food and
value, and a superb choice of wine".* / 10.45 pm; closed Sat & Sun;
smart casual; no smoking area.

Harbour City W1   £26   ❷④⑤

46 Gerrard St   439 7859   4–3B
*"Varied, fresh, interesting" dim sum is the highlight at this
"tacky" Chinatown establishment.* / 11.15 pm, Fri & Sat 11.45 pm.

Hard Rock Café W1   £ 26   ③②①

150 Old Park Ln   629 0382   3–4B
"The oldest of the theme places, but still the most fun"
("providing you don't value your eardrums"), this Mayfair
fixture deserves its permanent queue and proves that such
venues don't have to rip you off. / 12.30 am, Fri & Sat 1 am;
no Switch; no smoking area.

Hardy's W1   £ 29   ③③③

53 Dorset St   935 5929   2–1A
"A fine and welcoming place", this "crowded but no hassle"
Marylebone wine bar offers "good traditional food (such as
proper fishcakes) and well chosen wines, mainly New World".
/ 10.30 pm; closed Sat & Sun.

The Havelock Tavern W14   £ 24   ②⑤③

57 Masbro Rd   603 5374   7–1C
"All the rage in W14", this Olympia gastropub offers
"yummy", "trad/mod Brit fare"; it gets "too crowded", and
service, though "friendly", can be very slow. / 10 pm, Sun 9.30 pm;
no credit cards; no booking.

Haweli SW13   £ 21   ②③④

7 White Hart Ln   0181-876 4441   10–1A
Indian food "worth travelling for" is the attraction of this
"friendly", if "worn", Barnes curry house. / Midnight.

Helter Skelter SW9   £ 23   ③⑤④

50 Atlantic Rd   274 8600   10–2D
Low on creature comforts it may be, but this colourful Brixton
café is "anxious to please" and high on youthful zest; modest
prices make it easy to overcome any quibbles with the
"interesting world cooking" – don't despair, it does come,
eventually. / 11 pm, Fri & Sat 11.30 pm; D only; no Amex.

Henry J Beans SW3   £ 20   ④③③

195 King's Rd   352 9255   5–3C
The "great outdoor area" is the special attraction of this
"loud, fun" dated Chelsea fixture, rather than the
"relatively cheap American food". / 10.30 pm; no booking.

Hilaire SW7   £ 48   ②②③

68 Old Brompton Rd   584 8993   5–2B
"Going strong" – this South Kensington establishment offers
"accomplished" cooking from an "inviting" modern French
menu; some do find the smart, but "cramped", setting
"romantic", but we're with those who find it rather like
"an Eastbourne hotel". / 11.30 pm; closed Sat L & Sun.

Hodgson's WC2   £ 32   ④④❸
115 Chancery Ln   242 2836   2–2D
Some think these unusual sky-lit, pillared premises, near
Fleet Street, a "stunning" location for a business lunch,
although the modern British cooking is "up and down";
the inexpensive cellar wine bar is a useful place in its
own right. / 10 pm; closed Sat & Sun.

Hope & Sir Loin EC1   £ 30   ❷❷④
94 Cowcross St   253 8525   9–1B
"Impeccably cooked breakfasts" and "the best fillet steak
money can buy" are the attractions of this "pricy", but
"always good quality", Smithfield pub grill room; "you usually
need a reservation". / L only; closed Sat & Sun; smart casual.

Hornimans SW4   £ 21   ❸④❸
69 Clapham Common S'side   0181-673 9162   10–2D
"Very friendly and very reasonable Clapham Common local";
the set menus are "good value", but service "can be hit
and miss". / 11 pm; no Amex.

Hothouse Bar & Grill E1   £ 25   ④④④
78/80 Wapping Ln   488 4797   1–3D
This converted Wapping warehouse may offer "the only
decent food in the area", but its initially promising modern
British cooking has rather "lost its way"; some say it's a
"beautiful" space, but it "lacks atmosphere when empty".
/ 11 pm; closed Sat L & Sun D.

House on Rosslyn Hill NW3   £ 31   ④④❷
34a Rosslyn Hl   435 8037   8–2A
This "fun and young" Hampstead scene may be "too busy
and with tables too close together" but it's "still the best
venue for Sunday papers", and still the place to be if you
want to hang out with the local in-crowd. / Midnight; no Amex.

Hujo's W1   £ 24   ❸❶❷
11 Berwick St   734 5144   3–2D
This "few frills" bistro, in the sleazier part of Soho, offers a
laudable combination of "unusual", "good value" modern
British cooking, "buzzy atmosphere" and "very friendly staff
and clientèle". / Midnight; closed Sun.

Hunan SW1   £ 27   ❶❷④
51 Pimlico Rd   730 5712   5–2D
"Very interesting, very spicy" cooking, with a real "spark", is
served by an "enthusiastic" owner and his "professional" staff
at this "dated" but "delightful" Chinese near Pimlico Green.
/ 11.15 pm; closed Sun L; no Switch.

Hyde Park Hotel
Park Room SW1   £ 17   ❸❷❷

Knightsbridge   235 2000   2–3A

This grand hotel dining room, with its "big picture window overlooking Hyde Park" is especially recommended for "power breakfasts" (to which the price shown relates); otherwise it's "very pricey for standard food". / 11 pm; eve, jacket & tie.

I Thai W2   £ 68   ④④④

31-35 Craven Hill Gdns   298 9001   6–2C

Lady Weinberg's new Bayswater hotel's ultra-minimalist dining room "pushes self-conscious design into the realms of parody"; some do find the Italian/oriental dishes "beautiful, like the waiters" – "incredibly light" and "interesting" – but, for the majority, this is just a "characterless" and "pretentious" place, charging "silly" prices. / 11 pm.

Ikkyu   £ 25   ❶④❸

67 Tottenham Ct Rd, W1   636 9280   2–1C
7 Newport Pl, WC2   439 3554   4–3B

You get "real Japanese food at sensible prices" (including "very fresh" sushi) at the "authentically dingy" Nipponese basement-original, by Goodge Street tube (though "staff are sometimes quite rude"); its lesser-known, Chinatown offshoot offers the same formula in a brighter setting. / 10.30 pm, WC2 Fri & Sat 11.30 pm; W1, closed Sat & Sun L; W1 no Switch, WC2 no Amex; WC2 no smoking area; set weekday L £15(FP).

Imperial City EC3   £ 33   ❷❷❷

Cornhill   626 3437   9–2C

A "top City venue to entertain clients" and "good value, for where it is", too – "authentic Chinese food" is served in the "interesting surroundings" of the cellar of the Royal Exchange. / 8.30 pm; closed Sat & Sun; smart casual.

Inaho W2   £ 27   ❶④❸

4 Hereford Rd   221 8495   6–1B

This "tiny" Bayswater café has a justified reputation for "great, affordable Japanese food"; service can be "very slow" though, and "it would help if someone spoke English". / 11 pm; closed Sat L & Sun; no Amex & no Switch; set weekday L £14(FP).

L'Incontro SW1   £ 52   ④⑤⑤

87 Pimlico Rd   730 6327   5–2D

Reporters "can't really understand why anyone goes" to this "overrated" and "ridiculously expensive" Pimlico Italian, which numbers sometimes "rude" service amongst its many drawbacks; neither can we, though some tip lunch as "excellent" value. / 11.30 pm; closed Sat L & Sun L; smart casual.

F S A

India Club WC2   £19   ❷❷④
143 Strand   836 0650   2–2D
*Though the setting is "reminiscent of a school hall" this
Aldwych institution's "outstanding food" – good curries and
the "best dosas in town" – has a devoted following; "BYO –
the hotel bar is not to be recommended!"* / 10 pm; closed Sun;
no credit cards; need 6 to book.

Indian Ocean SW17   £21   ❷❷④
216 Trinity Rd   0181-672 7740   10–2C
*"Cheap" and comfortable Wandsworth Indian, that's superior
of its type.* / 11.30 pm.

Inmala EC2   £32   ❸❸④
9 Liverpool Arc   623 5750   9–2D
*Useful, if tacky, standby near Liverpool Street, offering "steady
and interesting" Malaysian cooking.* / 10 pm; closed Sat & Sun.

Interlude W1   £56   ❸❸④
5 Charlotte St   637 0222   2–1C
*Despite the departure of M Chavot, this "grownup" Fitzrovia
establishment continues, on the evidence of a September '97
visit, to offer accomplished cuisine and attentive, "very
French" service; it is "expensive", though, and its "soulless",
banqueting suite-style décor largely limits its appeal to
business.* / 10.45 pm; closed Sat L & Sun; set weekday L £23(FP).

Isfehan W2   £23   ❸❷❸
3-4 Bouverie Pl   460 1030   6–1D
*Old-school Paddington Persian, whose jolly "traditional" setting
(buoyed by "lively music") and well prepared grub make it a
good choice in a thin area; there's a bargain lunchtime buffet.*
/ Midnight; set weekday L £14(FP).

Italian Kitchen   £27   ❸❷❷
43 New Oxford St, WC1   836 1011   2–1C
17-21 Tavistock St, WC2   379 9696   4–3D
*"Wholesome", "rustic" cooking is making quite a success
of these "cramped" and "unpretentious" Bloomsbury and
Covent Garden establishments; for top value, "stick to the set
menus".* / WC1 11 pm, WC2 Midnight; WC1 Fri & Sat restricted booking,
WC2 no booking.

THE IVY WC2　　　　　　　　£ 42　　❷❶❶

1 West St　836 4751　4–3B

*"Just everything a restaurant should be" – reporters go
glassy-eyed about this panelled Theatreland classic; it's not
just that it's "the definitive place for star-gazers" (though
that helps) – the British menu, if "not revolutionary",
is "wonderfully executed", and service is "charming,
without being too formal". / Midnight; set Sat & Sun L £23(FP).*

Iznik N5　　　　　　　　£ 19　　❷❷❶

19 Highbury Pk　354 5697　8–2D

*"Excellent Ottoman grub, presented with care and served
amid exotic oriental décor" wins unanimous local support for
this "Turkish family-run restaurant close to Arsenal FC";
the day-time fry-ups come highly recommended, too.
/ 11 pm; no credit cards.*

James R SW6　　　　　　　£ 25　　④④④

175 New King's Rd　731 6404　10–1B

*This Parson's Green local has serious aspirations but
"never quite seems to make it", despite constant acclaim in
some quarters as "a great neighbourhood spot". / 11 pm;
closed Sun D; no smoking area.*

Japanese Canteen EC1　　　£ 18　　④④⑤

394 St John St　833 3222　8–3D

*Some praise this budget Japanese near Angel as a "good,
quick, cheap" venue, though the food is rather "fake" and the
setting a touch uncomfortable. / 11 pm; closed Sun L; no credit cards;
no smoking area; to book need 6+.*

Jason's W9　　　　　　　　£ 37　　❶❸❸

Opposite 60 Blomfield Rd　286 6752　8–4A

*"Fantastic fish quality" and Mauritian cooking "with a punch"
makes this unpretentious café in Maida Vale one of the most
interesting seafood places in town; "in summer, book a canal-
side table". / 10.30 pm; closed Sun D.*

Jenny Lo's Teak House SW1　£ 15　　④❸④

14 Eccleston St　259 0399　2–4B

*"Cheap", "charming" snackery near Victoria Coach Station;
some like the "steaming, nutritious bowls of oriental fare",
but we sympathise with complaints of "no-taste English Asian
food". / 10 pm; closed Sun; no credit cards; no booking.*

Jim Thompson's SW6 £ 26 ④⑤❶

617 King's Rd   731 0999   5–4A

"Great atmosphere" makes this large Fulham oriental pub-conversion a *"good venue"* for a *"fun, lively time"*; service is *"very slow"*, though, and the South East Asian cooking is *"ordinary"* and *"expensive"*. / 11 pm.

Jimmy Beez W10 £ 37 ❸④❸

303 Portobello Rd   0181-964 9100   6–1A

"Very Portobello – a great place to chill out at the weekend", this *"funky"* diner is a top brunching hang-out with an eclectic menu realised well. / 11 pm.

Jindivick N1 £ 28 ❷❷❷

201 Liverpool Rd   607 7710   8–3D

Islington-fringe yearling which provides a *"good all round package"* combining an *"airy"* setting, *"tasty"* modern British cooking and *"attentive"* service; its out-of-the way location means it can be *"quiet"* but it *"deserves to be more popular"*, and brunch comes recommended. / 10.45 pm; closed Mon L & Sun D; no Amex; set weekday L & early eve £17(FP).

Joe Allen WC2 £ 31 ④❸❷

13 Exeter St   836 0651   4–3D

The *"exciting buzz"* is the chief asset of this well-known subterranean Covent Garden hang-out that's *"excellent for B-list star-spotting"*; fans praise the *"solid and dependable"* American fare (particularly the famous 'off-menu' burgers), but we're with those who say it's *"unexciting"*. / 12.45 am; no smoking area; set weekday L £19(FP).

Joe's Brasserie SW6 £ 28 ❸❸❸

130 Wandsworth Br Rd   731 7835   10–1B

"Very Fulham" bar-restaurant, liked by a younger crowd (particularly in groups) for its raucous atmosphere and reasonable modern British food. / 10.45 pm.

Joe's Café SW3 £ 38 ❸④❷

126 Draycott Ave   225 2217   5–2C

For the *"smart set"* of Brompton Cross, this *"reliable"* *"standby"* is perhaps best known as a brunch rendezvous; the *"good, relatively straightforward"* modern British fare is on the pricey side, and service can be *"slow"*. / 11 pm; closed Sun D.

Julie's W11 £40 ④❸❶
135 Portland Rd   229 8331   6–2A
*The "gorgeous brothel-esque setting" of this subterranean
Holland Park "old favourite" – "like stepping back to the
'70s" – maintains its ranking as a top romantic choice;
"the bill is always a shock", however, for such "so-so" cooking.*
/ 11.15 pm; closed Sat L; no Switch.

Julie's Bar W11 £29 ❸❸❶
137 Portland Rd   727 7985   6–2A
*The rambling seductive styling which makes its parent
restaurant so popular spills over into the neighbouring bar –
lower prices here mean "the quality of the food is less of a
problem"; a fave rave for afternoon tea.* / 10.45 pm; no Switch.

Justin de Blank W1 £25 ❸❷④
120-122 Marylebone Ln   486 5250   3–1A
*Sparse, characterless new Marylebone space brightened up
by "friendly and helpful" staff; some find the "very good",
simple modern British cooking one might hope for from this
well-known name – we're with those who found it "so-so".*
/ 10.30 pm; closed Sat & Sun.

Kalamaras, Mega W2 £25 ④❸❷
76-78 Inverness Mews   727 9122   6–2C
*It's "not quite what it once was" – the cooking is now
decidedly average – but this Bayswater taverna (tucked away
in a mews off Queensway) retains its "romantic" intimacy.*
/ Midnight; closed Sat L & Sun L; no Switch; smart casual.

Kalamaras, Micro W2 £19 ❸④④
66 Inverness Mews   727 5082   6–2C
*"Cosy", shabby little brother to next door 'Mega', where the
change of ownership has had a less negative impact on the
"cheap" nosh; BYO.* / 11 pm; D only; closed Sun; no Switch.

Kartouche SW10 £34 ④④❸
329-331 Fulham Rd   823 3515   5–3B
*"Sloppy standards all round" mar this "noisy", "always
packed", "oh so trendy" Chelsea hang-out; "fun" and
"buzzy", it may be, but a "boring" modern British menu
and too often "awful" service make it "a place to be seen,
not to eat".* / Midnight.

FSA

Kaspia W1   £44 ❷❷❸

18-18a Bruton Pl   493 2612   3–2B
*"The caviar is incredible", say the loyal regulars of this
Mayfair parlour (discreetly hidden in a mews), who laud the
"delicious short menu", the "spacious calm" of the setting,
and the "attentive and friendly" service; it's "overpriced",
"... but then caviar is expensive". / 11.30 pm; closed Sun; no Switch;
smart casual.*

Kastoori SW17   £16 ❶❶④

188 Upper Tooting Rd   0181-767 7027   10–2C
*"Wonderfully interesting South Indian-East African food"
offers a "taste explosion" at this "unbeatable", family-run
Tooting veggie – it's "worth the trip, from anywhere";
service is "attentive" and "knowledgeable". / 10.30 pm; closed
Mon L & Tue L; no Amex & no Switch.*

Kavanagh's N1   £28 ❸❷❷

26 Penton St   833 1380   8–3D
*"Fresh, bright décor", "charming service" and consistent
modern British cooking make this hospitable Islingtonian a
local favourite. / 10.30 pm; closed Mon & Tue L; no Amex.*

Ken Lo's Memories SW1   £40 ❷❷④

67-69 Ebury St   730 7734   2–4B
*"The guru's memory lives on" at this quality Pimlico Chinese,
where "superb" cooking with "distinctive flavours" make for a
real "culinary experience"; the setting, "simple and quiet" to
some, is merely "stale" to others. / 10.15 pm; closed Sun L;
smart casual.*

Ken Lo's Memories of China W8   £36 ④❸④

353 Kensington High St   603 6951   7–1D
*Ken Lo's undercharged new Kensington sibling (on the site
of Al Gallo Doro, RIP) is "not a patch on Ebury Street",
and "way overpriced". / 11.15 pm; closed Sun L; no smoking area.*

KENSINGTON PLACE W8   £39 ❷❸❷

201-205 Kensington Ch St   727 3184   6–2B
*"The din is deafening" at this "vibrant" modern British
brasserie near Notting Hill Gate – a perennial smart crowd
favourite; some (ourselves included) gripe of "bland" cooking
that's "resting on its laurels", but, for its many loyalists,
"sheer reliability" and "Al atmosphere" carry the day.
/ 11.45 pm, Sun 10.15 pm; set weekday L £23(FP), Sun L £25(FP).*

Kettners W1   £21   ④④❷
29 Romilly St   437 6437   4–2A
*"Great building – dull food, dull service" is the depressing
verdict on this Soho landmark, which trades on the "faded
grandeur" of its magnificent Edwardian premises rather than
the quality of its pizzas-and-more menu; the upstairs rooms
remain useful for a large budget West End get-together.*
/ Midnight; smart casual; no booking.

Khan's W2   £16   ❸⑤❸
13-15 Westbourne Grove   727 5420   6–1C
*There's "no chance of a leisurely dinner" at this "manic"
Bayswater Indian, but it's certainly "cheap", and most find
that the "stressful" nature of a visit – complete with
"abusive staff" – is all part of the "fun". / 11.45 pm.*

Khan's of Kensington SW7   £22   ❷❸④
3 Harrington Rd   581 2900   5–2B
*"Excellent value" South Kensington Indian whose "good
variety" of "delicate" dishes continues to make it a
"favourite"; service can be "off", though, and the ambience
is nothing to write home about. / 11.15 pm, Fri & Sat 11.45 pm.*

Khun Akorn SW3   £36   ④④④
136 Brompton Rd   225 2688   5–1C
*"Quality food and presentation" have never in our view
compensated for the ambitious prices of this thinly
commented-on Knightsbridge Thai. / 10.30 pm; closed Sun L.*

Khyber Pass SW7   £19   ❸❸④
21 Bute St   589 7311   5–2B
*"Who cares about the décor?", say fans of the "inexpensive"
quality curries at this long-established, tatty South Kensington
Indian. / 11.30 pm; no Switch; set weekday L £11(FP).*

King's Road Café SW3   £19   ④❷④
206 King's Rd   351 6645   5–3C
*"Good, friendly service" and "reasonably priced" light
Mediterranean dishes, coffee and cakes make Habitat's
first-floor café a good refuge for Chelsea shoppers. / open shop
hours only, with L till 5 pm; no Amex; no smoking area.*

Kolossi Grill EC1   £18   ❷❷❸
56-60 Roseberry Ave   278 5758   8–4D
*"Excellent Greek family-run establishment" in Clerkenwell,
especially popular for its top-value set lunches. / 11 pm;
closed Sat L & Sun; no Switch.*

Krungtap SW10   £ 18   ❸❸❸
227 Old Brompton Rd   259 2314   5–2A
"Cheap and reliable" Earl's Court Thai – "rather tatty
surroundings, but good food and very reasonable". / 10.30 pm;
D only; no Amex.

The Ladbroke Arms W11   £ 21   ❸❸❸
54 Ladbroke Rd   727 6648   6–2B
"If you can get a seat" this "laid back", leafily located pub,
off Notting Hill Gate, provides "yummy", "inventive" grub
(especially the "fabulous sausages"); it's not, however, as
good as it was. / 9.45 pm; no Amex; no booking.

Lahore Kebab House E1   £ 15   ❷⑤⑤
2 Umberston St   488 2551   1–2D
Famous East End canteen offering "food at its most basic" –
if you like "authentic rather than nice", its "excellent cheap
curries and kebabs" are for you; BYO. / 1.30 am; no credit cards.

The Landmark Hotel NW1   £ 47   ❸④❷
222 Marylebone Rd   631 8000   8–4A
Bored with London? – head for the soaring atrium of this
Marylebone hotel which might as well be in Singapore or
Los Angeles; the 'Winter Garden' offers pleasant but "pricey"
all-day dining in "relaxing", "airy" comfort. / 10 pm; closed Sat L
& Sun D; smart casual; no smoking area.

The Lanesborough W1   £ 45   ④❷❶
Hyde Pk Corner   259 5599   2–3A
"Very good value dinner dances", "excellent afternoon teas",
"fantastic English breakfasts" – it is the various set 'deals'
which commend the OTT conservatory dining room of this
hyper-luxurious landmark hotel to reporters; those who lunch
or dine à la carte may find "exorbitant" prices for lacklustre
modern British cooking (though veggies are well catered for).
/ Midnight; no Switch; smart casual.

Langan's Bistro W1   £ 29   ④❸④
26 Devonshire St   935 4531   2–1A
Some feel Marylebone's intimate, parasol-lined sibling of
Langan's Brasserie to be a "reliable" bistro standby; it's
never going to set the world on fire though, and some find
it "disappointing". / 11.30 pm; closed Sat L & Sun.

F S A

Langan's Brasserie W1   £36   ④❷❶
Stratton St   493 6437   3–3C
*This famously "buzzing", grand Mayfair brasserie – "a place
to see and be seen" – is still "relying on past glories", and still
attracts more than its share of out-of-towners; that said, in
the face of competition from all the new mega-brasseries, the
cooking here is at last showing signs of recovery, and service is
now "slick and friendly". / 11.45 pm, Sat 12.45 am; closed Sat L & Sun.*

Lansdowne NW1   £23   ❸⑤❷
90 Gloucester Ave   483 0409   8–3B
*"Consistently good", "hearty" food at reasonable prices
ensures this trendy Primrose Hill super-pub is "always
packed"; under pressure, the service can appear
"contemptuous". / 10 pm; closed Mon L; no Amex; book Sun L only.*

Latymers W6   £19   ❷❸⑤
157 Hammersmith Rd   0181-741 2507   7–2C
*Ignore the "gin palace" look, say fans of this Hammersmith
pub – the "reliable", "very good" Thai food is "well worth the
smoke and wait". / 10 pm; closed Sun; no Switch; no booking at lunch.*

Launceston Place W8   £40   ❷❷❶
1a Launceston Pl   937 6912   5–1B
*"Gracious but unintimidating", this "romantic" Kensington
townhouse received rapturous recommendations this year;
the "unhurried" drawing room atmosphere combines with
"very discreet service" and "distinguished", "simple" modern
British cooking to produce an "excellent all rounder".
/ 11.30 pm; closed Sat L & Sun D.*

Laurent NW2   £21   ❶❷⑤
428 Finchley Rd   794 3603   1–1B
*The "best cous-cous outside of Morocco" makes it "worth the
trip" to this "excellent" family-run Cricklewood café; so what
if it's "not comfortable"? / 11 pm; closed Sun; no Switch.*

The Lavender SW11   £22   ❸④❷
171 Lavender Hill   978 5242   10–2C
*"Good for chilling out", this "bustling" Battersea local offers a
"limited", but "interesting and varied" modern British menu.
/ 11 pm, Sat 11.30 pm.*

Leadenhall Tapas Bar EC3   £19   ④❸❸
27 Leadenhall Mkt   623 1818   9–2D
*A "pleasant outlook", from under the eaves of Leadenhall
Market, helps make this "relaxed" un-Citified bar an
agreeable rendezvous. / 9 pm; closed Sat & Sun; need 6+ to book.*

Legend of India SW10   £ 22   ❸❷❸
430a King's Rd   376 8969   5–3B
*Soothingly decorated basement Indian, at World's End,
whose competent standards and reasonable prices make it
useful in a pricey part of town. / 11 pm; no smoking area.*

Leith's W11   £ 54   ④❸❸
92 Kensington Pk Rd   229 4481   6–2B
*Opinions are more mixed than ever about this long-
established modern Briton, which occupies an impressive
Notting Hill townhouse; some do rate the cooking as
"supremely accomplished", but those who are irritated by
"obsequious" service and who find the place "overpriced
and utterly pretentious" are becoming ever more voluble.
/ 11.30 pm; closed Mon L, Sat L & Sun; closed Sat L & Sun; set weekday L
£35(FP).*

Leith's at the Institute EC2   £ 34   ④⑤④
Moorgate Pl   920 8626   9–2C
*With its "well spaced tables", this "sanitised" City basement
makes "a good business lunch venue"; the modern British
cooking is mixed, though, and service can be "very slow".
/ L only; closed Sat & Sun.*

Lemonia NW1   £ 24   ❸❷❷
89 Regent's Pk Rd   586 7454   8–3B
*"All-year-round holiday atmosphere" and "fab", "friendly"
staff ensure this phenomenal Primrose Hill mega-taverna is
"always buzzing"- "be sure to book"; the "solid Greek" nosh
is "variable", though, and some fear the place risks being
"a victim of its own success". / 11.30 pm; closed Sat L & Sun D;
no Amex; set weekday L £14(FP).*

Leonardo's SW10   £ 27   ❷❷❸
397 King's Rd   352 4146   5–3B
*It "may look faded and very '70s", but many find this
"welcoming" World's End trattoria "surprisingly good";
it offers "quality cooking", with fish dishes especially
recommended. / 11.45 pm; closed Sun D.*

The Lexington W1   £ 29   ❸❷❸
Lexington St   434 3401   3–2D
*A slightly "odd atmosphere" – not helped by railway-carriage
proportions – does little to put off followers of this "intimate"
Soho spot; the modern British grub has its moments, and the
evening prix-fixe, in particular, is "excellent value". / 11 pm;
closed Sat L & Sun.*

Lindsay House W1
21 Romilly St   439 0450   4–3A
Irishman Richard Corrigan – one of the leading exponents of
truly British cooking – is, from October '97, taking over the
stove at this Soho townhouse; what used to be the place's
main selling point – its olde worlde look – is being pitched out
in favour of something more contemporary; this is one to
watch. / *Midnight, Sun 10 pm; no Switch; smart casual.*

Lisboa Patisserie W10   **£ 5**   ❶❸❸
57 Golborne Rd   0181-968 5242   6–1A
"Magnificent pasteis de nata" (custard tarts to you and me) –
"just like in Lisbon" – plus "great coffee" and a cast of "local
characters" project the fame of this "fab" pâtisserie far
beyond North Kensington. / *8 pm; no credit cards; no booking.*

Little Bay   **£ 12**   ④④❸
147 Lupus St, SW1   834 9075   5–3D
228 Belsize Rd, NW6   372 4699   1–2B
"Tolerable budget fare" served "in a mildly chaotic way"
makes these "basic" "shoestring efforts" popular with the
impecunious; Pimlico's former super-budget bistro, Brahms,
has taken on the branding of the Kilburn original. / *11.45 pm;*
no credit cards.

Little Italy W1   **£ 28**   ④❷❸
21 Frith St   734 4737   4–2A
This tightly-packed and "lively" Soho Italian yearling started
off so well, and some still say it's a "super late eatery"
offering "good fun and value"; ratings, though, are sliding,
thanks to complaints of "boring" and "overpriced" food.
/ *4 am, Sun midnight.*

LIVEBAIT SE1   **£ 34**   ❶❷④
43 The Cut   928 7211   9–4A
"Fantastic" and "imaginative" seafood made this Waterloo
parlour this year's top choice for fish-eaters – be warned that
it's a "gutsy eating, smoking, drinking place", and some
"expect more comfort at the price"; the big question is "what
will happen under the new owners?" (Groupe Chez Gérard) –
we hope the answer is 'nothing', but the October '97 arrival
of a new Covent Garden sibling (21 Wellington St, WC2)
hardly augurs well. / *11.30 pm; closed Sun; no Amex.*

Lobster Pot SE11 £35 ❶❷❷
3 Kennington Ln 582 5556 1–3C
To come across a kitsch 'sunken galleon' in the wasteland surrounding Elephant & Castle is implausible enough; but to find that the place serves "wonderful", "imaginative seafood" and "ultra fresh" fish can make an encounter with this "cosy" family-run establishment seem little short of surreal. / 11 pm; closed Mon & Sun; smart casual; set weekday L £22(FP).

Lola's N1 £32 ❸❸④
359 Upper St 359 1932 8–3D
We agree with those who hail a "very auspicious" beginning for Juliet Peston's "quality" Islington newcomer (in the 'graveyard' site above the Antiques Market); others find the 'global eclectic' menu plain "odd", and the décor is not to all tastes. / 11 pm; closed Sun D.

The Lord Palmerston N19 £20 ❸❷❷
Dartmouth Park Hill 485 1578 8–1B
"Glad I don't live too close or I'd never cook", says one of the fans of the "cheap and tasty" modern British fare (and "good beer, too") on offer at this ultra-stripped-down Archway boozer. / 10 pm; closed Mon L; no Amex; no booking.

Los Remos W2 £21 ❸❸④
38a Southwick St 723 5056 6–1D
Fans say this no-frills Paddington basement serves "some of the best tapas in London", and it's certainly "consistent", if "a bit expensive"; the extensive wine list is also worth checking out – the upstairs restaurant less so. / Midnight; closed Sun; no Switch.

Lou Pescadou SW5 £36 ❷④❸
241 Old Brompton Rd 370 1057 5–3A
"Abrupt" service is still too often encountered at this traditional Gallic fish restaurant in Earl's Court; culinarily speaking, however, the place is now – after a very sticky patch – back on its old form, offering "delicious", if rather "expensive", cooking. / Midnight; set weekday L £18(FP).

Luc's Brasserie EC3 £33 ❸❸❸
17-22 Leadenhall Mkt 621 0666 9–2D
"Hustle and bustle" makes for better than average City atmosphere at this "cramped", "smoky" and "noisy" Gallic fixture – a "dependable oasis in Leadenhall market"; "basic food is well served, with good value wines". / L only; closed Sat & Sun; no Switch.

Luigi Malones SW7   **£ 22**   ④❷❷

73 Old Brompton Rd   584 4323   5–2B
*Some go a bundle on this "loud and lively" South Kensington
joint, whose younger crowd following hails "good portions" of
pizza and burgers to "soak up those wicked cocktails";
we're with those who say it's a "grim diner". / 11 pm.*

Luigi's WC2   **£ 40**   ④④④

15 Tavistock St   240 1789   4–3D
*It's not unanimous, but we agree with those who think this
long-established, grand, old-style Theatreland Italian – with its
"tired" cooking and "anonymous" service – "seems now to
have accepted its tourist-trap status". / 11.30 pm; closed Sun;
smart casual; set pre-th. £21 (FP).*

Luigi's Delicatessen SW10   **£ 11**   ❶④❸

359 Fulham Rd   351 7825   5–3B
*"Excellent Italian food at Burger King prices" makes this
chaotic but fun Chelsea canteen a popular "local lunch
haunt"; Eurotrash-wise, le tout Londres congregates here
on Saturdays. / 8 pm, Sat 6 pm; closed Sun; no credit cards; no booking.*

Luna Nuova WC2   **£ 25**   ④❸④

22 Short's Gdns   379 3336   4–2C
*The name has changed (from Sol e Luna), but the pizza
and more package remains the same at this Covent Garden
shopping mall café-restaurant; fans praise its "relaxed" style
and "interesting" menu, but others find "disappointing food"
and a rather flat experience. / 11.30 pm; no smoking area.*

Ma Goa SW15   **£ 24**   ❷❷④

244 Upper Richmond Rd   0181-780 1767   10–2B
*The Goan cooking – "which relies on proper spicing, not chilli
powder" – is "out of this world", say vociferous supporters of
this "authentic" and "friendly" family-run Putney Indian.
/ 11 pm; D only, closed Sun.*

Mackintosh's   **£ 23**   ④❸❷

46 Moreton St, SW1   821 1818   2–4C
142 Chiswick High Rd, W4   0181-994 2628   7–2B
*"What Pimlico has been crying out for", say fans of the
new offshoot to the popular Chiswick café-brasserie; both
branches are praised for their "very wide ranging menu"
and "bright and cheery" décor, but some think them rather
lacklustre. / W1 11 pm – W4 midnight; no smoking area; SW1 book
L only – W4 no booking.*

Mad Dog Café W1   £ 22   ④❸④
35 James St   486 1511   3–1A
*If (and, in our view, only if) you're looking to escape from
Oxford Street for a hot dog (various styles, including veggie)
and a bottle of beer, this loud, younger-scene place has
its attractions. / 10.30 pm.*

Made in Italy SW3   £ 22   ❸❸❸
249 King's Rd   352 1880   5–3C
*"Cheap pizza" and pasta "and good value for Chelsea" make
this "no pretence" diner very popular locally, even if it can
be a touch "hit and miss". / 11.30 pm; no Amex; to book need 8+.*

Maggie Jones's W8   £ 34   ④❸❶
6 Old Court Pl   937 6462   5–1A
*"Like being in a county cottage", this "mellow", "retreat" near
Kensington High Street is particularly "good in winter";
"great home cooking" can sometimes be had, though too
often it tends to "average", and the weekday set lunches –
formerly a top bargain – are no more. / 11 pm; set Sun L £22(FP).*

Magno's Brasserie WC2   £ 31   ⑤❸④
65a Long Acre   836 6077   4–2D
*Canny Magno sold his Covent Garden brasserie – always
best known as a pre-opera pit stop – just as the ROH went
AWOL; the place has now gone from indifferent to worse.
/ 11.30 pm; closed Sat L & Sun.*

Maison Bertaux W1   £ 5   ❷❷❷
28 Greek St   437 6007   4–2A
*"Dingy but classic" – London's oldest patisserie (Soho, 1871)
may "need a facelift", but partisans still say it's "wonderful".
/ 8.30 pm (Sun, closed 1 pm - 3 pm); no credit cards; no smoking area.*

Maison Novelli EC1   £ 49
29 Clerkenwell Gn   251 6606   9–1A
*As we go to press the ground-floor brasserie – the good bit –
of Maison Novelli is being relaunched, next door, as Novelli
EC1 (see also); the upstairs restaurant – the "pompous" and
"overpriced" bit – will now take over the whole building here.
/ 11.30 pm; closed Sat & Sun; no Switch.*

Malabar W8   £ 25   ❷❷❸
27 Uxbridge St   727 8800   6–2B
*"Dependably good" cooking with "fabulous colours and
spices" continues to make this Mediterranean-looking
Indian, just off Notting Hill Gate, one of the best curry
houses in town. / 11.15 pm.*

Malabar Junction WC1　　　　£ 23　　③②②
107 Gt Russell St　580 5230　2–1C
"Good Indian food, pleasant décor and attentive service"
ought to create more interest in this Bloomsbury
conservatory-restaurant, which still doesn't have the
following it deserves. / 11.30 pm; no Switch; no smoking area.

Mamta SW6　　　　　　　£ 18　　②②⑤
692 Fulham Rd　371 5971　10–1B
Fulham's "best Indian veggie for miles" is up for sale as we go
to press; such a shame that it's always been let down by some
of the ugliest décor in west London. / 10.30 pm; closed Mon L, Tue L
& Sun L; no Switch; no smoking area.

Mandalay W2　　　　　　　£ 15　　②①④
444 Edgware Rd　258 3696　8–4A
"Fantastic service from friendly owners" and "fresh", "lightly
spiced" food "for almost no money" make this Burmese
(Indian with oriental twists) a top cheap and cheerful choice;
it's just round the corner from Lord's. / 10.45 pm; closed Sun;
no Switch; no smoking.

Mandarin Kitchen W2　　　　£ 29　　①④④
14-16 Queensway　727 9012　6–2C
"Stick to the seafood and you will have a fine meal" at this
"first class" Bayswater Chinese which uses "the freshest
possible fish" to produce "sublime" dishes; the rest of the
performance is ordinary. / 11.30 pm.

Mandeer W1　　　　　　　£ 21　　②②②
21 Hanway Pl　323 0660　4–1A
For 30 years, this basement Indian (near Tottenham Court
Road tube) has served "delicious", "excellent value" vegan
fare in its characterful, almost Moorish restaurant; in the
'refectory', a "wonderful" lunchtime buffet is served – one of
the best deals in town. / 10 pm; closed Sun; no smoking; set weekday L
£9(FP).

Mandola W11　　　　　　　£ 22　　③⑤③
139 Westbourne Grove　229 4734　6–1B
"Tasty" ("very spicy if you want") cooking can be had at
this "cheap and cheerful" BYO Sudanese/Somalian café in
Bayswater; service is often "bad", but this is a "laid back"
type of place, and "they're lovely people, so it doesn't matter".
/ 11.30 pm; closed Sun L; no credit cards.

FSA

Mange 2 EC1 £ 38 ❸❸④
2 Cowcross St   250 0035   9–1A
*Though some approve the "dramatic" decoration and
"good value" cooking at this modern French restaurant in
Smithfield, others find the whole experience "bizarre";
lunchtime is preferable to the "quiet" evenings. / 10.30 pm;
closed Sat & Sun.*

Manna NW3 £ 23 ❷❸④
4 Erskine Rd   722 8028   8–3B
*Following its major refurb a couple of years ago, the UK's
oldest veggie, in Primrose Hill, is finally finding culinary form;
reporters applaud the "creative", "varied" cooking and the
"friendly" and "genuine", if sometimes "slow", service.
/ 11 pm; D only; no Amex & no Switch; no smoking area.*

Manorom WC2 £ 22 ❸❸④
16 Maiden Ln   240 4139   4–3D
*"Small and cosy" Theatreland Thai, where diners are made to
feel "welcome and unhurried". / 11 pm; closed Sat L & Sun.*

Manzara W11 £ 15 ❷❸❸
24 Pembridge Rd   727 3062   6–2B
*"Fabulous Turkish food at great prices" (especially meze)
makes this unpretentious café/bistro, off Notting Hill Gate,
a top budget standby. / 10.30 pm; no smoking area.*

Manzi's WC2 £ 37 ❷❷④
1 Leicester St   734 0224   4–3A
*"A good, old-fashioned restaurant", this cramped Theatreland
fish parlour "never fails to satisfy" traditionalists with its
"reliable", "well cooked" dishes and its amiable, if "mad",
service; some feel, as we do, that the whole formula "could do
with a freshen up". / 11.30 pm, Cabin Room 10.30 pm; closed Sun L; set
pre-th. £20(FP).*

Mao Tai SW6 £ 30 ❷❷❸
58 New King's Rd   731 2520   10–1B
*"Professional" Parson's Green Chinese whose "well flavoured
and clean tasting" Szechuan cooking guarantees a devoted
following; it's "much smarter than average", and "small
portions" are the only real gripe. / 11.45 pm; no Switch.*

Marine Ices NW3 £ 23 ❸❸❸
8 Haverstock Hl   485 3132   8–2B
*Since the '20s, "the best ice cream" and "good pasta
and pizza" have made this "old fashioned" Chalk Farm
institution a dependable destination for all the family.
/ 11 pm; no Amex; no smoking area.*

Maroush £ 30 ❷❷④

I) 21 Edgware Rd, W2   723 0773   6–1D
II) 38 Beauchamp Pl, SW3   581 5434   5–1C
III) 62 Seymour St, W1   724 5024   2–2A

*"Smart" Lebanese group, whose food is "mouth-watering,
but not cheap"; at I the late-night atmosphere, with "loud"
live music and dancing (minimum charge £48 after
10.30 pm), is the particular attraction, while at II, especially
in summer, it's the conservatory; the less expensive café/take-
away sections (at I and II) are among the best places in town
for a snack in the wee hours. / W2 1.30 am, SW3 3 am, W1
11.30 pm.*

The Marquis W1 £ 31 ❷❶④

121a Mount St   499 1256   3–3B
*"Really good", "unfussy" modern British food – at
"a reasonable price" – and "very attentive" service make this
relaunched old-timer "great value for Mayfair"; at lunchtime
it gets the following it deserves, but in the evenings the
"stark" setting can seem too "hushed". / 10.45 pm; closed Sat L
& Sun; smart casual.*

Mas Café W11 £ 28 ❷④❷

6-8 All Saints Rd   243 0969   6–1B
*"Excellent weekend brunches" are the highlight at this
"friendly", "relaxed" Notting Hill hang-out which attracts a
"diverse and hip" crowd; at other times a Mediterranean
menu is served. / 11.30 pm; closed Mon L; no Amex.*

Masako W1 £ 55 ❷❷❸

6 St Christopher Pl   935 1579   3–1A
*Little-known but very professionally run Japanese, in a cutesy
oasis just off Oxford Street; it serves some "wonderful food".
/ 10 pm; closed Sun.*

The Mason's Arms SW8 £ 21 ❷④❷

169 Battersea Park Rd   622 2007   10–1C
*Modishly converted boozer, in a grim location by Battersea
Park railway station, which provides a short menu of
"exceptional pub grub"; it can get "very noisy". / 10.10 pm;
no Amex.*

Matsuri SW1 £ 47 ❷❷④

15 Bury St   839 1101   3–3D
*The "entertaining" spectacle of this "great teppan-yaki"
in St James's makes it "perfect for introducing people to
Japanese cooking", and they do "good sushi" too; "shame
about the setting though" – "like a staff canteen". / 10 pm;
closed Sun; no Switch; smart casual.*

Mawar W2 £16 ❷❸⑤
175a Edgware Rd 262 1663 6–1D
*For "good cheap fill", few places rival this "excellent
authentic" Malaysian, in a cosily grim basement near the
Westway. / 10 pm; set always available £10(FP).*

Mekong SW1 £19 ❸④❸
46 Churton St 834 6896 2–4B
*"Reliable, if unadventurous, cooking" helps makes this long-
established Pimlico Vietnamese a cheerful "neighbourhood"
place. / 11.30 pm; no Amex.*

Melati W1 £22 ❷④④
21 Great Windmill St 437 2745 3–2D
*"One of the first and still the best", say fans of the "tasty"
and "good value" grub at this "cramped" South East Asian
canteen, just off Piccadilly Circus; service can be "iffy".
/ 11.30 pm, Fri & Sat 12.30 am; no Switch.*

Le Mercury N1 £15 ⑤④❸
140a Upper St 354 4088 8–3D
*"Candles everywhere" create an "intimate" atmosphere at
this "cramped" and "noisy" Islington super-budget bistro;
service is "shaky", though, and the cooking – never a strength
– is "not as good as it used to be". / 1 am, Sun 11.30 pm; no Amex
& no Switch; no smoking area.*

Mesclun N16 £24 ❸❷④
24 Stoke Newington Ch St 249 5029 1–1C
*"Already a favourite", this ambitious Stoke Newington
newcomer wins votes for its "high quality", imaginative
modern British cooking and enthusiastic, if "quirky", service;
not every dish is brilliant, however, and the slightly odd décor
is not to all tastes. / 11 pm; D only; closed Sun.*

Meson Don Felipe SE1 £23 ❸④❷
53 The Cut 928 3237 9–4A
*"A tiny space that jumps for joy", this "very smoky and
crowded" bar near the Old Vic is "worth the crush";
plusses include "extremely reliable tapas" and "good wine",
but beware the "guitar player from hell". / 11 pm; closed Sun;
no Amex; book pre 1 pm only.*

Le Metro SW3 £26 ❸❸❸
28 Basil St 589 6286 5–1D
*"A good stop for lunch", by Harrods, this coolly decorated
all-day wine bar ("incredible selection by the glass") offers
competent, simple modern British dishes and "friendly"
service. / 10.30 pm; closed Sun; no booking at L.*

Mezzaluna NW2   £ 34   ❸❸④
424 Finchley Rd   794 0452   1–1B
*This rather tacky trattoria on the way to Golder's Green is
"great for a local", if perhaps a touch expensive.*
/ 11 pm; closed Mon & Sat L; no Switch.

Mezzanine SE1   £ 27   ❸❸❸
National Theatre, South Bank   928 3531   2–3D
*"We'll go again – without going to the theatre", applaud
fans of the RNT's "underrated" in-house modern British
restaurant.* / 11 pm; closed Sun; no smoking area.

MEZZO W1   £ 42   ⑤④❸
100 Wardour St   314 4000   3–2D
*Conran's huge Soho "food factory" is "the ultimate triumph
of style over substance" – booking is "impersonal, like the
NHS", the setting is "slick, but unengaging", and, even at its
"high prices", the modern British cooking rarely rises above
"pedestrian".* / Mon-Wed midnight, Thu-Sat 1 am (crustacea till 3 am),
Sun 11 pm; closed Sat L; set pre-th. £24(FP), L £26(FP).

MEZZONINE W1   £ 32   ⑤④④
100 Wardour St   314 4000   3–2D
*Though some find the ground floor of Conran's Soho
behemoth "more consistent than Mezzo" (downstairs),
it scores no better overall; pan-Asian cooking comes in
"very small portions at very high prices", to be eaten
"crammed together", "like in a factory canteen".* / Mon-Thu
12.45 am, Fri-Sat 2.45 am; closed Sun; set pre-th. £16(FP), L £18(FP).

Mildreds W1   £ 17   ❷❷❸
58 Greek St   494 1634   4–2A
*"Health-giving", "imaginative", "delicious" and "filling" veggie
fare that offers "excellent value for money" ensures that this
"super-cramped" Soho café is always full to bursting.* / 11 pm;
closed Sun D; no credit cards; no smoking; no booking.

Mimmo d'Ischia SW1   £ 47   ❸❸❸
61 Elizabeth St   730 5406   2–4A
*"Mimmo is the best host in town", say devotees of this ageing
groover of a trattoria, who love its "vibrant atmosphere" and
its "expensive, but worth it" grub; critics bemoan bills that
are "wildly excessive", even for the purlieus of Eaton Square.*
/ 11.30 pm; closed Sun D; smart casual.

Mitsukoshi SW1   £ 60   ❶❸⑤
14-16 Regent St   930 0317   3–3D
*No one's heard of it, but some Japanese cognoscenti hold
the food here to be "unquestionably the finest in London",
especially the "wonderful, utterly fresh sushi"; the stark décor
seems "neglected".* / 9.30 pm; closed Sun; no Switch.

F S A

Miyama W1   £ 50   ❷❸⑤

38 Clarges St   499 2443   3–4B
*On the culinary front, this "straightforward", long-established
Mayfair Japanese is "a class act", though the "atmosphere
could be better". / 10.30 pm; closed Sat L & Sun L; smart casual; set
weekday L £20(FP).*

Momo W1   £ 33   ❸❸❶

25 Heddon St   434 4040   3–2C
*"The most happening place in London right now", this very
"attractive" new Moroccan, just off Regent Street, is currently
'It' (the basement bar in particular); the food is "well spiced",
if rather variable, and the amount of time spent in
self-contemplation makes service "slow". / 11.15 pm;
closed Sat L & Sun.*

Mon Plaisir WC2   £ 34   ❷❷❶

21 Monmouth St   836 7243   4–2B
*This Covent Garden "stalwart" has been "a little piece of
France", for over half a century; attractions include the
"very good", "no frills" cooking, the "friendly" service and
the "delightful" atmosphere; "lunchtime and pre-theatre
packages" offer top West End value. / 11.15 pm; closed Sat L
& Sun; set pre-th. £15(FP), always available £20(FP).*

Mona Lisa SW10   £ 12   ❸❷④

417 King's Rd   376 5447   5–3B
*This World's End "transport-caff" does "solid, and cheap
with it" Italian fare (including an incredible value £4.95 set
menu), as well as more traditional fry-ups; its appeal is
"age-blind, class-blind, and democratic". / 10.45 pm; closed Sun D;
no credit cards; to book need 10+.*

Mondo W1   £ 27   ❸④❷

13 Greek St   734 7157   4–2A
*"Funky" Soho basement bar/café/club, where the "Asian-y"
food is "more than beside the point", but "never the point
of going". / 11 pm, snacks till 2 am; D only, closed Sun; Fri & Sat
no booking after 9 pm.*

Mongolian Barbecue   £ 22   ⑤④④

12 Maiden Ln, WC2   379 7722   4–3D
31 Parson's Gn Ln, SW6   371 0433   10–1B
61 Gloucester Rd, SW7   581 8747   5–2B
1-3 Acton Ln, W4   0181-995 0575   7–2A
88-89 Chalk Farm Rd, NW1   482 6626   8–2B
*"A really good fun place to go" and "great in a large group",
cheer fans of the chain which pioneered the eat-all-you-can,
'pic 'n' mix', stir-fry concept; personally, we're in the "yuk",
"nasty", "never again" camp. / 11 pm; D only; no Amex.*

Monkeys SW3   £ 42   ❷❷❸

1 Cale St   352 4711   5–2C
*Rather grown-up Chelsea Green establishment which is
"romantic", "civilised" and "not too formal"; it is
particularly tipped as a "great winter restaurant", with the
"well-prepared" Anglo-French cooking including some
"exceptional game"; bills can mount alarmingly. / 11 pm;
closed Sun D; no Amex.*

Monsieur Max TW12   £ 32   ❷❸❸

133 High St, Hampton Hill   0181-979 5546   1–4A
*Max Renzland has exported his brand of bourgeois French
cooking to Hampton Hill; 'vaux le détour', if perhaps not le
voyage – it's good, honest stuff and, though the place is
licensed, the invitation to BYO (£5 corkage) may suit
œnophiles. / 11 pm; closed Sat L; credit cards to be accepted from Sep 97.*

Montana SW6   £ 36   ❷❸❷

125-129 Dawes Rd   385 9500   10–1B
*"Wild" south western USA cooking and a "trendy" vibe
(buoyed by quite serious jazz) bring punters from far and
wide to this deepest Fulham hang-out; arguably it offers
"the best brunch in town", and there's an interesting selection
of New World wines to boot; Notting Hill and Highgate sites
are planned. / 11 pm, Fri & Sat 11.30 pm.*

Montpeliano SW7   £ 41   ④❸❸

13 Montpelier St   589 0032   5–1C
*To its fans, this flash Knightsbridge trattoria is "a bit dated,
but fun and reliable", and has "very competent staff";
a large minority (including ourselves) think it "not at all up to
the standards of much cheaper places". / Midnight; set weekday L
£22(FP).*

Moro EC1   £ 28   ❷❸❸

34-36 Exmouth Mkt   833 8336   9–1A
*"Setting the trend in Clerkenwell", this North African
newcomer has had rapturous press reviews for its "extremely
tasty" and unusual cooking; perhaps we were disenchanted
by the "minimalist" setting, the "uncomfortable" seating
and the "rather slow" service, as we tended to the minority
"nothing special" school of thought. / 10.30 pm; closed Sat & Sun;
no Amex.*

Moshi Moshi Sushi £ 18 ❷❷❸

Unit 24, Liverpool St Station, EC2 247 3227 9–2D
7-8 Limeburner Ln, EC4 248 1808 9–2A
*A "great idea" – London's original conveyor-belt sushi chain
has spawned many imitators; both "very busy" branches offer
"good value" and "fun" – not qualities superabundant in the
Square Mile; many "hate the queues".* / 9 pm; closed Sat & Sun;
no Amex; EC2 no smoking, EC4 no smoking area; no booking.

Motcomb's SW1 £ 39 ❸❷❷

26 Motcomb St 235 9170 2–4A
*"Very friendly", tightly packed basement Belgravian,
whose "enjoyable" English fare is reasonably priced by local
standards.* / 11.15 pm; closed Sun D; smart casual; set weekday L £22(FP).

MPW E14 £ 31 ❷❷④

2nd Fl, Cabot Pl East 513 0513 1–3D
*At last – a tolerable business lunching venue for Canary
Wharf; this grand Deco-ish brasserie is branded as a
Marco Pierre White place, but the chef, Garry Hollihead,
has a reputation of his own – justifiably so, on the basis of our
early visit; the service could be emulated to good effect by
MPW's other establishments.* / 9 pm; closed Sat & Sun.

Mr Chow SW1 £ 42 ⑤④④

151 Knightsbridge 589 7347 5–1D
*Though a few say "I've put it back on my list", most feel
this relaunched Knightsbridge '60s-survivor would have been
better left to die, and deride the Chinese-food-from-Italian-
waiters formula as "mediocre" and "boring".* / 11.45 pm.

Mr Frascati W2 £ 36 ④❸④

34 Spring St 723 0319 6–1D
*Traditional Italian, a stone's throw from Paddington
Station, that offers a refuge from an unlovely quarter;
it's professionally run, with quality cooking, but "expensive
for what it is".* / 11 pm; closed Sat L & Sun L.

Mr Kong WC2 £ 20 ❷④⑤

21 Lisle St 437 7341 4–3A
*"One of the best in London", say fans of this "cramped"
Chinatown chow-house which has "very reasonable prices";
service can be "unwelcoming".* / 1.45 am; no Switch.

Mr Wing SW5   £ 34   ❸❸❶
242-244 Old Brompton Rd   370 4450   5–2A
*"Like sitting in a rain forest" – the "fab" jungle décor at
this "fun" Earl's Court Chinese makes a fantastic venue for
romance ("especially in one of the private seats") or a
celebration; the pricey food – like the service – "can be
excellent", but it's "inconsistent".* / Midnight; no smoking area.

Le Muscadet W1   £ 35   ❸❸④
25 Paddington St   935 2883   2–1A
*"Very authentic", "very French" Marylebone restaurant
offering a "varied menu" of bourgeois fare in rather dated
comfort.* / 10.45 pm, Sat 10 pm; closed Sat L & Sun; no Amex;
smart casual.

Museum St Café WC1   £ 29   ❷❷❸
47 Museum St   405 3211   2–1C
*Sometimes "stunning" modern British cooking ("at a
reasonable price") and "personable service" carry the day
at this "minimal" café, near the BM; few seem to mind the
"rather pokey" proportions and "uncomfortable chairs".*
/ 9.15 pm; closed Mon D, Sat & Sun; no smoking.

Mustards Brasserie EC1   £ 25   ④❸❸
60 Long Ln   796 4920   9–1B
*Though "nothing exciting", this brasserie and neighbouring
'bistro à vin', near Smithfield Market, offer "solid fare at
reasonable prices".* / 11 pm; closed Sat & Sun.

Naked Turtle SW14   £ 28   ④❷❷
505 Upper Richmond Rd   0181-878 1995   10–2A
*The "food is hit and miss but the whole experience is a lot of
fun" at this extremely popular East Sheen wine bar, where
the atmosphere is boosted by live music.* / 11 pm; no smoking area;
set weekday L £18(FP).

Nam Long SW5   £ 31   ❸④❶
159 Old Brompton Rd   373 1926   5–2B
*"Lethal cocktails" kick-start many "great evenings out" at
this buzzy and seductive South Kensington bar/restaurant;
the Vietnamese cooking, if no bargain, is more than
incidental, but service "needs improving".* / 11.30 pm;
closed Sat L & Sun; smart casual.

Nanking W6   £ 25   ❸❸❸
332 King St   0181-748 7604   7–2B
*"Tasty" Chinese cooking "in attractive surroundings" makes
this "reliable" Hammersmith oriental a good standby; its iffy
location means it's "rarely full".* / 11.30 pm; no Switch.

FSA

Nautilus NW6 £21 ❷❸④
27 Fortune Gn Rd 435 2532 1–1B
*"Excellent and honest" West Hampstead chippy serving
"fine matzo-battered fish and crispy chips". / 10.15 pm;
closed Sun; no credit cards; no booking.*

Nayab SW6 £25 ❷❸④
309 New King's Rd 731 6993 10–1B
*"Reliable", "well spiced" food makes this Parson's Green
Indian a local favourite, but its "unusual" décor finds little
favour. / 11.45 pm; smart casual.*

Neal Street WC2 £55 ④④④
26 Neal St 836 8368 4–2C
*Famous funghiphile Antonio Carluccio's well-known Covent
Garden Italian is, as ever, widely thought "a bit of a rip off";
the "A1 mushrooms", in particular can be "scrummy",
however – "if a friend or company is paying". / 11 pm;
closed Sun; smart casual.*

New Culture Revolution £17 ❸④④
305 King's Rd, SW3 352 9281 5–3C
42 Duncan St, N1 833 9083 8–3D
43 Parkway, NW1 267 2700 8–3B
*"Bright, clean and swift" noodle-bars – places "to grab a
nutritious meal and whizz out again". / 10.30 pm; N1 closed Sun;
no Amex; no smoking area; to book need 4+ .*

New World W1 £23 ④⑤④
Gerrard Pl 734 0677 4–3A
*"Like being in Hong Kong" – this gigantic Chinatown
institution is best visited for the "excellent" trolley-served dim
sum rather than "iffy" other fare. / 11.45 pm; no booking Sun L.*

Nico Central W1 £37 ❸❸④
35 Great Portland St 436 8846 3–1C
*"Good quality all round but a little uninspiring", fairly
summarises opinions on Nico Ladenis's upmarket Marylebone
bistro; even though "tables are too close together", it's most
often recommended for business. / 11 pm; closed Sat L & Sun;
smart casual.*

Nicole's W1 £41 ④④④
158 New Bond St 499 8408 3–3C
*"Very ladies-who-lunch" Mayfair fashion store basement
whose "amateurish" service and "pricey" fare hamper its
ambitions to be a 'real' modern British restaurant; still,
"for an indulgent shopping break"... / 10.45 pm; closed Sat D
& Sun; no smoking area.*

Nikita's SW10   £ 35   ④❸❷
65 Ifield Rd   352 6326   5–3B
"Memories are hazy" about this long-established Russian, probably due to the *"great vodkas"* – one of the best selections in town; you don't have to get hammered to eat the food – but it helps. / 11.30 pm; D only; closed Sun; smart casual.

NOBU W1   £ 50   ❷④❸
Metropolitan Hotel, Old Park Ln   447 4747   3–4A
"Magical" and *"amazing"* Japanese-meets-South American cooking has made Matsuhisa Nobu's *"breathtaking"* Mayfair newcomer – an import from LA and NYC – an instant hit; those who do not take to a place *"full of fashion industry people"* (and celebs) may find it *"precious"* and *"extremely expensive"*. / 10.30 pm; closed Sat L & Sun; no smoking area; set weekday L £31(FP).

Nontas NW1   £ 17   ❷❸④
14 Camden High St   387 4579   8–3C
Long-established taverna, near Mornington Crescent tube, whose regulars like the "cosy" atmosphere ("lovely cat!") and dependable cooking; some find it a touch "dingy", but in summer you can eat in the garden. / 11.30 pm; closed Sun; no Switch.

Noor Jahan SW5   £ 24   ❷❸④
2a Bina Gdns   373 6522   5–2B
"Consistently good", classic, *"no frills"* Indian with décor *"smart"* enough to satisfy its solid South Kensington following; service can be *"unfriendly"*. / 11.30 pm; no Switch.

C Notarianni & Sons SW11   £ 19   ❷④④
142 Battersea High St   228 7133   10–1C
"Reliable", family-owned Battersea fixture offering *"great" pizza and pasta*; its Art Deco-ish setting *"lacks atmosphere"*, though. / 11 pm; closed Sat L & Sun; no Amex & no Switch.

Noto   £ 19   ❸❸④
2/3 Bassishaw Highwalk, EC2   256 9433   9–3B
7 Bread St, EC4   329 8056   9–2C
"Huge bowls of tasty noodles" and *"good bento boxes"* are offered at these *"quick"*, *"enjoyable"* and *"cheap"* City Japaneses. / EC2 10 pm, Sat 9 pm – EC4 9 pm; EC2 closed Sat & Sun – EC4 closed Sat D & Sun; EC2 no Amex – EC4 no credit cards; EC2 no smoking at L; no booking.

Noughts 'n' Crosses W5 £30 ④④❸
77 The Grove   0181-840 7568   1–3A
*Ealing's posh restaurant, behind the Broadway Centre, is
"delightful", if in a rather suburban way; fans vaunt the
"imaginative" modern British cooking, but we're with those
who feel it "somehow just misses". / 10 pm; closed Mon; D only ex
Sun when L only; smart casual; no smoking area.*

Novelli EC1 EC1 £29
30 Clerkenwell Gn   251 6606   9–1A
*The "brilliant", "unbelievably good value" brasserie section of
Maison Novelli (see also) re-opens in autumn '97 in its 'own'
building (adjacent to its former site). /*

Novelli W8 W8 £32 ④④④
122 Palace Gardens Terrace   229 4024   6–2B
*J-C Novelli's replacement for the beloved Ark (RIP), off Notting
Hill Gate, offers "interesting" French cooking of "high calibre";
"aggressively" priced incidentals bump up the bill, though,
and given the absurdly "cramped" surroundings, it's not hard
to find this place "overhyped and overpriced". / 11 pm, Fri & Sat
midnight, Sun 10 pm; no smoking area.*

O'Conor Don W1 £27 ❸②②
88 Marylebone Ln   935 9311   3–1A
*This "very jolly" Marylebone tavern is "a great place all
round"; in the downstairs bar they serve good, simple
snacks; upstairs in the "relaxed" and comfortable restaurant,
the "meaty" Irish fare "rises well above 'bog' standards".
/ 10 pm; closed Sat L & Sun; smart casual.*

OAK ROOM MARCO PIERRE WHITE
HOTEL MERIDIEN W1 £106
Piccadilly   437 0202   3–3D
*Mr White's prices are the UK's highest, yet last year
(when he was at the Hyde Park) he achieved a risible 10th
position in reporters' nominations for their 'top gastronomic
experience of the year'; we were hoping that this glorious new
setting would inspire more impressive results (and perhaps
also help his "self-important" staff to lighten up a little), but
an early report is hardly encouraging. / 10.30 pm; closed Sat L
& Sun; set weekday L £51(FP).*

Oceana W1 £32 ❸④④
Jason's Ct, 76 Wigmore St   224 2992   3–1A
*"Trying hard and getting better", this "interesting new arrival",
"handy for Oxford Circus", offers competent modern British
fare; some say the basement setting (briefly Hollihead, RIP)
is "interestingly decorated" – we're with those who find it
"stilted". / 11.15 pm; closed Sat L & Sun.*

L'Odéon W1   £ 50   ④④④
65 Regent St   287 1400   3–3D
*"It started OK at first", but Bruno Loubet's departure and
rising prices have killed enthusiasm for this two-year-old
mega-brasserie, near Piccadilly Circus; it's still tipped as a
central business venue, but many now find it "expensive"
and "ordinary". / 11.30 pm; no smoking area; set pre-th. £25(FP).*

Odette's NW1   £ 39   ❸❷❶
130 Regent's Pk Rd   586 5486   8–3B
*"A wonderful local restaurant", this smart Primrose Hill fixture
is "a bit pricey, but irresistible"; the sound modern British
cooking is perhaps not currently up to its best past form,
but the "first class", richly decorated setting – the walls groan
with mirrors – still makes it a "romantic" favourite. / 11 pm;
closed Sat L & Sun; set weekday L £19(FP).*

Odin's W1   £ 33   ❸❶❶
27 Devonshire St   935 7296   2–1A
*This "opulent" and "comfortable" art-filled Marylebone
restaurant offers "courteous service" and "pampering of
the highest order" – few places in town are better suited
"to dining more conservative types"; the "solidly British,
and proud of it" cooking is "consistent" rather than exciting.
/ 11.30 pm; closed Sat & Sun; smart casual.*

Ognisko Polskie SW7   £ 27   ❸❸❷
55 Prince's Gt, Exhibition Rd   589 4635   5–1C
*The "great, old-fashioned" dining room makes a visit to this
South Kensington émigrés club an experience (and "on a hot
day, it's great on the terrace", too); the gutsy Polish grub is
acceptable – especially if you go for the "good value" set
menu – and "service is slow, but it's that kind of place".
/ 10.45 pm; no Switch; smart casual; set always available £14(FP).*

Oliveto SW1   £ 31   ❷❸❸
49 Elizabeth St   730 0074   2–4A
*"Good for a quick, satisfying meal in Belgravia", this "cool"
and "stylish", but "affordable" Italian offers "great pizza
and pasta". / 11.30 pm.*

Olivo SW1   £ 33   ❷❸❸
21 Eccleston St   730 2505   2–4B
*"Uncomplicated", "light Italian" (actually Sardinian) cooking
in "casual surroundings" makes for "easy, quality dining out"
at this "comfortable local" near Victoria station; some find
the setting a touch "airless". / 11 pm; closed Sat L & Sun L.*

On the Rise SW11   **£ 26**   ③③④

30 Battersea Rise   228 0611   10–2C
"Good value" Battersea "neighbourhood" newcomer, offering
"simple" modern British fare. / 11 pm, Fri & Sat 11.30 pm; no Amex.

1 Lawn Terrace SE3   **£ 36**

1 Lawn Terrace   0181-853 3151   1–4D
Blackheath's first attempt in recent years at a serious
restaurant is scheduled to make its appearance in October
'97; West End-style (and scale) modern British dining is
promised, with Sanjay Dwivedi (ex-Coast and the Atlantic)
at the stove. /

192 W11   **£ 34**   ④⑤❸

192 Kensington Pk Rd   229 0482   6–1A
It's the "exceptionally poor" service that really gets to
people at this "too trendy for its own good" Notting Hill wine
bar/restaurant, although the "expensive" modern British fare
is "nothing to write home about" either; the wine list is
excellent, though, and the place's "media luvvies" following
ensures it's "always buzzing". / 11 pm; set weekday L £20(FP).

Opus 70 W1   **£ 37**   ④❸⑤

70 Stratton St   344 7070   3–3C
Those with fond memories of the Mayfair Hotel's former
Château restaurant are wont to decry its "dreadfully sad
replacement"; those untainted by prior experience seem to
find an "unexpectedly pleasant" hotel dining room, if one
whose "uninspiring décor" limits its appeal to business.
/ 11 pm; closed Sat L; no smoking area.

L'ORANGER SW1   **£ 43**   ❶❶❷

5 St James's St   839 3774   3–4D
This "gem in St James's" (hailed by some as "a cheaper
Aubergine" – same owners) is now one of the top places
in town thanks to Marcus Wareing's "sophisticated and
polished" modern French cooking, the excellent service
and the fine, rather traditional setting (with charming
conservatory); if there is a complaint, it is of a "slightly stiff
ambience". / 11.15 pm; closed Sun L.

Oriel SW1   **£ 27**   ④④❷

50-51 Sloane Sq   730 2804   5–2D
Elegantly refurbished brasserie with "a very good
atmosphere"; its prominent location makes it a "good
meeting point", and it has a deserved reputation for
breakfasts – other fare is "plain" and "pricey".
/ 10.45 pm; no smoking area; no booking.

Orrery W1

Marylebone High St   616 8000   2–1A
The latest offering from the Conran stable is, in fact, to be sited in a C19 Marylebone stable! – it's set to open in autumn '97, and among the promised attractions are French provincial cuisine and views over a quiet churchyard. /

Orsino W11   £39   ④❸❷

119 Portland Rd   221 3299   6–2A
All applaud the "attractively cool and sophisticated" setting of Orso's Holland Park country cousin; far too many, though, feel the place "doesn't deliver on its potential", serving "slapdash" modern Italian food at "inflated prices". / 11 pm; no smoking area; set weekday L £23(FP).

Orso WC2   £37   ④④④

27 Wellington St   240 5269   4–3D
"Nothing like as wonderful as it used to be", this "jaded" Covent Garden basement Italian offers "unmemorable cooking, "brusque" service and a setting which – even if, post-theatre, it can show its old "buzz" – now risks becoming "dingy". / Midnight; no smoking area.

Oslo Court NW8   £35   ❶❶❸

Prince Albert Rd   722 8795   8–3A
Passions run high – "I just love this restaurant, I want to be buried there" – in praise of this jolly, dated institution at the base of a Regent's Park apartment block; the key is the "courteous staff" of real characters, but the International cooking gets amazingly strong support, too – and not just from the many who've been regulars for decades. / 11 pm; closed Sun; smart casual.

Osteria Antica Bologna SW11   £27   ❷④❷

23 Northcote Rd   978 4771   10–2C
"Great peasant food" – some of it "brilliant and inventive" – makes this "no fuss farmhouse Italian" "worth the trip", even unto the environs of Clapham Junction; service can be "very slow". / 11 pm, Fri & Sat 11.30 pm.

Osteria Basilico W11   £28   ❷❸❶

29 Kensington Pk Rd   727 9957   6–1A
"Great pizza at affordable prices" and "fresh Italian home cooking" are just part of the appeal of this "fun" Italian which is permanently packed with Notting Hill trendies; the odd complaint of staff "attitude" is perhaps inevitable. / 11 pm; no Amex; no booking Sat L

Osteria del Parco W11   £27   ❸❸❷

148 Holland Pk Ave   221 6090   6–2A
*Locals like the new "faster, livelier and noisier" look of
this reformatted Holland Park venture (formerly La Fenice);
the Franco/Italian cooking is "reasonable". / 10.30 pm; no Switch.*

Osteria Le Fate SW3   £37   ⑤⑤❸

5 Draycott Ave   591 0070   5–2D
*Opinions on this small and "intimate" Chelsea Italian divide
starkly – true, some do proclaim an "interesting", "romantic"
place with "very good" Ligurian cooking, but too many decry
"minute" portions of "average" food, and "dreadful" service.
/ 11.30 pm; closed Sun; smart casual.*

OXO TOWER SE1   £42   ④④❷

Barge House St   803 3888   9–3A
*It may have a "staggering" river view, but this eighth-floor
bar/brasserie/restaurant yearling – reporters' most-mentioned
place of the year – is widely dismissed as "really average and
very expensive"; more was expected than "predictable",
"designer" food – and why are the staff so "snotty" and
"unsmiling"? / 11.15 pm.*

LE PALAIS DU JARDIN WC2   £34   ❷❸❷

136 Long Acre   379 5353   4–3C
*"Urbane, professional – and packed", this huge Covent
Garden brasserie is "wonderful value" and one of the best
all-rounders in town; its many fans hail its "superb bustling
atmosphere" and the "desirable menu that delivers" (with
"excellent seafood platters" particularly praised). / Midnight.*

Palio W11   £31   ⑤④❸

175 Westbourne Grove   221 6624   6–1B
*This "loud, brash" Notting Hill standby "has gone right off" –
its modern British cooking now "lacks imagination", and
service is at best up-and-down. / 11.30 pm; set weekday L £18(FP).*

Paparazzi Café SW3   £25   ④❸❷

58 Fulham Rd   589 0876   5–2C
*"Loud live music" contributes to the "amazing" atmosphere
of this Chelsea Euroscene pizzeria – "they really do dance
on the tables". / 1 am; no Switch; smart casual.*

Park Inn W2   £26   ❸❷④

6 Wellington Ter, Bayswater Rd   229 3553   6–2B
*Affordable Chinese nosh – with seafood the speciality – and
"welcoming staff" make this a "reliable" Bayswater standby
(located opposite the entrance to Kensington Gardens).
/ 11.30 pm; no Amex.*

The Parson's Nose SW6   £ 25   ❸❸④
803 Fulham Rd   731 7811   10–1B
"Hearty bowlfuls of rustic nosh" are generally praised at this
welcoming, slightly suburban Fulham newcomer. / 11 pm.

Pasha SW7
1 Gloucester Rd   589 7969   5–1B
The latest venture from Mogens Tholstrup (of Daphne's and
The Collection fame) is to pay homage to the current vogue
for North Africa; opening in November '97, it will take over
the South Kensington site left vacant by the unlamented
Establishment (RIP). /

Pasha N1   £ 22   ❸❷❸
301 Upper St   226 1454   8–3D
This Popular Islington Turk is liked for its *"excellent set
menus"*, *"friendly staff"* and *"relaxed atmosphere"*. / 11.30 pm,
Fri & Sat midnight; no Switch; set weekday L £14(FP).

Pâtisserie Valerie   £ 19   ❷❷❷
105 Marylebone High St, W1   935 6240   2–1A
44 Old Compton St, W1   437 3466   4–2A
RIBA Centre, 66 Portland Pl, W1   631 0467   2–1B
8 Russell St, WC2   240 0064   4–3D
215 Brompton Rd, SW3   823 9971   5–2C
"Coffee and croissants adored even by French people" and
a *"very comforting"* atmosphere make this *"great"* pâtisserie
chain a *"dependable"* choice; branches other than the lovely,
"tatty" Soho original offer light snack food too – these
include the characterful Maison Sagne in Marylebone, a
smart branch at RIBA, and the very convenient rendezvous
near Harrods. / 6 pm-8 pm, Sun earlier; Portland Pl, closed Sun;
no smoking area; no booking.

Paulo's W6   £ 23   ❸❷❸
30 Greyhound Rd   385 9264   7–2C
"Great fun and good food" make a happy combination at
jovial Paulo's *"all-u-can-eat"* Brazilian buffet (with lots for
veggies) – you *"get treated like a member of the family"*;
if you OD on the red-hot salsa, Charing Cross hospital is just
next door. / 10.30 pm; D only – Sun L only, closed Mon; no credit cards.

The Peasant EC1   £ 29   ❸❸④
240 St John St   336 7726   8–3D
"Upstairs formal dining – downstairs grand boozer", at
this *"decent"* Clerkenwell gastropub, whose *"fashionably
Mediterranean"* menu still has its fans. / 10.45 pm; closed Sat L
& Sun.

Pélican WC2 £30 ④❸❸

45 St Martin's Ln 379 0309 4–4C

"Good pre-theatre or post-opera", this well known, cavernous central fixture, by the Coliseum, provides OK brasserie fare. / 12.30 am, Sun 10.30 pm; smart casual.

The Pen SW6 £28 ❸❸❷

51 Parson's Green Ln 371 8517 10–1B

The "cosy and intimate" first-floor dining room of this trendified Parson's Green pub (opposite the tube) provides decent modern British grub of some ambition. / 11 pm; closed Sat L, summer closed Sun L; no Amex.

The People's Palace SE1 £35 ④❸④

South Bank Centre 928 9999 2–3D

Though some still find "exciting" modern British cooking in this cavernous, "slightly soulless" Royal Festival Hall chamber, the consensus view is that it's only "OK"; there's no doubting the "exceptional view over the Thames", however, and the pre-performance menu is fair value. / 11 pm.

The Pepper Tree SW4 £16 ❸❷❸

Clapham Common S'side 622 1758 10–2D

"Cheap", "tasty", "quality" cooking wins an enormous following for this "canteen-style", "good budget Thai", by Clapham Common tube. / 11 pm, Mon 10.30 pm; no Amex; no smoking area; no booking.

La Perla WC2 £23 ❸❸④

28 Maiden Ln 240 7400 4–4D

If this fun Covent Garden Mexican bar-café (a chip off the Café Pacifico block) was done slightly less on the cheap it could be very atmospheric; service is efficient (if, in our experience, brusque) and decent food comes at modest prices. / 11 pm, Sun 7.30 pm; closed Sun D.

Le P'tit Normand SW18 £26 ❸❷④

185 Merton Rd 0181-871 0233 10–2B

The "tacky décor is part of the charm" at this "exceptionally friendly" Southfields Gallic local (though its "dinginess" is not to all tastes); the "good value regional fare" commands general support, and Sunday lunch is recommended. / 10 pm, Sat 11 pm; closed Sat L; smart casual; set weekday L £16(FP).

Phoenicia W8 £30 ❷❶④

11-13 Abingdon Rd 937 0120 5–1A

"Really warm" service and carefully prepared food (especially "great meze" and the "superb lunchtime buffet") make this "timeless" Lebanese, off Kensington High Street", a "great neighbourhood restaurant". / 11.45 pm; smart casual; set weekday L £17(FP), Sun L £19(FP).

Phoenix Bar & Grill SW15 £ 30 ❸❷❸
Pentlow St 0181-780 3131 10–1A
*It's "not yet up to the standard of Sonny's (its parent)", but
this "clean, bright", perhaps rather "stark", Putney yearling
wins thumbs-almost-up for its "good but not outstanding"
modern British grub.* / 11.30 pm, Sun 10 pm; closed Sat L;
set weekday L £16(FP), Sun L £19(FP).

Phuket SW11 £ 18 ❸❷④
246 Battersea Pk Rd 223 5924 10–1C
*"Friendly", reliable Battersea Thai; "the recent redecoration
is an improvement".* / 10.50 pm; D only.

Picasso SW3 £ 18 ❸❸❸
127 King's Rd 352 4921 5–3C
*"Coffee and Bob Geldof" are the key attractions at this
Chelsea diner, where designer-stubbled trendies ostentatiously
work off their hangovers.* / 11.15 pm.

PIED À TERRE W1 £ 55 ❶❷❸
34 Charlotte St 636 1178 2–1C
*"Very good but not pretentious" Fitzrovia foodie hotspot,
now moving into the Premier League, as Tom Aikens's
"outstanding" modern French cooking "continues to improve"
– "smarter décor" and "much better service" also play their
part.* / 10.30 pm; closed Sat L & Sun; smart casual.

La Piragua N1 £ 17 ❸❷❷
176 Upper St 354 2843 8–2D
*"Gargantuan platefuls" of "muy autentico" grub and
"brusquely chaotic" macho service make this "very cheap
and cheerful" Islington Columbian an above-average budget
choice.* / Midnight; no credit cards.

Pitcher & Piano £ 22 ④❸❷
69-70 Dean St, W1 434 3585 4–2A
40-42 King William IV St, WC2 240 6180 4–4C
214 Fulham Rd, SW10 352 9234 5–3B
871-873 Fulham Rd, SW6 736 3910 10–1B
18-20 Chiswick High Rd, W4 0181-742 7731 7–2B
69 Upper St, N1 704 9974 8–3D
8 Balham Hill, SW12 0181-673 1107 10–2C
*Pheromone-charged twentysomething bars, where the grub
is much better than it ought to be, given that it is utterly
incidental; also popular for breakfast.* / 10 pm - 11 pm; W1
closed Sun.

FSA

Pizza Chelsea SW3 £21 ③④④
93 Pelham St   584 4788   5–2C
*"Interesting pizzas and salads", reasonably priced by the
standards of Brompton Cross, make this a shopping standby
worth knowing about. / 11 pm; no Amex; no smoking area.*

Pizza Metro SW11 £22 ❶❶❸
64 Battersea Rise   228 3812   10–2C
*"Pizza by the metre from a wood-burning oven" is the special
attraction of this "informal" (some might say tacky) and "very
friendly" Battersea pizzeria; "all the Italians recommend it,
and it's really worth the journey". / 11 pm; closed Mon; no Amex.*

Pizza On The Park SW1 £19 ❸❸❷
11 Knightsbridge   235 5273   2–3A
*"Space and the location" – together with dependable pizza,
and a "superb brekkie" too – make this stylish Hyde Park
Corner institution one of the top budget places in town; the
basement houses a major jazz/cabaret venue (substantial
music charge). / Midnight; no smoking area; no booking.*

Pizza Pomodoro £22 ④④❶
51 Beauchamp Pl, SW3   589 1278   5–1C
7 Steward St, E1   377 6186   9–1D
*The original Pomodoro – seedily located in a Knightsbridge
basement – is a "fun filled", "too crowded" pizza-dive, that
hops till late thanks to the "great live music"; the Spitalfields
offshoot, though not nearly as special, makes a "reliable night
spot in the City". / SW3 1 am – E1 midnight; E1 closed Sat & Sun; E1
no Amex; SW3 book only till 7.30 pm.*

Pizza the Action SW6 £18 ❸❷❸
678 Fulham Rd   736 2716   10–1B
*"Cheerful, relaxed" Fulham local offering "lots of choice"
from a "reliable" pizza, pasta and grills menu. / Midnight.*

122

PizzaExpress £19 ❸❸❸

154 Victoria St, SW1   828 1477   2–4B
10 Dean St, W1   437 9595   3–1D
133 Baker St, W1   486 0888   2–1A
20 Greek St, W1   734 7430   4–2A
21-22 Barrett St, W1   629 1001   3–1A
23 Bruton Pl, W1   495 1411   3–2B
29 Wardour St, W1   437 7215   4–3A
7-9 Charlotte St, W1   580 1110   2–1C
30 Coptic St, WC1   636 3232   2–1C
9-12 Bow St, WC2   240 3443   4–2D
363 Fulham Rd, SW10   352 5300   5–3B
6-7 Beauchamp Pl, SW3   589 2355   5–1C
895 Fulham Rd, SW6   731 3117   10–1B
137 Notting Hl Gt, W11   229 6000   6–2B
7 Rockley Rd, W14   0181-749 8582   7–1C
26 Porchester Rd, W2   229 7784   6–1C
252 Chiswick High Rd, W4   0181-747 0193   7–2A
35 Earl's Ct Rd, W8   937 0761   5–1A
335 Upper St, N1   226 9542   8–3D
85-87 Parkway, NW1   267 2600   8–3B
194 Haverstock Hill, NW3   794 6777   8–2A
70 Heath St, NW3   433 1600   8–1A
39-39a Abbey Rd, NW8   624 5577   8–3A
Chapter Ho, Montague Cl, SE1   378 6446   9–3C
230 Lavender Hill, SW11   223 5677   10–2C
46 Battersea Br Rd, SW11   924 2774   5–4C
305 Up Richmond Rd W, SW14   0181-878 6833   10–2A
144 Up Richmond Rd, SW15   0181-789 1948   10–2B
539 Old York Rd, SW18   0181-877 9812   10–2B
43 Abbeville Rd, SW4   0181-673 8878   10–2D
125 London Wall, EC2   600 8880   9–2B
*"King amongst chain pizza restaurants", this remarkable
group is a case-study in achieving "consistent standards"
across the board; Chelsea has always been an odd gap in
coverage, to be rectified in late-'97 with an opening in the
King's Road's long-neglected Pheasantry building. / 11 pm-
Midnight, Greek St Wed-Sat 1 am, Chapter Hs 4.30 pm, London Wall Sat
8 pm; Chapter Hs & Bruton Pl closed Sat & Sun (Chapter Hs open Sat in
summer); not all branches take bookings.*

Pizzeria Castello SE1 £16 ❷❷❷
20 Walworth Rd   703 2556   1–3C
*"Magnifico pizzas" and "very good value for money" ensure
a loyal fan-club for this famous pizzeria, horribly located near
the Elephant & Castle; "office parties predominate
sometimes". / 11 pm; closed Sat L & Sun; smart casual.*

Pizzeria Condotti W1   £19   ③③②
4 Mill St   499 1308   3–2C
*"Fresh and flavourful pizza in smart surroundings", and at
reasonable prices for Mayfair, draws a fashionable following
to this smart PizzaExpress in disguise. / Midnight; Mon-Fri
no booking at L after 12.30 pm.*

PJ's SW3   £30   ⑤④③
52 Fulham Rd   581 0025   5–2C
*A "great brunch" is the highlight at this "relaxed", "buzzing"
Chelsea hang-out; at other times, the "lousy" American grub
means the place is best enjoyed as a bar. / 11.30 pm; smart casual.*

The Place Below EC2   £14   ②③③
St Mary-le-Bow, Cheapside   329 0789   9–2C
*For a "healthy lunch in the City", the veggie self-service café
in the crypt beneath St Mary-le-Bow is "always worth a visit";
"prices are a bit toppy", though, and beware "long queues".
/ L only; closed Sat & Sun; no Amex; no smoking; no booking.*

Planet Hollywood W1   £31   ⑤④③
13 Coventry St   287 1000   4–4A
*Some are "pleasantly surprised" by this huge West End
theme-diner that's "great for kids"; more, though, find a
"tacky, tacky, tacky", "touristy" "insult" of a place, where
"they should be paying us to eat". / 1 am; no smoking area;
no booking.*

Plummers WC2   £24   ③②④
33 King St   240 2534   4–3C
*It's not what you'd call chic, but this "cosy", cramped
Covent Garden standby has its fans who find "good value",
dependable British fare (with "interesting choices for
vegetarians"). / 11.30 pm.*

Poissonnerie de l'Avenue SW3   £44   ②③③
82 Sloane Av   589 2457   5–2C
*"Excellent", if "expensive", fish and "good seafood" win much
support for this Brompton Cross fixture, where "quality is
maintained in a rather quaint and old fashioned setting";
reservations include "squashed" seating and sometimes
"iffy" service. / 11.30 pm; closed Sun; smart casual.*

Pollo W1   £14   ④④③
20 Old Compton St   734 5917   4–2A
*"Huge portions" of "quick and cheap pasta" feed the
impecunious and the mean at this "fun", studenty Soho
pit stop; you're "rushed" and "treated like cattle" – but
"at prices like these, who's complaining?" / Midnight;
no credit cards.*

Polygon Bar & Grill SW4   £ 29   ②③②
4 The Polygon, Clapham Old Town   622 1199   10–2D
*This "smart" and "trendy" Clapham newcomer "feels more
like a central London restaurant"; the "nice food" (mainly
grills) and "interesting wine list" are "reasonably priced",
too, though "failures in execution" are not unknown. / 11 pm;
no Amex.*

Pomegranates SW1   £ 35   ④④❸
94 Grosvenor Rd   828 6560   2–4C
*"A time-warp, but a pleasurable one", say supporters of this
dated Pimlico basement whose "illicit" atmosphere attracts
"eloping couples" and MPs; the eclectic cooking is agreeable
enough. / 11.15 pm; closed Sat L & Sun; no Switch.*

La Pomme d'Amour W11   £ 29   ❸①②
128 Holland Pk Av   229 8532   6–2A
*"Very attentive and accommodating service" and a "calming",
slightly middle-aged atmosphere win continuing praise for this
"sweet" Holland Park rendezvous – "an especially lovely place
à deux"; the "reasonably priced" Gallic fare tends to the
"unexceptional". / 10.45 pm; closed Sat L & Sun; no Switch; smart casual.*

LE PONT DE LA TOUR SE1   £ 54   ❸④②
36d Shad Thames   403 8403   9–4D
*With its "dramatic surroundings", Conran's "slick" riversider –
with its "A1 position" overlooking Tower Bridge – is still
reporters' top tip for business (and also popular for pleasure);
the "first class" modern French cooking can be "uneven",
though, and service continues to attract complaints of
"inattention" and "attitude". / 11.30 pm; closed Sat L; set pre- & post-
th. £31 (FP).*

Le Pont de la Tour Bar & Grill SE1   £ 34   ❸❸②
36d Shad Thames   403 8403   9–4D
*"Delicious shellfish" (plus steaks and other superior snacks)
and the "outlook over the Thames" – especially from the
outside tables – make this Conran riversider a popular
non-expense account destination. / 11.30 pm; no booking.*

Poons WC2   £ 18   ❸❸④
4 Leicester St   437 1528   4–3A
*This well-known Theatreland standby is still, for many
reporters, "the best Chinese, and the most accessible",
offering smart-enough décor, reasonably civil service and
"decent food at a fair price"; it's "variable", though. / 11.30 pm.*

Poons in the City EC3   **£ 14**   ❷❷④

2 Minster Pavement   626 0126   9–3D
*The main restaurant at this City Chinese is, to many,
"grim" and "mediocre"; the "fast food", canteen-style section
however – to which our prices and ratings relate – offers
"exceptional value", "particularly for the Square Mile".*
/ 10.30 pm; closed Sat & Sun.

Poons, Lisle Street WC2   **£ 19**   ❷❸④

27 Lisle St   437 4549   4–3B
*The inauspicious-looking Chinatown cradle of the Poon
dynasty remains, in its own way, rather "wonderful", offering
"most enjoyable", "very authentic" and "cheap" chow.*
/ 11.30 pm; no credit cards.

Popeseye W14   **£ 26**   ❶❸④

108 Blythe Rd   610 4578   7–1C
*"Carnivores' heaven" – a "great formula" of "steak, frites,
salad" and "good value wine" awaits those who venture to
this "no-frills" Brook Green bistro.* */ 10.30 pm; D only; closed Sun;
no credit cards.*

La Porchetta Pizzeria N4   **£ 16**   ❷❷❷

147 Stroud Green Rd   281 2892   8–1D
*"Brilliant, cheap, happening" Finsbury Park Italian – the
epitome of a local institution – where "the queues form
from early on" (no booking); "mad staff" bear down with
"huge, tasty pizzas", "fab risotti" and so on, and all at
extremely "reasonable prices"; "great with the kids".*
/ Midnight; closed Sat D & Sun D.

La Porte des Indes W1   **£ 43**   ❸④❸

32 Bryanston St   224 0055   2–2A
*Some swoon over the "wow" setting of this extravagantly
themed Indian near Marble Arch, and praise the "fab
flavours" of its Indian/French colonial fare; "arrogant"
and "lackadaisical" staff can spoil the experience, though,
and many find "high prices" for food which is "exact rather
than exciting" (though the buffet lunch is an undoubted
bargain).* */ Midnight, Sun 10.30 pm; closed Sat L; smart casual;
no smoking area; set L £25(FP).*

Porters WC2   **£ 20**   ④⑤⑤

17 Henrietta St   836 6466   4–3D
*Its "good, traditional" pies still have their supporters, but
the consensus is that this Covent Garden English restaurant,
which is usually "full of tourists", "seems to be going
downhill".* */ 11.30 pm.*

La Poule au Pot SW1   £39   ④❸❶

231 Ebury St   730 7763   5–2D
*This candle-lit Pimlico Green "old favourite" is once again
reporters' top choice for a romantic tête-à-tête; it's the setting,
rather than the "ropy, old-fashioned cooking", which is the
attraction, though, and as for the service – "hassle/shout/joke
in French to get the best results". / 11.15 pm; set weekday L £24(FP).*

Prego TW9   £31   ④④❸

100 Kew Rd   0181-948 8508   1–4A
*An "excellent Italian with a touch of class", claim loyal
Richmond fans of what is just about the only serious
restaurant thereabouts; it's "erratic when busy" – which is to
say just about always. / 11 pm, Fri & Sat 11.30 pm; no smoking area.*

Pret A Manger   £9   ❸❶❸

12 Kingsgate Pd, Victoria St, SW1   828 1559   2–4B
75b Victoria St, SW1   222 1020   2–4C
120 Baker St, W1   486 2264   2–1A
163 Piccadilly, W1   629 5044   3–3C
173 Wardour St, W1   434 0373   3–1D
18 Hanover St, W1   491 7701   3–2C
298 Regents St, W1   637 3836   4–1A
54-56 Oxford St, W1   636 5750   3–1C
63 Tottenham Court Rd, W1   636 6904   2–1C
7 Marylebone High St, W1   935 0474   2–1A
122 High Holborn, WC1   430 2090   2–1D
240-241 High Holborn, WC1   404 2055   2–1D
77/78 St Martins Ln, WC2   379 5335   4–3B
80 King's Rd, SW3   225 0770   5–2D
8-10 King St, W6   0181-563 1985   7–2C
Kensington Arcade, W8   938 1110   5–1A
27 Islington High St, N1   713 1371   8–3D
157 Camden High St, NW1   284 2240   8–3B
10 Leather Ln, EC1   831 7219   9–2A
140 Bishopsgate, EC2   377 9595   9–2D
17 Eldon St, EC2   628 9011   9–2C
28 Fleet St, EC4   353 2332   9–2A
*"Great coffee and snacks" and "cheerful staff" win a large
following for these shiny café/take-aways; affections are
ebbing, though, and even those praising their "high quality"
bemoan the "tired" and "boring" selection; (only branches
with seating are listed). / 3.30 pm-11 pm; closed Sun except some more
central branches; no credit cards; no smoking area; no booking.*

The Prince Bonaparte W2   £ 19   ❸④❸

80 Chepstow Rd   229 5912   6–1B
"Unusual pub food" – "fresh salads and healthy soups"
included – win a lot of support for this "lively" Bayswater
boozer; it's "too trendy and crowded" for some, though,
and "better ventilation would help". / 10.20 pm; closed Tue L;
no credit cards; no booking.

Princess Garden W1   £ 45   ④④④

8 North Audley St   493 3223   3–2A
"Stuffy", characterless Mayfair Chinese, voted 'most
overpriced restaurant' by all but one of those who mentioned
it this year – the exception thought it "corporate, but
reliable". / 11.45 pm; smart casual.

Prost W11   £ 25   ❸❷④

35 Pembridge Rd   727 9620   6–2B
Terribly low-key but "intimate" and "friendly" Notting Hill
local, with a rather unusual Teutonic menu and a "good
authentic beer list"; "everything sounds nicer than it is",
but prices are not demanding. / 11 pm; D only, ex Sat & Sun open
L & D; no Switch.

Pucci Pizza SW3   £ 19   ④④❶

205 King's Rd   352 2134   5–3C
"Cult", "fun" Chelsea pizzeria "always crammed full" of
pulchritudinous teenagers and twentysomethings – "you pay
for the atmosphere, not the food". / 12.30 am; closed Sun;
no credit cards.

Putney Bridge SW15   £ 40   ⑤⑤❸

Embankment   0181-780 1811   10–1A
"A real shame, given the setting and style"; rarely has
somewhere failed so utterly to live up to expectations as this
externally stunning new building overlooking the Thames;
the modish fare "lacks zip" and is "horrendously overpriced",
and "supercilious" service adds insult to injury. / 11 pm; no Amex.

QUAGLINO'S W1   £ 41   ④④❷

16 Bury St   930 6767   3–3D
"An experience" – as it approaches its fifth birthday,
this "always buzzing", "slick" and "glamorous" St James's
brasserie is, for many, "the nicest of the Conran factories";
results from a menu majoring in grills and crustacea are
"average, for what they charge", though, and service is
"amateurish". / Midnight, Fri & Sat 1 am, Sun 11 pm; set weekday L
& pre-th. £25(FP).

The Quality Chop House EC1   £31   ❸❸❸
94 Farringdon Rd   837 5093   9–1A
*"Bum-numbing benches" and shared booths are famed
masochistic delights of this restored Clerkenwell 'Working
Class Caterer'; it's an "interesting space", with "charming",
"cheerful" staff, but the "plain, but good" food is getting
"rather pricey".* / 11.30 pm; closed Sat L; no credit cards.

Quincy's NW2   £32   ❷❶❷
675 Finchley Rd   794 8499   1–1B
*This "extremely reliable" French bistro/restaurant in Finchley,
"presided over by the very friendly (English) proprietor",
offers "good value" cooking from an "excellent fixed-price
menu"; the "cosy, if cramped" accommodation is a touch
"uncomfortable".* / 11 pm; D only; closed Mon & Sun.

Quo Vadis W1   £40   ❸❸④
26-29 Dean St   437 4809   4–2A
*The involvement of not one but two 'enfants terribles' has
hardly led to a wild revamp of this Soho landmark; avant-
garde the "boring" Damien Hirst-influenced décor most
certainly is not, and though some do say the grand brasserie
cooking, 'overseen' by Marco Pierre White, is "wonderful",
fireworks seem most notable by their absence.* / 11 pm;
closed Sat L & Sun L.

Ragam W1   £19   ❸④⑤
57 Cleveland St   636 9098   2–1B
*"Good, simple" south Indian food is the attraction of this
long-established subcontinental near the Telecom Tower;
its furnishings are somewhere between "plain" and
"a disgrace".* / 11.30 pm; no Switch.

The Rainforest Café W1   £27   ④❸❷
20 Shaftesbury Avenue   434 3111   3–3D
*The newest of the West End theme-behemoths has had
rather a grudging reception – the food's not the point, of
course, but we thought the animated jungle setting really
quite impressive (and more so than the Minneapolis original);
"what exactly are they doing for the rainforests?"* / 10.45 pm, Fri
& Sat 11.45 pm; no smoking; no booking.

Randall & Aubin W1   £23   ❸④❸
16 Brewer St   287 4447   3–2D
*"Simple", "fresh" rôtisserie fare and seafood is eaten at the
counter of this atmospheric Soho deli-turned-diner; it's quality
fast food, or would be if the staff were more on the ball.*
/ 11 pm; closed Sun D.

Rani   £ 23   **❸❷**④

7 Long Ln, N3   0181-349 4386   1–1B
3 Hill St, TW9   0181-332 2322   1–4A
*Opinions divide on this South Indian vegetarian mini-chain –
for some, the food is "intriguing" and "aromatic", but for
others it's "bland" and comes in "small" portions; there is
consensus about the "lack of atmosphere". / 10 pm, Fri & Sat
10.30 pm; N3 D only – TW9 Mon-Fri closed L; no smoking areas, Sat
no smoking.*

Ranoush W1   £ 14   **❶**④④

43 Edgware Rd   723 5929   6–1D
*Late-night café/take-away offering "wonderful" Lebanese fast
food (meze, kebabs and so on), until very late; remember –
'readies' only. / 3 am; no credit cards.*

Ransome's Dock SW11   £ 34   **❷❷❷**

35 Parkgate Rd   223 1611   5–4C
*"Just an all-round good place", this modern British brasserie,
near Battersea Park, wins a loyal following for its "consistently
reliable", "good simple fare", its "relaxed" atmosphere and its
"friendly" welcome; all this and an "awesome" wine list.
/ 11 pm; closed Sun D; smart casual.*

Raoul's Café W9   £ 24   **❷❸❸**

13 Clifton Rd   289 7313   8–4A
*"Good anytime, day or evening" this recently enlarged
Maida Vale pâtisserie/bistro has "the best cappuccino" and
"great home-made dishes, too". / 10.30 pm; closed Sun D;
no smoking area; book eve only.*

Rasa N16   £ 19   **❶❶❸**

55 Stoke Newington Ch St   249 0344   1–1C
*Even non-veggies hail the "tremendous and exotic" South
Indian cooking served here, and "at rock bottom prices";
"shame it's in Stoke Newington". / 11 pm, Fri-Sat midnight; closed
Mon L; no smoking.*

Rebato's SW8   £ 22   **❷❶❷**

169 South Lambeth Rd   735 6388   10–1D
*"Like being in Spain", this "wonderful" Vauxhall tapas bar,
with its "well flavoured dishes", is a great experience, and its
characterfully macho service is the icing on the cake; there is
an agreeably tacky restaurant at the back. / 10.30 pm;
closed Sat L & Sun; smart casual.*

Red Fort W1   **£ 35**   ❸❸④
77 Dean St   437 2525   4–2A
*Soho subcontinental "stalwart" which – in spite of its size and
reputation – "still captures the gloomy essence of a proper
curry house"; as ever there are gripes that the cooking is only
"OK" and "too expensive", but no one doubts that their
regional cuisine festivals are worth seeking out. / 11.30 pm;
no smoking area.*

The Red Pepper W9   **£ 28**   ❷④❸
8 Formosa St   266 2708   8–4A
*The "best pizza this side of Venice" (and other good
Mediterranean fare) wins much praise for this "small" and
"cramped" Maida Vale Italian; some, though, complain it's
"run like a wartime factory", and "vastly overrated despite its
quite extraordinary popularity". / 10.45 pm; no Amex.*

Redmond's SW14   **£ 32**   ❸❷❷
170 Upper R'mond Rd West   0181-878 1922   10–1A
*Highly popular Sheen newcomer – a quality neighbourhood
restaurant with a "simple, colourful space", charming
service and a well-chosen wine list; we thought Mr Hayward's
"inventive" modern British grub promised rather more than it
delivered. / 10.30 pm; closed Sat L & Sun; no Amex.*

Reynier Wine Library EC3   **£ 15**   ❸❷❸
43 Trinity Sq   481 0415   9–3D
*"Brilliant", "very civilised" idea whereby a simple quality
buffet is provided to accompany wine at merchant's prices
plus £1 corkage – book ahead for a perch in this atmospheric
cellar. / L only; closed Sat & Sun.*

Rib Room
Hyatt Carlton Tower Hotel SW1 **£ 48**   ❸❷④
2 Cadogan Pl   858 7053   2–4A
*With its "good English food", "nice spacious tables" and
"a quiet enough atmosphere to have a serious discussion",
this long-established Knightsbridge grill-room is "perfect for
deal-making"; "prices are high", of course. / 11.15 pm; no Switch;
smart casual.*

Riccardo's SW3   **£ 24**   ❸⑤④
126 Fulham Rd   370 6656   5–3B
*An "appealing selection of Mediterranean starter-size dishes",
at reasonable prices, makes this Chelsea local "always full
and deservedly so"; service – always "a little stretched" –
"has slipped lately". / Midnight.*

Ristorante Italiano W1   £ 27   ❸❸❸
54 Curzon St   629 2742   3–3B
"Timewarp" Mayfair Italian, near Shepherd Market, that offers "solid and dependable" cooking at "reasonable prices". / 11.15 pm; closed Sat L & Sun; no smoking area.

The Ritz W1   £ 65   ④❷❶
150 Piccadilly   493 8181   3–4C
With its "flamboyant" Louix XVI décor, the "prettiest dining room in Europe" provides an "unbeatably romantic" mis-en-scène; some vaunt its Anglo/French cuisine, too, but we had a dire meal – and our "school food" experience was by no means unique; perhaps the new chef will throw off the curse which afflicts the kitchens here. / 11 pm; jacket & tie; set weekday L £38(FP).

Riva SW13   £ 33   ❷❸④
169 Church Rd, Barnes   0181-748 0434   10–1A
Foodie plaudits continue to rain down for the "challenging" cooking at this "real Italian" in Barnes, which remains "very popular"; "good but not as good as some say" is not an unknown reaction, however, and the atmosphere is rather "chilly". / 11 pm, Fri & Sat 11.30 pm, Sun 9.30 pm; closed Sat L; smart casual.

THE RIVER CAFÉ W6   £ 45   ❶❸❷
Thames Whf, Rainville Rd   381 8824   7–2C
"Still the best Italian in town", say devotees of this distinguished Hammersmith destination, where "quality ingredients" and "inspirational cooking" can produce "sensational results"; "buy the books instead", say those whose gripes of "stupid prices" leave the food-rating a whisker away from a downgrade. / 9.30 pm; closed Sun D.

Rôtisserie   £ 25   ❸❸④
56 Uxbridge Rd, W12   0181-743 3028   7–1C
134 Upper St, N1   226 0122   8–3D
"Results are good, especially if compared to the bill" at these simple steaks and seafood joints, in Shepherd's Bush and Islington; "excellent value" set meals. / 11 pm; W12 closed Sat L & Sun – N1 Mon-Fri closed L.

Rôtisserie Jules   £ 18   ④❸④
338 King's Rd, SW3   351 0041   5–3C
6-8 Bute St, SW7   584 0600   5–2B
133 Notting Hill Gate, W11   221 3331   6–2B
"Nice if you like chicken" (you can order lamb, too, if you call ahead) – the "tasty, French and cheap" formula makes these no-frills cafés "dependable" standbys; the food can be "bland". / 11 pm.

Rowley's SW1   **£ 40**   ⑤④④
113 Jermyn St   930 2707   3–3D
*Though it's an "old favourite" to some, this conveniently
located standby, near Piccadilly Circus, offers a grills and so
on menu which is widely thought "expensive and run-of-the-
mill".* / 11.30 pm; smart casual.

Royal China W2   **£ 29**   ❶❸❸
13 Queensway   221 2535   6–2C
*"Fantastically cheesy" black and gold styling is the only real
drawback at this outstanding Bayswater Chinese, which
serves the "best dim sum in London" (and above average
evening meals, too); the new branch (40 Baker Street W1,
tel 487 4688) has "equally good food, but the same '70s
décor!"* / 10.30 pm, Fri & Sat 11.30 pm; no booking Sun L.

Royal China SW15   **£ 28**   ❷❸❸
3 Chelverton Rd   0181-788 0907   10–2B
*Putney's Royal China shares the "nightclub atmosphere" of
its distant cousins (from whom it parted company some
years ago); its following may be largely local, but it serves
some "good food" – and "not just the dim sum".* / 10.30 pm;
no Visa or Mastercard.

RSJ SE1   **£ 27**   ❷❷❸
13a Coin St   928 4554   9–4A
*The "reliably good" modern British cooking at this
comfortable, if unexciting, South Banker, near the Festival
Hall, is somewhat eclipsed by its list of Loire wines, which
reads "like a PhD thesis".* / 11 pm; closed Sat L & Sun.

Rudland & Stubbs EC1   **£ 30**   ④④④
35 Cowcross St   253 0148   9–1A
*It's difficult to get too excited about this large tiled Smithfield
fish parlour, which gives rise to pretty ambivalent reactions –
"food and service both OK" is fairly typical.* / 10.45 pm;
closed Sat L & Sun.

La Rueda SW4   **£ 25**   ❸❷❷
66-68 Clapham High St   627 2173   10–2D
*"Top food, top laugh", say fans of this "very Spanish"
Clapham tapas bar, where "one bottle of Rioja quickly
becomes two or three"; the other branches in Chelsea and
Fitzrovia (not listed) are OK but lack the spark of the original.*
/ 11 pm; book only in restaurant.

Rules WC2   £ 40   ❸❷❷

35 Maiden Ln   836 5314   4–3D

*The capital's oldest restaurant (1798) pulls off a rare
double-act – it's "very London, but not too touristy"; the
panelled premises retain much period charm and the menu
of "good old English stodge" ("treacle pudding to die for")
"delivers what is promised very well"; all this, and "efficient"
service, too.* / 11.30 pm.

Rupee Room EC2   £ 25   ❸❸④

10 Copthall Ave   628 1555   9–2C

*A "decent City curry" ("but overpriced") is to be had in this
garish basement, near London Wall.* / 10 pm; closed Sat & Sun;
no smoking area.

S Bar SW11   £ 29   ❸❸❸

37 Battersea Bridge Rd   223 3322   5–4C

*Vaguely gothic Battersea pub-conversion newcomer, which is
already heaving with "trendy" locals; the modern British food
may not try too hard, but it's enjoyable.* / 11 pm; closed Sun D.

S&P   £ 28   ❷❷④

181 Fulham Rd, SW3   351 5692   5–2C
9 Beauchamp Pl, SW3   581 8820   5–1C

*"Always reliable", these Chelsea and Knightsbridge twins
provide "fresh tasting", "good value" Thai cooking; their
"simple" décor is a touch characterless.* / 10.30 pm;
no smoking areas at Beauchamp Pl.

Sabai Sabai W6   £ 23   ❷❷④

270-272 King St   0181-748 7363   7–2B

*"Brilliant, unpretentious Thai food" – and in "good sized
portions" – makes it worth braving this Hammersmith spot,
in spite of its "spartan" décor and "lack of atmosphere".*
/ 11.30 pm; closed Sun L.

Sabatino W8   £ 40   ④❷④

1 Palace Gt   589 9992   5–2B

*Welcoming but uninspired, would-be grand Italian newcomer,
by Kensington Gardens, whose "attentive and discreet"
service is its best point; the surroundings "have no ambience",
and the cooking is perfectly OK, but no match for the prices.*
/ 11 pm; closed Sun.

Le Sacré-Coeur N1   £ 19   ❸❸❷

18 Theberton St   354 2618   8–3D

*"Crowded and spirited" Islington Gallic bistro that is open
late, "serves decent but oily food" and "can get smoky" –
in short, it's pretty close to the genuine article.* / 11.30 pm;
set weekday L £11(FP).

Saint WC2   £ 30   ④④❷

8 Great Newport St   240 1551   4–3B
This West End scene "for young trendies" is more like a
nightclub than a restaurant; some do think its 'French Pacific'
grub "better than it ought to be for such a groovy place",
but others complain of "tiny, overpriced portions". / 11.30 pm;
closed Sat L & Sun.

St John EC1   £ 31   ④❸④

26 St John St   251 0848   9–1B
Dramatically converted, stark Smithfield ex-smokehouse
which offers a "not-for-weak-stomachs" modern British menu
(majoring in offal); the ideas may be "fresh and innovative",
but the realisation this year was too often found "dull".
/ 11.30 pm; closed Sun.

St Moritz W1   £ 26   ❸❷❸

161 Wardour St   734 3324   3–1D
"Fantastic fondue" is just one of the culinary attractions of
Soho's "cosy corner of the Alps"; appropriately – even at
current exchange rates – some find it "rather pricey for
what it is". / 11.30 pm; closed Sat L & Sun.

Sale e Pepe SW1   £ 36   ❸❸❶

9-15 Pavilion Rd   235 0098   2–3A
This "wonderful, boisterous Italian", near Knightsbridge,
wins particular support for its "noisy and vibrant"
atmosphere; given the area, what's more remarkable is that
it's "reasonably priced and reliable", too. / 11.30 pm; closed Sun.

Salloos SW1   £ 45   ❷④⑤

62-64 Kinnerton St   235 4444   2–3A
"It's irritatingly expensive, but you can't get away from
the quality" of the cooking at this once smart Pakistani,
off Knightsbridge; drawbacks include "zero ambience" and
service "whose attentiveness slips away on every visit".
/ 11.15 pm; closed Sun; smart casual; set weekday L £26(FP).

Sambuca SW3   £ 33   ❸❶④

6 Symons St   730 6571   5–2D
"Always reliable, always good service and great value" –
it's surprising that this long-established Italian, by Peter Jones,
isn't rather better known; perhaps it's because it's so cramped
– "go early or late to avoid other customers". / 11.30 pm;
closed Sun.

San Carlo N6　　　　　　£33　❸❷❸
2 Highgate High St　0181-340 5823　8–1B
*This grand Highgate trattoria has "improved"; it's
"expensive", but the "attentive" staff serve "good food" in a
spacious and comfortable atmosphere.* / 11 pm; closed Mon;
no jeans; no smoking area.

San Frediano SW3　　　　　£34　⑤④④
62 Fulham Rd　584 8375　5–2C
*"Now it's posh, it's lost all of its charm" – the many who
remember this Chelsea trattoria's cramped and friendly past
are most unforgiving about its grander new incarnation.*
/ Midnight.

San Lorenzo SW3　　　　　£50　⑤⑤④
22 Beauchamp Pl　584 1074　5–1C
*Regulars at this famed Knightsbridge trattoria think of it
"like a club, to see and be seen"; it's certainly "no place for
outsiders" – as staff attitude can make abundantly clear.*
/ 11.30 pm; closed Sun; no credit cards; smart casual.

San Martino SW3　　　　　£36　④❸❸
103 Walton St　589 3833　5–2C
*The "great atmosphere" and "personalised", "friendly"
service of this "fun" Chelsea trattoria make it an "ideal place
for a laugh"; but while fans praise the "excellent fresh food",
others say it's a "rip off" – "astronomical prices" for "very
mediocre" cooking that's "stuck in the '80s".* / 11.30 pm;
closed Sun L; smart casual; no smoking area.

Sandrini SW3　　　　　　£37　❸❸❸
260 Brompton Rd　584 1724　5–2C
*With its pleasant street-side tables, this long-established, once
very glamorous Italian is still, for its fans, "the garden-like
heart of Brompton Cross buzz"; recently it's too often been
"average", but there are signs of improvement.* / 11.30 pm.

Santini SW1　　　　　　£52　⑤④④
29 Ebury St　730 4094　2–4B
*"If the food matched the prices" at this "smart and discreet"
Belgravia Italian, "they could be on to a winner"; sadly,
though, the cooking is "disappointing", the service "arrogant"
and the ambience "sterile".* / 11.30 pm; closed Sat L & Sun L;
smart casual; set weekday L £32(FP).

Sarastro WC2 £ 26 ⑤⑤❶
126 Drury Ln   836 0101   2–2D
Even those who say "the food was terrible" admit they'll
"probably go back" to this "absolutely weird" and "wacky"
Covent Garden "circus", where the "flamboyant owner"
(King Richard) subdues the inmates with "loud opera".
/ 11.30 pm.

Sarcan N1 £ 16 ❷❸❸
4 Theberton St   226 5489   8–3D
"Cheap but very pleasant" Islington Turk, which serves
"delicious" meaty fare and "lovely, fresh meze"; when the
place is "very busy" service can be "overstretched". / Midnight.

Sash SW6 £ 19 ❸④❸
825 Fulham Rd   736 9429   10–1B
"Cheap and fun" Fulham "hang-out" where the "nice mix"
of inexpensive Chinese/Thai dishes, if not really the main
point, is perfectly well done; as we go to press, a more
ambitious Clapham offshoot opens at 32 Abbeville Road SW4
(tel 0181-673 9300). / 11 pm.

Les Saveurs W1 £ 57 ❸❷④
37a Curzon St   491 8919   3–4B
A turbulent year has seen three different chefs at the stove of
this grand Gallic Mayfair basement – the current incumbent,
Mark Wishart, was installed in June '97; as you might expect,
reports are mixed, but a "lack of atmosphere" is a perennial
complaint. / 11 pm; closed Sat L & Sun; jacket & tie.

SAVOY GRILL WC2 £ 60 ④❷❷
Strand   836 4343   4–3D
"Reeking of power", this "classic" dining room is "still the
tops for business and politics", and service is appropriately
"ever-present and discreet"; the rather "heavy" traditional
fare has come in for increasing stick of late, but a new chef is
taking the helm as we go to press. / 11.15 pm; closed Sat L & Sun;
jacket & tie.

Savoy River Restaurant WC2 £ 66 ④❸❷
Strand   420 2699   4–3D
The grand Anglo-French cuisine "may not always be as good
as it ought to be", but this "wonderful room" makes a
"sensuous venue" for a "classy", "old-fashioned" celebration –
especially if you get a window seat; also a top tip for
breakfast. / 11.30 pm; jacket & tie.

Scalini SW3 £ 41 ❸❸❷

1-3 Walton St   225 2301   5–2C

"The best for a noisy dinner", this "pricey but enjoyable"
Knightsbridge Italian was rated more highly this year; if you
are not in the party mood, you may find it "cramped, smoky
and over-loud". / 11.30 pm; smart casual.

The Scarsdale W8 £ 20 ④❸❷

23a Edwardes Sq   937 1811   7–1D

Wonderfully situated pub whose tiny, "pretty garden"
overlooks Kensington's nicest square; the grub is "average".
/ 9.45 pm; no Amex & no Switch; smart casual.

Scoffers SW11 £ 22 ❸❷❷

6 Battersea Rs   978 5542   10–2C

This "busy local brasserie" in Battersea is very popular with
local twentysomethings, who say it's a "charming", "friendly"
and "sympathetic" place – and one which does quite good
food, too. / 11 pm.

Scott's W1 £ 39 ❸❸❸

20 Mount St   629 5248   3–3A

Though some hail the "chic" new look at this grand Mayfair
seafood parlour and praise the "wonderfully fresh fish",
we're with the minority who say it's "rather disappointing"
and "overpriced", and find its aspirations to glamour largely
unfulfilled. / 11.15 pm; Sat L only oyster terrace open, closed Sun;
smart casual.

Seafresh SW1 £ 18 ❷❸④

80-81 Wilton Rd   828 0747   2–4B

The "superb fish 'n' seafood menu and an acceptable wine
list" maintain the following for this "traditional" Pimlico
chippy's dining room. / 10 pm; closed Sun.

Searcy's Brasserie EC2 £ 35 ❸④④

Level II, Barbican Centre   588 3008   9–1B

Though some say it serves "good" modern British food, this
City venue (overlooking the Barbican 'lake') is also thought
"expensive" and "inconsistent" – for the money, you could
expect a lot more in the way of creature comfort, too.
/ 10.30 pm; closed Sat L & Sun L.

Seashell NW1 £ 22 ❶❸④

49 Lisson Grove   723 8703   8–4A

There are "no pretensions" – indeed, there's very little
character of any kind – at this famous chippy behind
Marylebone Station; the "good value fish and chips", though,
are still widely tipped as "the best". / 10.30 pm; closed Sun D;
no smoking area; no booking.

Seattle Coffee £ 7 ②④❸

137 Victoria St, SW1   233 5170   2–4B
14 James St, W1   495 6680   3–1A
27 Berkeley St, W1   629 5779   3–3C
3 Grosvenor St, W1   495 5534   3–2B
34 Gt Marlborough St, W1   434 0778   2–2D
333-359 The Strand, WC2   836 5166   2–2D
51-54 Long Acre, WC2   836 2100   4–2D
"Massively pricey coffee, but the best" makes this "very American" chain (which actually only operates in the UK) reporters' top recommendation for a caffeine fix – it does superior sandwiches and muffins, too; service, if "friendly", could be more efficient. / 6 pm – 11 pm; some branches closed Sat and/or Sun; no Amex; no booking.

755 SW6 £ 34 ❷❷⑤

755 Fulham Rd   371 0755   10–1B
Even fans can find this "comfortable" (if "cramped") Fulham yearling "a bit too subdued"; the "reasonably priced" modern British menu, though, offers "such a choice" of "really good" and "consistent" nosh that they keep coming back anyway. / 11 pm; closed Mon L & Sun D.

Shampers W1 £ 27 ❸❸④

4 Kingly St   437 1692   3–2D
"Personable service", a "great selection of wines" and decent "bistro-style" food make this popular traditional Soho wine bar "a very reliable haunt". / 11 pm; closed Sun (Aug also Sat).

Shaw's SW7 £ 48 ❸❷❸

119 Old Brompton Rd   373 7774   5–2B
The 'ayes' applaud "an overlooked gem" of a modern British restaurant in South Kensington with "superb food and service" and a "very elegant", "bustle-free" setting; for the 'noes', it's just "staid", "stuffy" and "very overpriced". / 11 pm; closed Sat L & Sun D; smart casual.

Sheekey's WC2 £ 47 ④④④

28-32 St Martins Ct   240 2565   4–3B
"So old-fashioned as to be almost a museum piece", this "crowded" Theatreland fish parlour offers cooking that is "enjoyable enough, but overpriced for what you get". / 11.30 pm; closed Sun; set weekday L & pre-th. £29(FP).

Sheekey's EC4 £ 38 ⑤❸④

11 Queen Victoria St   489 8067   9–3C
Though some claim this City fish specialist is "better than suggested in your last edition", it scores poorly all round for its "dull atmosphere" and indifferent cooking; we continue to believe it survives only as a result of a "captive audience". / L only; closed Sat & Sun; smart casual.

Shepherd's SW1   £ 33   ❸❷❸

Marsham Ct, Marsham St   834 9552   2–4C

*"Unpretentious, good value and welcoming", this "traditional,
English" Westminster restaurant is a model of "consistency";
being "dependable" and "discreet" makes it "great for
business", too.* / 11.30 pm; closed Sat & Sun.

The Ship SW18   £ 27   ❸❸❷

41 Jews Row   0181-870 9667   10–2B

*"Good in the summer" – the outside terrace at this riverside
pub by Wandsworth Bridge starts heaving the moment it gets
warm; the barbecue, and the all-year restaurant, provide a
"pretty good package" of simple dishes.* / 10.30 pm; no booking for
Sun L.

Shoeless Joe's SW6   £ 29   ⑤④❷

555 King's Rd   384 2333   5–4B

*Opened with a wave of hype a couple of years ago, this two-
year-old, celebrity-backed American sports bar-restaurant
in Fulham now provokes little comment – such as there is
practically all negative; "for the right sporting event",
though, the downstairs bar is still the place.* / 11 pm.

Shogun W1   £ 50   ❷❸❸

Adam's Rw   493 1255   3–3A

*This "good value Japanese" (in the basement of Mayfair's
Britannia hotel) wins specific praise both for its sushi, and for
its atmosphere – uniquely for a traditional Nipponese in
London, it has some of the latter.* / 11 pm; D only; closed Mon;
no Switch.

Le Shop SW3   £ 19   ❸❸❸

329 King's Rd   352 3891   5–3C

*"Cheap and cheerful" Chelsea crêperie, with "tasty"
"pancakes galore" and "friendly" staff; loud classical music
raises the tone.* / Midnight; no Switch; set weekday L £11(FP).

Shree Krishna SW17   £ 18   ❶④④

192-194 Tooting High St   0181-672 4250   10–2D

*"Really superb" cooking, much of it vegetarian, at
"knockdown prices" explains the more than local reputation
of this Tooting southern Indian; service is "variable", though,
and you must "bring your own ambience".* / Mon-Thu 10.45 pm,
Fri & Sat 11.45 pm; no Switch.

Signor Sassi SW1   £ 43   ❸❸❸

14 Knightsbridge Gn   584 2277   5–1D

*"Crowded" Knightsbridge Italian – "very lively, great service
and fun, but totally overpriced".* / 11.30 pm; smart casual.

Silks & Spice W1   £ 22   ❷❸❷

23 Foley St   636 2718   2–1B
*"Cramped and pokey" it may be, but it's the "tucked away
corners" which give this Fitzrovia oriental its atmosphere;
the mixture of dishes from across South East Asia is well
prepared, providing a "big choice for all budgets". / 11 pm.*

Simply Nico SW1   £ 36   ❷❷⑤

48a Rochester Rw   630 8061   2–4C
*Nico Ladenis's "very reasonably priced" Pimlico bistro enjoys a
"deserved reputation" for traditional Gallic fare of copper-
bottomed quality, with service to match; too bad it's such a
"ghastly", "bright and cramped" space – "like the café of an
Italian railway station". / 11 pm; closed Sat L & Sun; smart casual.*

Simply Nico Chelsea SW10   £ 35   ❷❶❸

7 Park Wk   349 8866   5–3B
*Chelsea yearling Christoph's signed up with the Nico empire
in the autumn of '97, but the "charming" personnel remain;
little needs to change to meet the Nico blueprint – the
cooking was already "well presented" and "deeply flavoured",
and the setting was already a touch "insipid". / 11 pm; closed Sun.*

Simpson's of Cornhill EC3   £ 21   ❸❷❸

38 1/2 Cornhill   626 9985   9–2C
*The "best pit stop in the City", say devoted fans of this
Dickensian chop-house, where "wholesome" stodge is doled
out by cheery Cockney matrons. / L only; closed Sat & Sun;
no booking.*

Simpsons-in-the-Strand WC2   £ 44   ④❸④

100 Strand   836 9112   4–3D
*The "cholesterol heaven" of "the definitive English breakfast"
is now, sadly, the only real reason to visit this "vestige of
Edwardian England"; once it was hallowed for its Roast Beef
lunches and dinners – now it's just a "tourist trap". / 11 pm, Sun
9 pm; no Switch; smart casual.*

Singapore Garden NW6   £ 29   ❷❸④

83-83a Fairfax Rd   328 5314   8–2A
*Tacky but welcoming Swiss Cottage oriental which attracts a
wider than local following for its "excellent", "fresh" South
East Asian dishes. / 10.45 pm, Fri & Sat 11.15 pm; set weekday L
£16(FP).*

Singapura £ 32 ❸❸④

Thomas Neal Centre, WC2 240 1083 4–2C
78/79 Leadenhall St, EC3 929 0089 9–2D
1-2 Limeburner Ln, EC4 329 1133 9–2A

*These South East Asian restaurants – an expanding chain –
come recommended, especially as "excellent lunch places",
on account of their "dependable" cooking and service "with
a smile"; a "lack of ambience" is a handicap, however.
/ 9.30 pm, WC2 11 pm; closed Sat & Sun; smart casual.*

606 Club SW10 £ 30 ④❸❷

90 Lots Rd 352 5953 5–4B

*"Wonderful jazz – palatable food", fairly summarises the
priorities of this "smoke-filled" Chelsea "hideaway" (entered
via an obscure entrance opposite Lot's Road power station);
those opting for basic dishes get the best value. / Mon-Thu
1.30 am, Fri & Sat 2 am, Sun 11.30 pm; D only; no Amex.*

Smollensky's £ 27 ④④❸

1 Dover St, W1 491 1199 3–3C
105 The Strand, WC2 497 2101 4–3D

*Looking after families is the forte of these large, lavishly
decorated American-theme establishments which suffer from
"boring" and "predictable" food; the Mayfair branch,
however, is undergoing a complete refit as we go to press,
prior to a major relaunch. / Midnight, Sun 10.30 pm – Strand Thu - Sat
12.30 am.*

Snows on the Green W6 £ 32 ❸❸④

166 Shepherd's Bush Rd 603 2142 7–1C

*An air of promise unfulfilled hangs over this Mediterranean
venture in Shepherd's Bush, which is "OK", "still pleasant",
"nothing special"; as ever, the "anonymous" atmosphere is
the least attractive feature. / 11 pm.*

Sofra £ 24 ❸❸④

1 St Christopher's Pl, W1 224 4080 3–1A
18 Shepherd Mkt, W1 499 4099 3–4B
18 Shepherd St, W1 493 3320 3–4B
17 Charing Cross Rd, WC2 930 6090 4–4B
36 Tavistock St, WC2 240 3773 4–3D

*"Fresh", "very tasty" Turkish nosh and "service with a smile"
mean this fast-growing chain always makes a useful standby,
though their bright, "over-exposed" décor is "not great
for lingering". / Midnight.*

Soho Soho W1 £34 ④④❸
11-13 Frith St   494 3491   4–2A
This Soho landmark's upstairs Mediterranean restaurant may be "lively", but it's the "vibrant", ground floor rôtisserie which really "buzzes"; some rate the cooking throughout as "consistent", but complaints about "uninspired" and "bland" food are up this year. / rotisserie 12.45 am, restaurant 11.45 pm; restaurant closed Sat L & Sun; no smoking area; no booking in rotisserie.

Soho Spice W1 £22 ❸❸❷
124-126 Wardour St   434 0808   3–1D
The Red Fort's café-like new off-shoot brings a "stylish, modern" approach to the Soho Indian experience; the menu offers "a small choice, but good food". / 11.30 pm; closed Sun; no smoking area.

Solly's NW11 £28 ❷④❸
148 Golders Green Rd   0181-455 0004   1–1B
"Reliable", "genuine Kosher food" and "lunatic" service make a visit to this tacky but endearing Golders Green Israeli quite an experience. / 11.30 pm; closed Fri D & Sat; no smoking area.

Sonny's SW13 £32 ❷❷❷
94 Church Rd   0181-748 0393   10–1A
"Classy" Barnes all-rounder that continues to please with its "relaxed" and "informal" attitude and its "interesting" modern British cooking – "when it's good it's brilliant". / 11 pm; closed Sun D; smart casual.

Sotheby's Café W1 £28 ❸❷❸
34 New Bond St   408 5077   3–2C
"Great for a light lunch with pals", this café yearling, off the foyer of the famous Mayfair auctioneers, is praised for "delicious", "fresh" cooking that offers fair value; "it's too small, so always fully booked". / L only; closed Sat & Sun, but May-Jul and Sep-Dec open Sun L; no smoking.

Le Soufflé
Inter-Continental Hotel W1 £60 ❷❷⑤
1 Hamilton Pl   409 3131   3–4A
Peter Kromberg's "very professional" repertoire of modern French fare – no prizes for guessing the speciality – wins limited but ardent support for this hotel dining room; shame about the "hardly sympathetic" setting – "rather like a '70s cinema". / 10.30 pm, Sat 11.15 pm; closed Mon, Sat L & Sun D; jacket; no smoking area; set Sun L £36(FP).

Soulard N1 £ 25 ❷❷❷

113 Mortimer Rd   254 1314   1–1C
*"The happiest proprietor in London" is just part of the
attraction of this "real find" on the fringes of Islington
and Hackney – a "tiny", cramped bistro serving "fine",
"traditional" French fare.* / 10.30 pm; D only, closed Sun & Mon;
no Switch.

South W11 £ 30 ④④❸

1-3 Elgin Cr   727 6667   6–1B
*New Notting Hill Scandinavian bar/brasserie that's good when
it's good – awful when it's bad; a characterful basement with
regular jazz, it's perhaps more a 'scene' than an eatery.*
/ 11.30 pm; ; closed Sun.

Spago SW7 £ 20 ❸④④

6 Glendower Pl   225 2407   5–2B
*Notwithstanding its "ugly" décor, this "small", "noisy" South
Kensington joint keeps "busy" and can be "good fun" thanks
to its "authentic pizza and pasta" and eminently reasonable
prices.* / 12.30 am; D only; no credit cards.

La Spighetta W1 £ 23 ❷④❸

43 Blandford St   486 7340   2–1A
*Quality, pizzas from the wood-burning oven – fairly priced –
are the high point of this cacophonous, basement Italian
newcomer (previously Sol e Stella, RIP); service is amicable,
but leisurely.* / 10.30 pm.

Sporting Page SW10 £ 20 ❸❸❷

6 Camera Pl   376 3694   5–3B
*Stylish Chelsea boozer, whose food which, if not remarkable,
is "good for a pub".* / 10 pm; no Amex & no Switch; no booking.

Springbok Café W4 £ 30 ❸❸④

42 Devonshire Rd   0181-742 3149   7–2A
*Most hail a "fascinating experience" at this small South
African "neighbourhood cafe", off Chiswick High Street,
thanks to its "innovative" cooking and "warm" service;
the menu is "a bit too unusual" for some, though, and
"bum-numbing chairs prevent lingering".* / 10.30 pm;
closed Sun D; no Amex.

THE SQUARE W1   £ 56   ❷❸❸

6-10 Bruton St   495 7100   3–2C
The grand, new Mayfair home of this "very grown up"
restaurant (formerly of St James's) is "more sweeping and
graceful" than the old; some find the modern British cooking
"transcendent", but even those who say that "on its day,
it's the best in town", admit it can be "variable". / 10.45 pm;
closed Sat L & Sun L; smart casual.

Sri India EC2

7-8 Bishopsgate Place   628 2826   9–2D
Potentially splendid, these listed Turkish baths (in a basement
near Liverpool Street) are being launched in late '97 as the
first subcontinental venture of the highly successful group
which owns the Sri Siam.

Sri Siam W1   £ 27   ❷❷❸

16 Old Compton St   434 3544   4–2A
One of the top orientals in town – this attractive Soho Thai
offers "beautifully presented" food and is a model of all-round
consistency. / 11.15 pm; closed Sun L.

Sri Siam City EC2   £ 31   ❷❷④

85 London Wall   628 5772   9–2C
"Reliable", "very busy" City basement Thai serving "great",
"fresh" food (if from a "slightly samey" menu). / 7.45 pm;
closed Sat & Sun.

Sri Thai EC4   £ 32   ❷④④

3 Queen Victoria St   827 0202   9–3C
This impressively designed City basement has not lived up
to its early promise; some still say it's a "bustling" place,
providing "good quality, genuine Thai cooking at acceptable
prices", but for others it's just "terribly expensive" and
"too noisy", with "almost aggressive" service. / 8.30 pm;
closed Sat & Sun.

The Stable SW13   £ 24   ❸④❸

373 Lonsdale Rd   0181-876 1855   10–1A
Little known Barnes dining room (behind the Bull's Head,
a major music pub) whose hearty, wholesome grub offers very
fair value; for a "cosy and romantic", away-from-it-all venue,
you could do much worse. / 11 pm; D only; closed Sun.

Standard Tandoori W2   £ 19   ❸❸④

21-23 Westbourne Grove   229 0600   6–1C
This large, "no-nonsense" Bayswater Indian lives up to its
name, providing "very reliable", "tasty and cheap" curries;
it "needs redecorating". / 11.45 pm; no smoking area.

Star Café W1 £15 ❸④❸

22 Gt Chapel St 437 8778 3–1D
*Superior Soho greasy spoon (just south of Oxford Street),
providing "huge portions of really well cooked food"; breakfast
is its forte.* / 4 pm; closed Sat & Sun; no credit cards; no smoking area.

Star of India SW5 £34 ❷④❷

154 Old Brompton Rd 373 2901 5–2B
*"Absolutely camp" décor (not to mention the "free cabaret
from the maître d'") makes this "bizarre but wonderful"
South Kensington Indian a perennial crowd-pleaser; the
cooking is "creative" and "tasty", too, with "excellent
specialities", but the rather "snooty" service may make
you wait for it.* / 11.45 pm.

Stephen Bull W1 £38 ❷❷❸

5-7 Blandford St 486 9696 2–1A
*"There's always some new delight", say the many fans of
the "fine" modern British cooking at Mr Bull's original
restaurant; "attentive" service is a further plus, but even the
faithful can find the "crisp" décor of its Marylebone premises
"rather stark", especially at night.* / 10.30 pm; closed Sat L & Sun.

Stephen Bull WC2 £33 ❷❷❸

12 Upper St Martin's Ln 379 7811 4–3B
*Stephen Bull's latest venture is a stylish transformation of
a 'graveyard' Theatreland site, offering "delicious",
"wonderfully competent" modern British cooking and
"helpful", very professional service; the room's odd
proportions can contribute to a "slightly sterile" atmosphere.*
/ 11.30 pm; closed Sat L & Sun.

Stephen Bull Bistro EC1 £32 ❷❸④

71 St John St 490 1750 9–1A
*"Thoroughly dependable" modern British cooking wins high
praise for this upmarket Smithfield canteen; the "harsh"
décor can be "too cramped and uncomfortable" for some.*
/ 10.30 pm; closed Sat L & Sun; no smoking area.

The Stepping Stone SW8 £32 ❷❶❸

123 Queenstown Rd 622 0555 10–1C
*It's the "unusually genuine feeling to the welcome" which
distinguishes this agreeably "sparse" Battersea modern Briton,
which delivers "delicious", "interesting" and "reasonably
priced" cooking.* / 11 pm, Mon 10.30 pm; closed Sat L & Sun D;
no smoking area.

Sticky Fingers W8   £ 22   ④❸❸

1a Phillimore Gdns   938 5338   5–1A

Those who think that "Bill Wyman should stick to his music"
are in a minority – most praise this Rolling Stone's "relaxed"
Kensington diner as a reasonable value venue that's "great for
children"; "excellent burgers" are the speciality. / 11.30 pm;
book L only.

Stock Pot   £ 12   ④❸❸

40 Panton St, SW1   839 5142   4–4A
18 Old Compton St, W1   287 1066   4–2B
50 James St, W1   486 9185   3–1A
273 King's Rd, SW3   823 3175   5–3C
6 Basil St, SW3   589 8627   5–1D

"Not gastronomic, but great anyway", this "basic" chain has
"no pretensions", and "it's used by all kinds of people";
"you get what you pay for – school dinners". /
11 pm-Midnight; no credit cards; booking restricted at some times.

Stone Mason's Arms W6   £ 21   ❷❷❸

54 Cambridge Grove   0181-748 1397   7–2C

Yet another new Hammersmith gastropub; don't let the busy
roadside location put you off – the simple but conscientiously
prepared grub, and in generous portions, should give its local
competitors a run for their money. / 10 pm.

Stratford's W8   £ 36   ❷❷④

7 Stratford Rd   937 6388   5–2A

Quietly situated Kensington local whose devoted fans sing
the praises of the "genuinely nice" service, "cosy and
comfortable" setting and "always good" fish and seafood;
we've never quite seen it. / 11 pm; set weekday L & pre-th. £20(FP).

The Sugar Club W11   £ 36   ❷❷❷

33 All Saints Rd   221 3844   6–1B

"Trendsville '97" – the fame of these obscurely located
Notting Hill premises has spread wide, and praise for
Peter Gordon's "imaginative but solidly well cooked" Pacific
Rim food runs deep; the setting, though quite stark, strikes
some as "romantic", especially in the summer courtyard.
/ 11 pm; no smoking area.

Suntory SW1   £ 72   ❸❸④

72 St James's St   409 0201   3–4D

London's longest established grand Japanese is still, for many,
"the best" – "seriously good food, beautifully presented and
served"; freer spirits can find its St James's premises a touch
too "formal" and "business-like". / 10 pm; closed Sun; smart casual.

Le Suquet SW3   £36   ②④②
104 Draycott Av   581 1785   5–2C
*"The best fruits de mer" in a setting "like the Côte d'Azur"
gained renewed support this year for this "crowded and
noisy" Brompton Cross stalwart; "if you don't speak French"
you may encounter "outrageously contemptuous" service.*
/ 11.30 pm; set weekday L £19(FP).

Sushi Wong W8   £27   ❸❸④
38c Kensington Church St   937 5007   5–1A
*Head for the basement (rather than the tiny upstairs) of
this Kensington Nipponese newcomer – a canteen for
well heeled locals; the dishes are "simple but excellent",
although the pricing and the meagre portions suggest a
somewhat grabbing attitude; given its size, the teppan-yaki
is an unusual feature.* / 10.30 pm; closed Sun.

Sushi-Say NW2   £29   ❷❷④
33b Walm Ln   0181-459 7512   1–1A
*This small, high quality Japanese near Willesden Green tube
benefits from "friendly service" and offers some excellent,
reasonably priced fare – "pity it's so far out".* / 10.30 pm; D only;
closed Mon; no Amex.

Sweetings EC4   £31   ❷❸❷
39 Queen Victoria St   248 3062   9–3B
*"Still a favourite in the City", this wonderfully "olde worlde"
Victorian fish parlour is now back on its old form, and
receives a resounding thumbs-up for "pricey but good fresh
produce".* / L only; closed Sat & Sun; no credit cards; no booking.

t'su SW3   £25   ❸❸❸
118 Draycott Ave   584 5522   5–2C
*Brompton Cross's latest newcomer could hardly be more
different from Waltons (RIP), its cosy predecessor;
another sushi-conveyor-café, it's the brainchild of Julian (Pret A
Manger) Metcalfe and has appropriately bright and modish
décor; high quality grub, but pricey for fast food.* / 11 pm;
no smoking; no booking.

Taberna Etrusca EC4   £31   ④④❸
9 Bow Churchyard   248 5552   9–2C
*Popular City Italian "which only succeeds because the
waitresses attract attention instead of the food"; it also
boasts a "lovely courtyard for summer dining".* / L only;
closed Sat & Sun; no Switch.

F S A

Tamarind W1   **£ 34**   **❶❷❷**
20 Queen St   629 3561   3–3B
Thanks to its "beautiful", "unusual", "nouvelle" Indian cuisine
and "efficient and charming" service, this "sophisticated"
Mayfair basement is emerging as one of the top
subcontinentals in town. / 11.30 pm; closed Sat L.

Tandoori Lane SW6   **£ 22**   **❷❶❷**
131a Munster Rd   371 0440   10–1B
"Rolls-Royce service" – "nothing is too much trouble" –
and "top class curry" make this "romantic" deepest Fulham
Indian "a considerable cut above the average". / 11 pm; no Amex.

Tandoori of Chelsea SW3   **£ 32**   **④❸❸**
153 Fulham Rd   589 7749   5–2C
"OK and reliable", this long-established, grand and
comfortable Indian still has its attractions – "if you happen to
be on the Fulham Road". / Midnight.

LA TANTE CLAIRE SW3   **£ 64**   **❶❶❸**
68-69 Royal Hospital Rd   352 6045   5–3D
Pierre Koffmann's "sublime" and "wonderful" French cooking
still makes his Chelsea dining room the tops for many, and
his "attentive" staff are heaped with praise; the perennial
complaint – the "very boring" décor, which "lets down
everything else" – persists, but, as ever, the lunch menu is
venerated for its "unbeatable" value. / 11 pm; closed Sat & Sun;
no Switch; dinner, jacket & tie; set weekday L £35(FP).

Tao EC4   **£ 32**   **④④❸**
11 Bow Ln   248 5833   9–2C
The "poor" oriental food and "sloppy" Italian service are
"not the reasons most people go" to this brash City scene;
the bar "gets mobbed in the evenings". / 10 pm; closed Sat & Sun;
smart casual.

Tate Gallery SW1   **£ 39**   **④❸❷**
Millbank   887 8877   2–4C
The famous Whistler murals of this gallery dining room and
the "wonderfully affordable wines" are still much more of an
attraction than the modern British cooking; let's see what
changes the second new chef in as many years can bring.
/ L only; closed Sun; no smoking area.

TATSUSO EC2   £ 63   **❶❸**④

32 Broadgate Circle   638 5863   9–2D
"Supreme sushi" ("the best in Europe!") and other
"wonderful" dishes makes this City Japanese, for many,
the best in town, with the "traditional" ("no ambience")
basement culinarily preferable to the more stylish upstairs
teppan-yaki; "exorbitant" bills make the place "too pricey
for private purposes". / 9.45 pm; closed Sat & Sun; smart casual.

Tawana W2   £ 21   **❷**④④

3 Westbourne Grove   229 3785   6–1C
"Consistently good, fresh and tasty" Thai fare is "let down
by the décor", and sometimes by the service, at this "low-key"
Bayswater café. / 11 pm.

The Tenth W8   £ 40   **❸❸❸**

Royal Garden Hotel, Ken' High St   361 1910   5–1A
With "superb views across Kensington Gardens", a "relaxing"
atmosphere and "friendly" service, this elevated dining room
attracts a steady following – thanks to the "adventurous"
modern British cooking, many are willing to overlook its
"airportish" décor. / 11.30 pm; closed Sat L & Sun; no smoking area.

Terraza-Est EC4   £ 25   **❸❸**④

109 Fleet St   353 2680   9–2A
It's hardly at the culinary cutting edge, but this City-fringe
Italian's formula – good standard fare, with operatic arias
for dessert – has kept it going for a good number of years
now. / 11 pm; closed Sat & Sun.

Texas Embassy Cantina WC2   £ 25   ④**❸❸**

1 Cockspur St   925 0077   2–2C
Even those who think this large Tex/Mex off Trafalgar Square
serves the best cooking of its type in town admit that that is
not saying much; it is "extremely lively", though, helping to
overcome the touristiness of its location. / 11 pm, Fri & Sat
midnight.

Texas Lone Star SW7   £ 22   ⑤⑤**❸**

154 Gloucester Rd   370 5625   5–2B
Though still "fun for kids", this large, loud American theme-
diner has "gone down badly over the years" – service is too
often "atrocious", and "cookery classes would help".
/ Sun-Wed 11.30 pm, Thu-Sat 12.30 am; no booking.

TGI Friday's £ 29 ⑤④❸
25-29 Coventry St, W1   839 6262   4–4A
6 Bedford St, WC2   379 0585   4–4C
96-98 Bishops Bridge Rd, W2   229 8600   6–1C
*"Large portions of bland food" combined with hallmark
"pushy", "over-eager" service mean that there's "not much
to recommend" this very "overpriced" American-theme chain.*
/ Midnight, W2 11.30 pm; smart casual; no smoking area; W1 & WC2,
no booking Fri D-Sat L.

Thai Bistro W4 £ 19 ❷❸④
99 Chiswick High Rd   0181-995 5774   7–2B
*"Very tasty", "plentiful" cooking (including "superb noodles
dishes" and some less familiar regional specialities) makes
for "excellent value" at this Chiswick oriental; the "noisy"
"canteen atmosphere" – you eat at long shared tables –
is "something of a drawback".* / 11 pm; closed Tue L & Thu L;
no Amex & no Switch; no smoking area.

Thai on the River SW10 £ 26 ❸④❸
15 Lots Rd   351 1151   5–4B
*This erratic and "very expensive" Chelsea Thames-sider
(near the power station) has the special attraction of good
views "as long as you sit near the river"; service can be
"terrible".* / 11 pm, Fri & Sat 11.30 pm; closed Sat L.

Thai Pot WC2 £ 24 ❸❸④
1 Bedfordbury   379 4580   4–4C
*"Reliable, mid-price" central Thai (behind the Coliseum) that's
handy for the theatre or for a group get-together; foodwise,
results are "a mix of good and average".* / 11.15 pm; closed Sun;
no smoking area.

Thailand SE14 £ 31 ❷❷❸
15 Lewisham Way   0181-691 4040   1–3D
*South easterly reporters claim this "very small" and
"cramped" Lewisham destination as "the best Thai in
London"; it certainly offers "unusually good food" and a
"great selection of Scotch whiskies".* / 10.30 pm; D only; closed Mon
& Sun; no Amex.

Thierry's SW3 £ 30 ④❸❷
342 King's Rd   352 3365   5–3C
*Some still approve the "reliable" Gallic bistro cooking at this
"very romantic" Chelsea "old favourite"; we're with those who
say it's "overpriced, mediocre and clichéed".* / 11 pm.

33 SW I   £ 45   ②③④
33 St James's St   930 4272   3–4C
"Small but striking" St James's two-year-old that may yet defy its detractors; its slightly odd décor is a touch "soulless", but the modern British cooking" – though "quite expensive" – is "well executed" and "very strongly flavoured". / 11.30 pm; closed Sat L & Sun; smart casual.

Thomas Goode Restaurant W1   £ 49   ⑤②③
19 South Audley St   409 7242   3–3A
"Totally over the top" dining room – part of a self-important Mayfair glass and china emporium – which offers the chance to eat from the prettiest plates in town; the outside-catering-style fare is totally "overrated", but "very attentive" staff "make you feel special". / L & tea only; closed Sat & Sun; no jeans.

Three Little Pigs SE I   £ 23   ⑤④⑤
89 Westminster Br Rd   928 5535   2–3D
"Bland" but "friendly" British standby worth knowing about in the wasteland near Lambeth North tube. / 10.30 pm, Fri & Sat midnight; closed Sat L & Sun.

Tiger Lil's   £ 22   ④③②
500 King's Rd, SW3   376 5003   5–3B
270 Upper St, N1   226 1118   8–2D
15a Clapham Common S'side, SW4   720 5433   10–2D
Supporters say these oriental "make-up-your-own-combinations" eateries are "good value" and a "great place for a loud crowd night out"; critics just find "long queues waiting for a pile of tasteless gloop!" / 11.30 pm, Fri & Sat Midnight; no Amex; no smoking areas.

Toff's N10   £ 26   ①②④
38 Muswell Hl Broadway   0181-883 8656   1–1B
"Marvellous fish and chips" have for a number of years made this Muswell Hill fixture "the best chippy in London" – "no atmosphere, but excellent fish"; let's hope the new owners have the same culinary gifts as the old. / 10 pm; closed Mon & Sun; no booking; set weekday L £14(FP).

Tokyo Diner WC2   £ 14   ③①③
2 Newport Pl   287 8777   4–3B
Reliable, "simple" food, with "good bento boxes", makes this "cheap", "no-fuss " central Japanese – mislocated in Chinatown – a good bet for a quick bite. / Midnight; no Amex; no smoking area; eve, Fri & Sat no booking.

Tootsies   **£ 20**   ④❸④

177 New King's Rd, SW6   736 4023   10–1B
107 Old Brompton Rd, SW7   581 8942   5–2B
120 Holland Pk Ave, W11   229 8567   6–2A
148 Chiswick High Rd, W4   0181-747 1869   7–2A
198 Haverstock Hill, NW3   431 7609   8–2A
147 Church Rd, SW13   0181-748 3630   10–1A

"Good food for a chain" (the *"superior burgers"* in particular)
make these *"supremely consistent"*, *"reasonably priced"*
diners a good choice for *"vegging out"* (especially if you have
the family in tow). / 11 pm - 11.30 pm, Fri & Sat Midnight; no Amex;
no booking.

Topsy-Tasty W4   **£ 20**   ❶❷④

5 Station Parade   0181-995 3407   1–3A
*Though eclipsed in fame by its sibling, the Bedlington Café,
this smarter, but less atmospheric, Thai café (opposite
Chiswick Station) provides the same "honest", "cheap"
and spicy grub. / 10.30 pm; D only; closed Sun; no credit cards.*

Toto's SW1   **£ 40**   ❷❷❷

Lennox Gardens Mews   589 2062   5–2D
"A true delight", this *"elegant"* and glamorous Knightsbridge
trattoria pleases with its *"consistent"*, *"solid"* cooking and its
staff's professional and unstuffy attitude; in summer, the
mews outside makes a *"great lunchtime spot"*. / 11.30 pm;
smart casual.

Townhouse Brasserie WC1   **£ 28**   ❸❸❸

24 Coptic St   636 2731   2–1C
*New owners haven't done much to this interestingly
converted, if oddly proportioned, Bloomsbury townhouse
(formerly Chiaroscuro, RIP); the modern British food's a bit
more mundane now, but the prices give little cause for
complaint. / 11.30 pm; no smoking area.*

Troika NW1   **£ 17**   ❸❸❸

101 Regents Pk Rd   483 3765   8–2B
"Good value for money" makes this *"buzzing"* Primrose Hill
local *"one to go back to"* for its *"unusual"* eastern European
dishes, *"cheap coffee"* and *"excellent strudel"*. / 10.30 pm;
no credit cards; no smoking area.

Troubadour SW5   **£ 14**   ④⑤❶

265 Old Brompton Rd   no tel   5–3A
"They should bottle the atmosphere" at this *"eccentric"*,
"mellow" Earl's Court coffee house, which attracts an
"interesting" Bohemian crowd; the cakes, omelettes and
salads are quite OK, but go prepared for *"miserable"* and
"cranky" service. / 10.30 pm; no credit cards; no booking.

Tui SW7 £ 28 ❶❸⑤
19 Exhibition Rd   584 8359   5–2C
"Exceptional", "authentic" spicy cooking makes this stark
South Kensington Thai "the best in town" for some reporters;
the "charmless" setting "needs a make-over". / 10.45 pm;
smart casual.

Tuk Tuk N1 £ 22 ❸❸⑤
330 Upper St   226 0837   8–3D
"Interesting and tasty" Thai grub at an "economical" price
makes this "stark, metallic" Islington café a "popular"
standby; it offers "nothing much by way of atmosphere".
/ 11 pm; closed Sat L & Sun L.

Turner's SW3 £ 55 ❸④❸
87-89 Walton St   584 6711   5–2C
It looks "dated", but this ambitious Knightsbridge restaurant –
presided over by TV chef, Brian Turner – has "improved" of
late; "reliable" modern French cooking, "comfortable"
surroundings and the undoubted value of the set lunches are
among the virtues which commend it. / 11 pm, Sun 8.30 pm;
closed Sat L; smart casual; set weekday L £27(FP).

Tusc SW5 £ 28 ④④④
256 Old Brompton Rd   373 9082   5–3A
Despite the odd report of "massive improvement" and
"interesting cooking" this revamped Earl's Court trattoria
(fka Pontevecchio) has yet to regain the form which once
made this site famous. / Midnight.

The Tuscan W11 £ 26 ④❸❸
116 Princedale Rd   792 9302   6–2A
"They try very hard to please" at this new Holland Park pub-
conversion, which serves simple fare – "which has nothing to
do with Tuscany" – in bright and airy surroundings; breakfasts
come recommended. / 11 pm; no Amex.

Two Brothers N3 £ 22 ❶❷④
297/303 Regent's Pk Rd   0181-346 0469   1–1B
"Very fresh fish and chips" ensure there's "nearly always a
queue" at this large "upmarket" Finchley chippy. / 10.15 pm;
closed Mon & Sun; no smoking area; book L only.

The Union Café W1 £ 30 ④④④
96 Marylebone Ln   486 4860   3–1A
Beware "increasing complacency" at this airy, "California-
style" Marylebone café; its "limited menu" has always come
in "smallish portions", but this year the "simple, fresh food"
was too often judged "mediocre", providing restricted
compensation for the "spartan" setting and "uppity" service.
/ 10.30 pm; closed Sat D & Sun; no Amex.

Uno SW1   £24   ❷❸❸
1 Denbigh St   834 1001   2–4B
*Pimlico locals rave – we use the word advisedly – about
this "outstanding", "fun and friendly" new Italian, where
"delicious" pizzas and "the best pasta ever" make for
"excellent value". / 11.30 pm; closed Sun; no credit cards.*

Upper Street Fish Shop N1   £19   ❷④④
324 Upper St   359 1401   8–2D
*"Homely" Islington chippy whose "surprisingly sophisticated",
"wonderfully fresh" fish and seafood at "low cost" have made
it a local institution; it may be "the friendliest place", but it's
"understaffed"; BYO. / 10.15 pm; closed Mon L & Sun; no credit cards;
no booking.*

Valhalla SW11   £26   ④❸❸
57 Battersea Bridge Rd   978 7272   5–4C
*Agreeable Battersea bar-restaurant distinguished by its
Sistine Chapel ceiling, rather than its "unadventurous",
"good to ordinary" modern British fare. / 11 pm.*

Vama SW10   £30   ④❷④
438 King's Rd   351 4118   5–3B
*Camp and "Chelsified", this Indian summer newcomer aims
for a fashionable following; it offers minimal personal 'space',
and our meal was underspiced to the point of tedium. / 10 pm.*

Vasco & Piero's Pavilion W1   £30   ❷❶❸
15 Poland St   437 8774   3–1D
*A "charming place", say devotees of this "offbeat" Soho
curiosity (whose décor was inherited from a now-demolished
theatre); it's the "courteous" service that really makes it
special, but the food – "a strange mix of traditional and
modern Italian" – also gets the thumbs-up, especially the
"excellent value set menu". / 11 pm; closed Sat & Sun
(open one Sat D monthly); no Switch; smart casual.*

Veeraswamy W1   £32   ❷❷❷
99-101 (Victory Hs) Regent St   734 1401   3–3D
*London's oldest Indian (1926) has been rescued from its
tourist-trap status – both food and service seemed set fair
on a visit soon after the September '97 relaunch; though the
place is now twinned with Chutney Mary, its colourful and
comfortable new look owes nothing to the Raj. / 11.30 pm;
closed Sun; smart casual; no smoking area; set weekday L £20(FP).*

The Vegetarian Cottage NW3   £ 17   ❸❷❸

91 Haverstock Hl   586 1257   8–2B

"It takes imagination to fake fish", shrill fans of this veggie Chinese in Belsize Park, outraged that we might suggest – as we still do – that the "good and healthy" cooking here can tend to bland. / 11.15 pm; D only ex Sun open L & D; no Amex.

Vegia Zena NW1   £ 27   ❶❸❸

17 Princess Rd   483 0192   8–3B

"Mouth-watering", "genuinely regional" Italian cooking wins a devoted following for this rather modest Primrose Hill destination, which has an "unusual, family atmosphere". / 11 pm; no Amex; set weekday L £13(FP).

Vendôme W1   £ 35   ❸❸❷

20 Dover St   629 5417   3–3C

"Dramatic reds and blacks create a very louche feel" at this "sexy", "elegant" and "intimate" Mayfair bar/restaurant; "after such drama", the modern British menu can seem "pedestrian", but it's quite "reliable", and some note "lots of improvements since last year's re-opening". / 11 pm; closed Sat L & Sun.

Veronica's W2   £ 29   ❸❷❸

3 Hereford Rd   229 5079   6–1B

The "innovative", historical English menu and "candlelit magic" of these "unusual" Bayswater premises win ecstatic support from its small band of admirers; there is a school of thought (which we share) which says it offers an "interesting menu, but not a lot else". / Midnight; closed Sat L & Sun.

Vic Naylors EC1   £ 24   ⑤⑤❸

40 St John St   608 2181   9–1B

The "good, rowdy" atmosphere of this brick-lined Smithfield bar/bistro is its attraction, not the "awful" food or poor service. / 10.30 pm; closed Sat L & Sun.

Il Vicolo SW1   £ 29   ❸❷④

3-4 Crown Passage   839 3960   3–4D

"Down a seedy St James's alleyway" – and useful to know about in a pricey part of town – this rather undiscovered trattoria "looks after you", and serves "standard fare that's nonetheless well made and flavoured". / 10.15 pm; closed Sat & Sun.

Vijay NW6 £ 18 ❷❸④

49 Willesden Ln   328 1087   1–1B
*Atmospheric, in a slightly dingy way, this long-established
Kilburn Indian draws more than just a local crowd with its
"great value", "interesting" vegetarian dishes (plus more
standard repertoire). / 10.45 pm, Fri & Sat 11.45 pm.*

Villa Bianca NW3 £ 33 ④❸❷

1 Perrins Ct   435 3131   8–2A
*"The food is only OK, but the fawning staff make up for it
(just)" at this chichi and "overpriced" Hampstead Italian,
delightfully situated in a cobbled lane. / 11.30 pm.*

Village Bistro N6 £ 33 ❸❸❸

38 Highgate High St   0181-340 5165   8–1B
*It may be a touch "precious" and "cramped", but this
friendly Highgate cottage's "limited" Gallic menu is "reliable";
some do find it "too expensive", though. / 11 pm.*

Villandry Dining Rooms W1 £ 39

170 Gt Portland St   631 3131   2–1B
*Foodie French favourite which – as we go to press –
is shifting from its cramped shop conditions to more
spacious traiteur-cum-restaurant premises; let's hope that
the "delicious" cooking survives the translation and that the
sometimes "unfriendly" service does not. / 11 pm; closed Sun D;
no smoking.*

Vincent's SW15 £ 23 ❸❷④

147 Upper Richmond Rd   0181-780 3553   10–2B
*"Well cooked, well presented food at moderate prices" makes
this "van Gogh theme-restaurant" a useful Putney standby –
"the interior's suburban, but the food isn't". / 10.30 pm;
closed Sat L & Sun.*

The Vine NW5 £ 27 ❸⑤❸

86 Highgate Rd   209 0038   8–1B
*"Tasty", well-executed modern British fare "in goodly-sized
amounts" has made this dolled up Kentish Town boozer
(with an "excellent garden") an instant hit; "staff struggle
poorly to cope", however, contributing to a somewhat
"impersonal" atmosphere. / 10 pm; closed Mon L; no smoking area.*

Vingt-Quatre SW10 £ 24 ❸❷❸

325 Fulham Rd   376 7224   5–3B
*Young Chelsea's "trendy" "Beach-scene" loves this 24-hour
diner with its "funky menu"; amazingly, the food and service
are really quite good. / open 24 hours; no booking.*

VONG SW1 £ 42 ❷❸❷

Wilton Pl   235 1010   5–1D

This Knightsbridge yearling is widely praised for its "plush" ambience and its "aromatic", "brilliantly blended" and "beautifully presented" French/Thai combinations – especially from the "wonderful tasting menu"; a small but belligerent minority, though, dismisses both food and setting as "heavy-handedly pretentious". / 10 pm; closed Sun L; no smoking.

Vrisaki N22 £ 23 ❷❸④

73 Myddleton Rd   0181-889 8760   1–1C

"Worth a visit when you are very hungry" – fans journey from all over north London to this obscurely situated Bounds Green Greek for the "brilliant value" meze special that comes in "unbelievable" quantities; you must book. / Midnight; closed Sun.

W11 W11 £ 30 ④④❷

123a Clarendon Rd   229 8889   6–2A

Atmospheric converted pub, on the fringe of Holland Park (with a great outside terrace in summer); "slapdash" service and "dull" modern British cooking may explain why it's not better known. / 11.30 pm; D only ex Sun, when open L & D; no Amex.

Wagamama £ 16 ❷❷❸

10a Lexington St, W1   292 0990   3–2D
4a Streatham St, WC1   323 9223   2–1C

"The only problem is the queues" at these "efficient" and "friendly" pioneers of the Japanese noodle-bar revolution; "consistently good", "healthy" grub served in stark but stylish refectory surroundings makes eating here a "speedy" (once you're in) and "entertaining" experience. / 11 pm; no Amex; no smoking; no booking.

Wakaba NW3 £ 40 ❷❸④

122a Finchley Rd   586 7960   8–2A

Little-known Japanese, opposite Finchley Road tube, which serves high quality grub (including good sushi) in stark and dated surroundings. / 10.45 pm; D only; closed Sun; no Switch; no smoking area.

The Waldorf Meridien WC2 £ 24 ④❷❷

Aldwych   836 2400   2–2D

The civilised attractions of its famous tea-dance (the price given) and rather newer buffet breakfasts are the occasions when this "pleasant", if somewhat touristique, hotel scores best; the restaurant is one of the many pies into which Marco Pierre White is rumoured to be sticking his fêted fingers, perhaps heralding higher culinary ambition. / Tea daily 3.30 pm-6 pm; for tea dance, jacket & tie; no smoking.

FSA

The Waterloo Fire Station SE1   £24   ④④❸
150 Waterloo Rd   401 3267   9–4A
At its best, this once-innovative, large and "buzzing" bar-refectory (near the Old Vic) still provides "robust and varied", "reasonably priced" modern British nosh; shortages of popular dishes and "hit and miss" service have been perennial problems, but the cooking is now "not always up to scratch". / 11 pm; closed Sun D; D need 15+ to book.

The Westbourne W2   £22   ❸⑤❷
101 Westbourne Park Villas   221 1332   6–1B
The "hip crowd" continue to pack this trendified Notting Hill boozer, which offers an "interesting range of tasty food" at "value for money" prices; the wait for your meal affords an opportunity to cultivate mellowness. / 10 pm; closed Mon L; no Amex.

White Cross Hotel TW9   £18   ❸④❷
Water Ln   0181-940 6844   1–4A
For a weekend lunch, it is hard to beat this very traditional Young's pub, near Richmond Bridge, which boasts a nice garden and whose real fires make it cosy in winter; for pub-grub, the "excellent menu" offers "good value". / L only; no Amex & no Switch.

The White Onion N1   £30   ❷❷❷
297 Upper St   359 3533   8–3D
"A new opening that has really taken off", this "very professional", "friendly and imaginative" modern British eatery in Islington offers "magic cooking, unpretentiously served". / 10.30 pm, Fri & Sat 11 pm; closed Mon L, Tue L & Sun D.

White Tower W1   £30   ❸❸❸
1 Percy St   636 8141   2–1C
"Old fashioned" and "predictable" Fitzrovia landmark whose relaunch a year or so ago leaves its devotees cold; the culinary standard of its hallmark "Greek nursery food" is not the issue – "an old world sanctuary has been turned into a run-of-the-mill eatery". / 11 pm; closed Sun.

Whittington's EC4   £37   ④④④
21 College HI   248 5855   9–3B
Characterful, if perhaps "dingy", cellars, below Dick's old home, that serves "unspectacular Anglo/French" fare that is, nonetheless, "superior for the neighbourhood". / L only; closed Sat & Sun.

159

Wilson's W14   **£ 29**   ❸❶❸

236 Blythe Rd   603 7267   7–1C
*This "cranky but enjoyable" Shepherd's Bush outfit ("with
eccentric kilted proprietor") gets strong support for its
"good Scottish food"; "rich" ingredients make it "a cold
winter's night" place. / 10 pm; closed Sat L & Sun D.*

Wiltons SW1   **£ 56**   ④④❸

55 Jermyn St   629 9955   3–3C
*This pillar of the St James's establishment exudes a
"serious and stuffy" air some find "a touch Jurassic",
and service can grate, too; many do praise the "dependable
oysters, game and fish", but even supporters feel prices
are "outrageous". / 10.30 pm; closed Sat; jacket & tie.*

**Windows on the World
Park Lane Hilton Hotel W1**   **£ 55**   ④④❸

22 Park Ln   208 4021   3–4A
*"Stunning views" across the metropolis and a "very good
brunch" ("the real McCoy") are the twin peaks of visits to
this 28th floor Mayfair eyrie; prices are "stratospheric",
though – especially for lacklustre Gallic fare which can be
"disastrous". / Mon-Thu 11 pm, Fri & Sat 11.30 pm; closed Sat L & Sun D;
dinner, jacket & tie.*

Windsor Castle W8   **£ 18**   ❸④❶

114 Campden Hl Rd   727 8491   6–2B
*"Lots of nooks and crannies" in winter and "the best" garden
make this "delightful", "quirky" pub near Notting Hill Gate
many a Londoner's favourite; the menu is a ragbag that
mostly comes off. / 10.30 pm; no smoking area (L only); no booking.*

Wine Gallery SW10   **£ 25**   ❸④❷

49 Hollywood Rd   352 7572   5–3B
*Wine at merchant prices provides a new reason to visit this
dated, characterful Chelsea wine bar (with charming garden),
which serves rather pricey comfort food; service can be
"overstretched". / 11.45 pm.*

Wódka W8   **£ 34**   ④❸❸

12 St Alban's Grove   937 6513   5–1B
*"Fun", slightly quirky Pole, tucked away in a Kensington
backwater; the "interesting", if "very heavy", cooking can be
"surprisingly good", but it's not consistent, and some feel that
"vodka is the main draw". / 11.15 pm; closed Sat L & Sun L;
smart casual; set weekday L £21(FP).*

Wok Wok   £ 24   ❸❸❸

10 Frith St, W1   437 7080   4–2A
140 Fulham Rd, SW10   370 5355   5–3B
*These smart Chelsea, and recently Soho noodle-parlours
have been well received for their "light and tasty food"
("ideal after the movies"); critics, ourselves included, say
they're "overpriced Wagamama wannabees". / W1 midnight,
Sun 10.30 pm – SW10 11 pm, Fri midnight; SW10 Sat & Sun no booking.*

Wolfe's WC2   £ 26   ❸④④

30 Gt Queen St   831 4442   4–1D
*Homesick Knightsbridge Americans will now have to trek to
Covent Garden for "the best burgers" in town – the better-
known branch of these family diners, behind Harrods,
closed as we went to press. / 11.30 pm; closed Sun.*

Wong Kei W1   £ 14   ❸⑤④

41-43 Wardour St   437 8408   4–3A
*"The experience lives on" at this large rambling Chinatown
den, where "diabolical" service – from the "rudest waiters
in town" – is "an institution"; the chow can be "surprisingly
good", but "don't even think about paying for it with cheque
or plastic". / 10.30 pm; no credit cards; no booking.*

Woodlands   £ 22   ❸④④

37 Panton St, SW1   839 7258   4–4A
77 Marylebone Ln, W1   486 3862   3–1A
*An "excellent value vegetarian buffet lunch" is an attraction
of these Theatreland and Marylebone South Indians; in the
evening, they can seem expensive. / 10.30 pm; no Switch; set
weekday L £12(FP).*

Woz W10   £ 30   ❸❷❷

46 Golborne Rd   0181-968 2200   6–1A
*Antony Worrall Thompson's congenial, if grimly located,
North Kensington newcomer (on the site of Tabac, RIP)
offers a no-choice, five-course 'dinner party' formula – plan to
spend all evening; an early visit found Mediterranean dishes
roughly on a par with the fruits of a successful raid on M&S.
/ 11.30 pm; closed Mon L & Sun D.*

Wren at St James's SW1   £ 10   ④④④

197 Piccadilly   437 9419   3–3D
*It's perhaps useful for veggies needing a fix, and has nice
outside tables for the summer, but this annex to Piccadilly's
famous Wren church "gets away with pretty toppish prices".
/ 5 pm, Sun 4 pm; no credit cards; no smoking; no booking.*

FSA

Yo! Sushi W1 £21 ④❷❷
52-53 Poland St 287 0443 3–1D
*"Conveyor belt mayhem" is "gimmicky but good fun" say fans
of this "space age" Soho newcomer (where food and some
drinks are delivered by robot); prices are "toppish".* / Midnight;
no smoking; no booking.

Yoahan Plaza food court NW9 £ 8 ❸❸⑤
399 Edgware Rd no tel 1–1A
*A "multi-variety of dishes", from every imaginable oriental
cuisine, makes for an interesting cultural safari at this "lively",
"noisy" food plaza – on the ground floor of a large and
intriguing Japanese shopping mall, 10 minutes walk from
Colindale tube.* / 6 pm; no credit cards; no booking.

Yoshino W1 £27 ❶④❸
3 Piccadilly Pl 287 6622 3–3D
*The "real sushi bar atmosphere" of this simple Japanese,
just off Piccadilly, is heightened by the absence of any menu
in English, and the food is excellent and reasonably priced;
the "deliciously minimal" décor is not to all tastes, though,
and credit card payments attract a surcharge.* / 10 pm;
closed Sun; no smoking.

Yum Yum N16 £23 ❷❷❸
30 Stoke Newington Ch St 254 6751 1–1C
*Superior, but "very reasonably priced" Stoke Newington Thai
whose reliable cooking (with an extensive veggie menu) and
happy buzz make it a local favourite.* / 10.45 pm, Fri & Sat
11.15 pm.

ZAFFERANO SW1 £35 ❶❷❷
16 Lowndes St 235 5800 2–4A
*River Café watch out – this "stylish" two-year-old Belgravian
is increasingly widely held to be "the best Italian in London",
serving "fabulous" and "different" food; some, though, do find
service a touch "snooty".* / 11 pm; closed Sun.

Zamoyski NW3 £17 ④❸❷
85 Fleet Rd 794 4792 8–2A
*"Informal", "friendly" service and "lively music" make for
a cosy atmosphere at this simple South Hampstead Pole;
generally, the grub is unexceptional, but the meze-special is
"great value".* / 10.30 pm, Fri & Sat 11 pm; D only ex Sun, when open all
day; no Switch; smart casual.

Zen SW3 £ 44 ❷❷❸
Chelsea Cloisters, Sloane Av   589 1781   5–2C
The Chelsea original of this Chinese chain remains
"expensive but consistent", providing "high quality" cooking
with "courteous service" in "well spaced" comfort. / 11.15 pm;
smart casual.

Zen Central W1 £ 48 ❸④⑤
20-22 Queen St   629 8089   3–3B
"Amazing food and good presentation" ("the best crispy
duck", in particular) continues to win some support for this
"overpriced", minimalist Mayfair Mandarin; "make sure you're
in pleasant company", though – the "cold" décor makes for a
"bleak" atmosphere. / 11.30 pm; smart casual.

Zen Garden W1 £ 40 ❸❷❸
15-16 Berkeley St   493 1381   3–3C
Fans of this datedly swish Mayfair basement tip it as
"one of the few chic and comfortable places for a Chinese";
the cooking is "good", if "expensive". / 11 pm; smart casual.

ZeNW3 NW3 £ 33 ❷❸❸
83 Hampstead High St   794 7863   8–2A
Though some complain of "tiny portions", the "simple",
"clean" and "tasty" cooking generally pleases at this
Hampstead Chinese; the sparse modernistic décor can be
found "cold". / 11.30 pm; smart casual.

Ziani SW3 £ 34 ④❸❸
45-47 Radnor Wk   352 2698   5–3C
Even those who find this Chelsea back street Italian
"too noisy and cramped" confess that it's "fun"; the cooking
is "standard" though, and service can grate. / 11.30 pm.

Zilli Fish W1 £ 40 ❷❸❸
36-40 Brewer St   734 8649   3–2D
"A definite gold star", say supporters of Signor Zilli's
prominent Soho newcomer, applauding the "light" and "tasty"
seafood, the "attentive and professional" staff and the al
fresco dining possibilities; it is "pricey", though and "too
'traditional Italian'" for some. / 11.45 pm; closed Sun.

Zinc W1 £ 28 ④❷④
20 Heddon St   255 8899   3–2C
It is hard not to be disappointed by this Conran 'bar and grill',
off Regent Street, which opened just before we went to press;
anodyne styling – it's probably better at lunch – and a tedious
menu made for a thoroughly forgettable visit. / 10.45 pm, Thu-Sat
12.45 am; closed Sun D.

Zoe W1   £ 32   ④④④
3-5 Barrett St   224 1122   3–1A
Though some cite this brightly decorated but curiously
anonymous café-restaurant, just off St Christopher's Place,
as a good West End rendezvous, too many find "surly"
service of "poor value" modern British fare. / 11.30 pm;
closed Sun; smart casual; no smoking area.

Zucca W11   £ 34   ❸❸❷
188 Westbourne Grove   727 0069   6–1B
"Good pasta and pizza" are among the attractions of this
starkly stylish, "nice and airy" Notting Hill newcomer. / 11 pm.

Zujuma's SW19   £ 26   ❷❷❸
58a Wimbledon Hill Rd   0181-879 0916   10–2B
"Imaginative and delicious Indian cooking" is already drawing
attention, even to distant Wimbledon, for this "attractive,
bright and modern", "very different" Hyderabadi newcomer.
/ 11 pm.

INDEXES

Chelsea Kitchen *(8.30, Sun 10)*
Coins *(8.30, Sun 10)*
Conrad Hotel *(7)*
The Crescent *(Sat 10)*
Dôme: *all branches (8)*
Ed's Easy Diner: *SW3 (Sat & Sun 9)*
Fat Boy's *(6.30)*
Fileric: *all branches (8)*
Francofill *(Sat & Sun 10)*
Ghillies: *SW6 (8)*
Häagen-Dazs: *SW7 (10)*
Halcyon Hotel *(7, Sun 7.30)*
I Thai *(7)*
Jason's *(9.30)*
Jimmy Beez *(9.30)*
King's Road Café *(10)*
Lisboa Patisserie *(8)*
Mackintosh's Brasserie: *all branches (8)*
Manzara *(7)*
Le Metro *(7.30, Sun 8.30)*
Mona Lisa *(7)*
Pâtisserie
Valerie: *SW3 (7.30, Sun 9)*
Picasso *(8)*
Pret A Manger: *W8 (7.30); SW3, W6 (8)*
Raoul's Café *(9, Sun 9.30)*
Le Shop *(Sat & Sun 11)*
Stock Pot: *King's Rd SW3 (7.45); Basil St SW3 (9.30)*
Tootsies: *W11 (8, Sat & Sun 9)*
Troubadour *(8.30)*
Vingt-Quatre *(always available)*
Woz *(Sat & Sun 9)*

North

Banners *(10)*
Bar Gansa *(10.30)*
Café Delancey *(8)*
Café Flo: *NW3 (10); N1 (9, Sat & Sun 8.30)*
Café Pasta: *NW3 (9); N1 (9.30)*
Café Rouge: *N6, NW8 (10)*
Calzone: *all branches (10)*
Cosmo *(8)*
Dôme: *all branches (8)*
Ed's Easy Diner: *NW3 (Sat & Sun 9)*
Häagen-Dazs: *NW3 (10)*
House on Rosslyn
Hill *(Sat & Sun, 10)*
Iznik *(Sat & Sun 9)*
The Landmark Hotel *(7)*
Nontas *(8)*
Pret A Manger: *NW1 (6); N1 (8)*
Tootsies: *NW3 (8, Sat & Sun 9)*
Troika *(9)*

South

Belair House *(9.30)*
Bistrot 2 Riverside *(8)*

Boiled Egg *(9, Sun 10)*
Le Bouchon Bordelais *(9.30)*
Café de la Place *(8, Sat 9, Sun 9.30)*
Café Portugal *(10)*
Café Rouge: *SE1, Parkgate Rd SW11, SW14, SW15, SW4 (10)*
Dixie's Bar & Grill *(Sat & Sun 10)*
Fileric: *all branches (8)*
Gastro *(8)*
Hornimans *(Sun 8)*
Scoffers *(10.30, Sat & Sun 10)*

East

Al's *(8, Sat & Sun 10)*
Beauchamp's *(9)*
Brick Lane Beigel Bake *(24 hr)*
Café Flo: *EC4 (9)*
Café Rouge: *all east branches (10)*
Café Sofra: *all branches (7)*
Carnevale *(10)*
Dôme: *all branches (8)*
Fox & Anchor *(7)*
Futures *(7.30)*
Futures *(7.30)*
Hope & Sir Loin *(7)*
Mustards Brasserie *(9.30)*
The Place Below *(7.30)*
Pret A Manger: *both EC2 (7); EC1, EC4 (7.30)*

Brunch places

Central

Balans
Le Caprice
Christopher's
Circus
Coast
The Ivy
Joe Allen
La Perla
Scott's
Zinc

West

Anonimato
Balans West
Beach Blanket Babylon
La Belle Epoque
Bistrot 190
Bluebird
La Brasserie
Cactus Blue
Café Grove
Chelsea Bun Diner
Coins
Conrad Hotel
The Crescent
The Cross Keys
Jimmy Beez

INDEXES

Rani: *N3 (hm)*
Rôtisserie: *N1 (h)*
Sarcan *(h)*
Seashell *(hm)*
Singapore Garden *(h)*
Solly's *(h)*
Tiger Lil's: *all branches (hp)*
Tootsies: *all branches (hmo)*
Troika *(hp)*
Tuk Tuk *(m)*
Upper St Fish Shop *(h)*
The Vegetarian Cottage *(h)*
Vijay *(h)*
Village Bistro *(hp)*
Vrisaki *(h)*
Yum Yum *(h)*
Zamoyski *(p)*

South
Alma *(p)*
Antipasto e Pasta *(h)*
Bah Humbug *(p)*
Battersea Rickshaw *(hp)*
Belair House *(h)*
Bellinis *(h)*
Bengal Clipper *(h)*
Boiled Egg *(hme)*
Le Bouchon Bordelais *(hm)*
La Bouffe *(h)*
Brady's *(p)*
Buona Sera *(h)*
The Butlers Wharf Chop-
   house *(h)*
Café Rouge: *SE1, SW14, SW15 (hm)*
Caffè Uno: *all branches (hm)*
Cantina del Ponte *(h)*
Del Buongustaio *(p)*
The Depot *(h)*
Eco *(h)*
Fina Estampa *(p)*
La Finca: *all branches (he)*
Gastro *(p)*
Ghillies: *SW17 (hp)*
Le Gothique *(hcp)*
Gourmet Pizza Co.: *all
   branches (hm)*
Helter Skelter *(hp)*
Hornimans *(hm)*
Kastoori *(p)*
The Lavender *(p)*
Lobster Pot *(p)*
Mezzanine *(h)*
Monsieur Max *(hm)*
Naked Turtle *(hm)*
C Notarianni & Sons *(p)*
On the Rise *(hp)*
Ost. Antica Bologna *(p)*
The People's Palace *(p)*
Pizza Metro *(h)*

PizzaExpress: *SE1, Lavender Hill
   SW11, SW14, SW15, SW18 (h); 46
   Battersea Br Rd SW11, SW4 (ho)*
Pizzeria Castello *(h)*
Le Pont de la Tour Bar &
   Grill *(h)*
Prego *(h)*
Ransome's Dock *(hp)*
Riva *(hm)*
La Rueda *(h)*
S Bar *(h)*
Scoffers *(hm)*
Sonny's *(h)*
The Stepping Stone *(h)*
Tiger Lil's: *all branches (hp)*
Tootsies: *all branches (hmo)*
The Waterloo Fire
   Station *(hp)*
White Cross Hotel *(h)*

East
Babe Ruth's *(hm)*
The Bar *(hp)*
Bleeding Heart *(h)*
Café Flo: *all branches (h)*
Café Spice Namaste: *E1 (h)*
The Clerkenwell *(p)*
The Eagle *(p)*
Frocks *(hp)*
Futures *(p)*
George & Vulture *(p)*
Gourmet Pizza Co.: *all
   branches (hm)*
Inmala *(p)*
MPW *(h)*
PizzaExpress: *EC2 (h)*
The Quality Chop House *(p)*
St John *(h)*
Searcy's Brasserie *(h)*

Entertainment
(Check times before you go)

Central
Atlantic Bar & Grill
   (jazz club, Sun)
The Avenue
   (jazz, Sun L)
Balans: *W1
   (music, nightly not Sun)*
Bar Madrid
   (DJ & dancing, Mon, Wed & Thu)
Blues
   (jazz, Fri & Sat)
Boulevard
   (blues/jazz, Wed-Fri)
Café Bohème
   (jazz, nightly)
Café de Paris
   (DJ nightly)
Café Latino
   (music Tue, Fri & Sat)
Calabash
   (African band, Fri or Sat)

Capital Radio Restaurant
(resident DJ)
Claridges Restaurant
(dinner dance, Sat)
Deals: *W1*
(music, Fri & Sat)
Dover St Wine Bar
(band, DJ & dancing, nightly)
Down Mexico Way
(DJ in bar Thu-Sat; 2nd floor, resident band)
Efes Kebab House: *2) 175-177 Gt Portland St W1 (belly dancer, nightly)*
Fifth Floor (Café)
(jazz, nightly)
Football Football
(sports screens)
The Foundation
(jazz Fri pm)
Garlic & Shots
(troubador, Fri & Sat)
The Halkin
(music, nightly)
Hamine
(karaoke, Mon-Sat)
The Lanesborough
(supper dances, Fri - Sat; jazz Sun brunch)
Langan's Brasserie
(jazz, nightly)
The Lexington
(pianist, Tue-Fri)
Mezzo
(music, Thu-Sat)
Mondo
(DJ nightly)
L'Odéon
(jazz, nightly)
Opus 70
(jazz, Sun L)
Oriel
(cabaret thu)
Pélican
(jazz, nightly)
Pizza On The Park
(jazz, nightly)
PizzaExpress: *Dean St W1 (jazz, nightly); Greek St W1 (jazz, Thu-Sat)*
La Porte des Indes
(folk dancing, Sun brunch)
Quaglino's
(bar-jazz, nightly)
The Ritz
(band, Fri & Sat)
Savoy River Restaurant
(dinner dance, nightly ex Sun)
Smollensky's: *W1*
(music, nightly)
Smollensky's, Strand: *WC2*
(music every night; dancing, Thu-Sat)
Sofra: *Tavistock St WC2*
(music, Mon-Sat)
Soho Soho
(music, rôtisserie nightly)
Le Soufflé
(string trio, Sun L)
Il Vicolo
(music, Fri)
The Waldorf Meridien
(jazz, Sun L)

Windows on the World
(dinner dance, Thu-Sat)

West
All Bar One: *all west branches*
(jazz, Sun pm)
Anonimato
(bossa nova, Sun)
Bar Central: *SW3*
(jazz or soul, Thu-Sat)
Big Easy
(band, nightly)
Bombay Brasserie
(piano & singer nightly and wkend D)
Brook
(jazz, Sun)
Café Lazeez
(music, Wed, Fri & Sat)
Café O
(Greek music, Thu-Sat)
Cambio de Tercio
(guitarist, Wed)
Chicago Rib Shack
(music Wed, Thu & Fri)
Chutney Mary
(jazz, Sun L)
Conrad Hotel
(singer & pianist, nightly)
Da Mario
(disco, nightly ex Sun)
First Floor
(jazz, Sun)
Isfehan
(music, nightly)
Los Remos
(guitarist & singer, Thu, Fri & Sat)
Maroush: *W2*
(music & dancing, nightly)
Montana
(jazz, Thu-Sat)
Nikita's
(Russian music, weekends)
Palio
(jazz, Tue & Thu eves)
Paparazzi Café
(music, nightly)
Pizza Pomodoro: *all branches*
(music, nightly)
PizzaExpress: *W8 (jazz, Fri & Sat); W14 (jazz, Sat); SW3 (jazz, Sat & Sun)*
Shoeless Joe's
(video screens)
606 Club
(jazz, nightly)
South
(jazz, Mon)
Star of India
(music, Tue-Fri)

North
Banners
(music, Mon D)
China Blues
(jazz, nightly)
Cuba Libre
(dancing, Fri & Sat)
Don Pepe
(singing & organist, nightly)

La Finca: *N1*
(rhumba & flamenco, Wed; salsa some Fri)

The Fox Reformed
(conjuror, Fri; regular wine tasting and backgammon evenings)

Greek Valley
(bouzouki music, Fri)

House on Rosslyn Hill
(karaoke, Mon; Winter – music, Fri & Sat)

The Landmark Hotel
(harpist, Sat eve; jazz, Sun L)

Lola's
(jazz, Sun L)

Troika
(Russian gypsy music, Fri & Sat)

Villa Bianca
(guitar twice weekly)

Zamoyski
(gypsy music, Fri & Sat)

South

Archduke Wine Bar
(jazz, nightly)

Batt. Barge Bistro
(guitarist, Thu-Sat)

Côte à Côte
(music, Wed-Sat)

Fina Estampa
(music, Fri & Sat)

La Finca: *SE11*
(Latin music, Sat)

Hornimans
(jazz, Sun)

Meson Don Felipe
(flamenco guitar, nightly)

Naked Turtle
(jazz, nightly & Sun L)

PizzaExpress: *SW18*
(large sports TV)

Pizzeria Castello
(guitarist, nightly)

Rebato's
(music, Wed-Sat)

La Rueda
(disco, Fri & Sat)

S Bar
(jazz, weekends)

East

Al's
(DJ, Fri)

Babe Ruth's
(basketball; games area)

Café du Marché
(music, nightly)

Café Indiya
(jazz, Thu)

The Fence
(music, Thu)

Fuego
(disco, Tue-Fri)

Hothouse Bar & Grill
(jazz & blues, Mon - Sat)

Pizza Pomodoro: *all branches*
(music, nightly)

Sri Siam City
(music, Thu)

Sri Thai
(music, Wed)

Terraza-Est
(opera singers, nightly)

Vic Naylors
(jazz, Sat)

Late
(open till midnight or later as shown; may be earlier Sunday)

Central

Atlantic Bar & Grill *(bar food until 2.30 am)*

The Avenue *(Fri & Sat 12.30 am)*

Balans: *W1 (Mon-Thu 4 am, Fri & Sat 6 am, Sun 1 am)*

Bar Italia *(4 am, Fri & Sat 24 hours)*

Bar Madrid *(2.30 am)*

Benihana: *all branches (Fri & Sat only)*

Blues *(Thu-Sat only)*

Boulevard

Café Bohème *(2.45 am, Thu-Sat open 24 hours)*

Café de Paris *(bar 3 am)*

Café du Jardin

Café Emm *(Fri & Sat 12.30 am)*

Café Latino *(Thu-Sat 1 am)*

Café Sofra: *all central branches*

Caffè Uno: *all branches*

Capital Radio Restaurant

Le Caprice

Circus *(midnight, Fri & Sat 12.30 am)*

Coast

The Criterion *(midnight, not Sun)*

Deals: *W1 (Fri & Sat 1 am)*

dell'Ugo

Dover St Wine Bar *(2 am)*

Ed's Easy Diner: *all central branches (midnight, Fri & Sat 1 am)*

Efes Kebab House: *Gt Portland St W1 (Fri & Sat 3 am)*

Fakhreldine

Garlic & Shots *(Fri & Sat 12.15 am)*

The Gaucho Grill *(ex Sun)*

Golden Dragon *(Fri & Sat only)*

Häagen-Dazs: *Covent Gdn WC2 (midnight, Fri & Sat); Leicester Sq WC2 (midnight, Fri & Sat 1 am)*

Hamine *(2.30 am, Sat 1.30 am, Sun midnight)*

Hard Rock Café *(12.30 am, Fri & Sat 1 am)*

Hujo's

Italian Kitchen: *WC2*

The Ivy

Joe Allen *(12.45 am)*

Kettners

The Lanesborough

Langan's Brasserie *(11.45 pm, Sat 12.45 am)*

Lindsay House *(not Sun)*

Little Italy *(4 am, Sun midnight)*

Tiger Lil's: *all branches (Fri & Sat only)*
Tootsies: *all branches (Fri & Sat)*
Vrisaki

South
Buona Sera
Caffè Uno: *all branches*
Gastro
Haweli
PizzaExpress: *Lavender Hill SW11, SW14, SW15, SW18*
Three Little Pigs *(Fri & Sat only)*
Tiger Lil's: *all branches (Fri & Sat only)*
Tootsies: *all branches (Fri & Sat)*

East
Al's *(Mon–Tue midnight, Wed–Sat 1.30 am (bar 3 am))*
Babe Ruth's *(Fri & Sat 12.30 am)*
Brick Lane Beigel Bake *(24 hr)*
Canteloupe
Lahore Kebab House *(1.30 am)*
Pizza Pomodoro: *all branches (1 am)*

No-smoking areas
(* completely no smoking)

Central
Ajimura
Atrium
Au Jardin des Gourmets
Bertorelli's: *all branches*
Café Emm
Café Fish
Café Pacifico
Café Sofra: *all branches*
Caldesi
Capital Radio Restaurant
Caravan Serai
Chez Gérard: *all branches*
Chicago Pizza Pie Factory
China City
Chor Bizarre
Chuen Cheng Ku
Connaught*
Cranks: *all branches**
Fashion Café
Fifth Floor (Café)
Food for Thought*
Football Football
Footstool
The Foundation
Garden Café
Gopal's of Soho
Gourmet Pizza Co.
Grissini
Häagen-Dazs: *all branches**
Hanover Square
Hard Rock Café
Ikkyu: *WC2*

Joe Allen
Luna Nuova
Mackintosh's Brasserie: *all branches*
Maison Bertaux
Malabar Junction
Mandeer*
Mildreds*
Museum St Café*
Neal's Yard Dining Rooms*
Nicole's
Nobu
L'Odéon
Opus 70
Oriel
Orso
Pizza On The Park
Planet Hollywood
La Porte des Indes
Pret A Manger: *both SW1, Regents St W1, Oxford St W1, Tottenham Court Rd W1, Wardour St W1, Hanover St W1, Piccadilly W1, Baker St W1, both WC1, WC2*
The Rainforest Café*
Red Fort
Ristorante Italiano
Soho Soho
Soho Spice
Sotheby's Café*
Le Soufflé
Star Café
Tate Gallery
TGI Friday's: *all branches*
Thai Pot
Tokyo Diner
Townhouse Brasserie
Veeraswamy
Villandry*
Vong*
Wagamama: *all branches**
The Waldorf Meridien*
Wren at St James's*
Yo! Sushi*
Yoshino*
Zoe

West
Big Easy
Bombay Palace
Cactus Blue
Café Lazeez
Café Pasta: *all west branches*
Chelsea Kitchen
Chicago Rib Shack
Chutney Mary
Clarke's
Daquise
Fats*
Francofill
Häagen-Dazs: *all branches**

Private rooms
(see also Big Group Bookings;
for the most comprehensive
listing of venues for functions –
from palaces to pubs – see
Harden's London Party Guide,
available in all good bookshops)
* particularly recommended

INDEXES

INDEXES

CUISINES

An asterisk (*) after an entry indicates exceptional or very good cooking

EUROPE

Belgian

Central
Belgo Centraal *(WC2)*

North
Belgo Noord *(NW1)*

East
Abbaye *(EC1)*

British, Modern

Central
Alastair Little *(W1)*
Alfred *(WC2)*
All Bar One *(W1, WC2)*
Andrew Edmunds *(W1)*
Atelier *(W1)*
Atlantic Bar & Grill *(W1)*
Atrium *(SW1)*
Aurora *(W1)**
The Avenue *(SW1)*
Bank *(WC2)*
Blues *(W1)*
Café de Paris *(W1)*
Café du Jardin *(WC2)*
Le Caprice *(SW1)**
Circus *(W1)*
Coast *(W1)*
dell'Ugo *(W1)*
Drones *(SW1)*
Ebury Street Wine Bar *(SW1)*
The Fifth Floor *(SW1)*
Fifth Floor (Café) *(SW1)*
The Foundation *(SW1)*
French House *(W1)*
Gabriel *(W1)*
Hodgson's *(WC2)*
Hujo's *(W1)*
The Ivy *(WC2)**
Justin de Blank *(W1)*
The Lanesborough *(W1)*
Langan's Brasserie *(W1)*
The Lexington *(W1)*
Lindsay House *(W1)*
The Marquis *(W1)**
Mezzo *(W1)*
Museum St Café *(WC1)**
Nicole's *(W1)*
Oceana *(W1)*
Opus 70 *(W1)*
Plummers *(WC2)*

Quaglino's *(W1)*
Saint *(WC2)*
Scott's *(W1)*
Sotheby's Café *(W1)*
The Square *(W1)**
Stephen Bull *(W1)**
Stephen Bull *(WC2)**
Tate Gallery *(SW1)*
33 *(SW1)**
Thomas Goode *(W1)*
The Union Café *(W1)*
Zinc *(W1)*
Zoe *(W1)*

West
The Abingdon *(W8)*
Alastair Little W11 *(W11)*
All Bar One *(SW6, W4)*
Anglesea Arms *(W6)**
Anonimato *(W10)**
Arcadia *(W8)*
Bar Central *(SW3)*
Beach Blanket Babylon *(W11)*
Belvedere *(W8)*
Bistrot 190 *(SW7)*
Bluebird *(SW3)*
Blythe Road *(W14)*
Boyd's *(W8)**
The Brackenbury *(W6)**
Brinkley's *(SW10)*
Brook *(W6)*
Café Med *(SW10, W11)*
The Canteen *(SW10)**
Charco's *(SW3)*
Chelsea Ram *(SW10)**
Chelsea Square *(SW3)*
Chiswick *(W4)**
Clarke's *(W8)**
The Collection *(SW3)*
The Cow *(W11)**
The Crescent *(SW3)*
The Cross Keys *(SW3)*
Dan's *(SW3)*
English Garden *(SW3)*
English House *(SW3)*
Fables *(SW6)*
Ffiona's *(W8)*
First Floor *(W11)*
Gilbert's *(SW7)*
Goolies *(W8)**
Halcyon Hotel *(W11)**
The Havelock Tavern *(W14)**
Hilaire *(SW7)**
James R *(SW6)*
Jimmy Beez *(W10)*
Joe's Brasserie *(SW6)*
Joe's Café *(SW3)*
Kartouche *(SW10)*
Kensington Place *(W8)**
The Ladbroke Arms *(W11)*

Launceston Place *(W8)**
Leith's *(W11)*
Mas Café *(W11)**
Le Metro *(SW3)*
Noughts 'n' Crosses *(W5)*
192 *(W8)*
The Parson's Nose *(SW6)*
The Pen *(SW6)*
The Prince Bonaparte *(W2)*
Raoul's Café *(W9)**
755 *(SW6)**
Shaw's *(SW7)*
Simply Nico Chelsea *(SW10)**
606 Club *(SW10)*
Snows on the Green *(W6)*
Stone Mason's Arms *(W6)**
The Sugar Club *(W11)**
The Tenth *(W8)*
Vingt-Quatre *(SW10)*
W11 *(W11)*
The Westbourne *(W2)*
Wilson's *(W14)*

North
All Bar One *(N1, N6, NW8)*
The Blenheim *(NW8)*
Bradley's *(NW3)*
Byron's *(NW3)*
Café des Arts *(NW3)*
The Chapel *(NW1)*
Crown & Goose *(NW1)*
Cucina *(NW3)*
The Engineer *(NW1)*
Euphorium *(N1)*
Granita *(N1)**
Gresslin's *(NW3)**
Jindivick *(N1)**
Kavanagh's *(N1)*
Lansdowne *(NW1)*
Lola's *(N1)*
The Lord Palmerston *(N19)*
Mesclun *(N16)*
Odette's *(NW1)*
Quincy's *(NW2)**
The Vine *(NW5)*

South
The Apprentice *(SE1)**
Bar Central *(SE1, TW9)*
Belair House *(SE21)*
Blue Print Café *(SE1)*
Buchan's *(SW11)*
Chez Bruce *(SW17)**
The Cook House *(SW15)*
The Depot *(SW14)*
Glaisters *(SW11)*
Helter Skelter *(SW9)*
The Lavender *(SW11)*
The Mason's Arms *(SW8)**
Mezzanine *(SE1)*

On the Rise *(SW11)*
1 Lawn Terrace *(SE3)*
Oxo Tower *(SE1)*
The People's Palace *(SE1)*
Phoenix *(SW15)*
Le Pont de la Tour *(SE1)*
Putney Bridge *(SW15)*
Ransome's Dock *(SW11)**
Redmond's *(SW14)*
RSJ *(SE1)**
S Bar *(SW11)*
Scoffers *(SW11)*
Sonny's *(SW13)**
The Stable *(SW13)*
The Stepping Stone *(SW8)**
Three Little Pigs *(SE1)*
Valhalla *(SW11)*
Vincent's *(SW15)*
The Waterloo Fire
    Station *(SE1)*
White Cross Hotel *(TW9)*

East
All Bar One *(E14, EC4)*
The Bar *(EC4)*
Canteloupe *(EC2)*
City Brasserie *(EC3)*
City Rhodes *(EC4)**
The Fence *(EC1)*
Frocks *(E9)*
Gladwins *(EC3)*
Hothouse Bar & Grill *(E1)*
Leith's at the Institute *(EC2)*
The Peasant *(EC1)*
The Quality Chop
    House *(EC1)*
St John *(EC1)*
Searcy's Brasserie *(EC2)*
Stephen Bull Bistro *(EC1)**
Whittington's *(EC4)*

British, Traditional

Central
Brown's Hotel *(W1)*
Claridges Restaurant *(W1)*
Connaught *(W1)*
Dorchester Grill *(W1)**
Fryer's Delight *(WC1)**
Green's *(SW1)*
Greenhouse *(W1)*
Grenadier *(SW1)*
The Guinea *(W1)*
Odin's *(W1)*
Porters *(WC2)*
Rib Room *(SW1)*
The Ritz *(W1)*
Rules *(WC2)*
Savoy Grill *(WC2)*
Savoy River Restaurant *(WC2)*

Seafresh *(SW1)* *
Shepherd's *(SW1)*
Simpsons-in-the-Strand *(WC2)*
Wiltons *(SW1)*

West
Basil St Hotel *(SW3)*
Costa's Fish *(W8)* *
Geale's *(W8)* *
Maggie Jones's *(W8)*
Monkeys *(SW3)* *
Turner's *(SW3)*
Veronica's *(W2)*
Windsor Castle *(W8)*

North
Nautilus *(NW6)* *
Seashell *(NW1)* *
Toff's *(N10)* *
Two Brothers *(N3)* *
Upper St Fish Shop *(N1)* *

South
Brady's *(SW18)* *
The Butlers Wharf Chop-
  house *(SE1)*

East
The Bow Wine Vaults *(EC4)*
Fox & Anchor *(EC1)* *
George & Vulture *(EC3)*
Hope & Sir Loin *(EC1)* *
Reynier *(EC3)*
Simpson's of Cornhill *(EC3)*

Czech

North
Czech Club *(NW6)*

East/West

Central
Mezzonine *(W1)*
Nobu *(W1)* *
Vong *(SW1)* *

West
I Thai *(W2)*

South
Bistrot 2 Riverside *(SE1)* *

Fish & seafood

Central
Bank *(WC2)*
Belgo Centraal *(WC2)*
Bentley's *(W1)*
Café Fish *(SW1)*
Cave *(W1)* *
Fung Shing *(WC2)* *

Green's *(SW1)*
Manzi's *(WC2)* *
Motcomb's *(SW1)*
Le Palais du Jardin *(WC2)* *
Quaglino's *(W1)*
Scott's *(W1)*
Sheekey's *(WC2)*
Wiltons *(SW1)*
Zilli Fish *(W1)* *

West
L'Altro *(W11)*
La Belle Epoque *(SW3)*
Bibendum Oyster Bar *(SW3)* *
Big Easy *(SW3)*
La Dordogne *(W4)* *
Ghillies *(SW6)*
Jason's *(W9)* *
Lou Pescadou *(SW5)* *
Mandarin Kitchen *(W2)* *
Poissonnerie de
  l'Avenue *(SW3)* *
Stratford's *(W8)* *
Le Suquet *(SW3)* *

North
Belgo Noord *(NW1)*
Bradley's *(NW3)*
Chez Liline *(N4)* *
Fisk *(N1)*

South
Ghillies *(SW17)*
Livebait *(SE1)* *
Lobster Pot *(SE11)* *
Le Pont de la Tour Bar &
  Grill *(SE1)*

East
Aquarium *(E1)*
Beauchamp's *(EC3)*
Gow's *(EC2)*
Rudland & Stubbs *(EC1)*
Sheekey's *(EC4)*
Sweetings *(EC4)* *

French

Central
L'Artiste Musclé *(W1)*
Au Jardin des Gourmets *(W1)*
Beotys *(WC2)*
Bistrot Soho *(W1)*
Boudin Blanc *(W1)*
Café Bohème *(W1)*
Café des Amis du Vin *(WC2)* *
Café Flo *(SW1, W1, WC2)*
Café Rouge *(W1, WC2)*
Café Royal Grill *(W1)*
Cave *(W1)* *

The Chelsea
  Restaurant *(SW1)**
Chez Gérard *(W1, WC2)*
Chez Nico *(W1)**
Claridges Restaurant *(W1)*
Connaught *(W1)*
The Criterion *(W1)*
Elena's L'Etoile *(W1)**
Entrecote *(SW1)*
L'Escargot *(W1)**
L'Estaminet *(WC2)*
Four Seasons *(W1)**
Le Gavroche *(W1)**
Interlude *(W1)*
Langan's Bistro *(W1)*
Magno's Brasserie *(WC2)*
Mon Plaisir *(WC2)**
Le Muscadet *(W1)*
Nico Central *(W1)*
Oak Room MPW *(W1)*
L'Odéon *(W1)*
Odin's *(W1)*
L'Oranger *(SW1)**
Orrery *(W1)*
Le Palais du Jardin *(WC2)**
Pélican *(WC2)*
Pied à Terre *(W1)**
La Poule au Pot *(SW1)*
Quo Vadis *(W1)*
Randall & Aubin *(W1)*
The Ritz *(W1)*
Les Saveurs *(W1)*
Savoy River Restaurant *(WC2)*
Simply Nico *(SW1)**
Soho Soho *(W1)*
Le Soufflé *(W1)**
Townhouse Brasserie *(WC1)*
Villandry *(W1)*
White Tower *(W1)*
Windows on the World *(W1)*

West
Au Bon Accueil *(SW3)*
Aubergine *(SW10)**
La Belle Epoque *(SW3)*
Bibendum *(SW3)*
La Bouchée *(SW7)*
Brass. du Marché *(W10)**
La Brasserie *(SW3)*
Brasserie St Quentin *(SW3)*
Café Flo *(SW6, W8)*
Café Rouge *(SW3, SW6, SW7, W11, W2, W4, W6, W8, W9)*
Capital Hotel *(SW3)**
Chavot *(SW3)*
Chez Moi *(W11)*
Chezmax *(SW10)**
Chinon *(W14)**
La Ciboulette *(SW3)**
La Dordogne *(W4)**

Emile's *(SW6)*
L'Escargot Doré *(W8)*
Francofill *(SW7)**
Grill St Quentin *(SW3)*
Lou Pescadou *(SW5)**
Monkeys *(SW3)**
Novelli W8 *(W8)*
Poissonnerie de
  l'Avenue *(SW3)**
La Pomme d'Amour *(W11)*
Stratford's *(W8)**
Le Suquet *(SW3)**
La Tante Claire *(SW3)**
Thierry's *(SW3)*
Turner's *(SW3)*

North
L'Aventure *(NW8)**
Café Flo *(N1, NW3)*
Café Rouge *(N6, NW1, NW3, NW8)*
La Cage Imaginaire *(NW3)*
Camden Brasserie *(NW1)*
Frederick's *(N1)*
Le Mercury *(N1)*
Oslo Court *(NW8)**
Le Sacré-Coeur *(N1)*
Soulard *(N1)**
Village Bistro *(N6)*
The White Onion *(N1)**

South
Le Bouchon Bordelais *(SW11)*
La Bouffe *(SW11)*
Café de la Place *(SW11)*
Café Rouge *(SE1, SW11, SW14, SW15, SW4)*
Emile's *(SW15)*
Gastro *(SW4)**
Le Gothique *(SW18)*
Lobster Pot *(SE11)**
Monsieur Max *(TW12)**
Le P'tit Normand *(SW18)*

East
Ashtons *(EC3)*
Bleeding Heart *(EC1)**
Bubb's *(EC1)*
Café du Marché *(EC1)**
Café Flo *(EC4)*
Café Rouge *(EC4)*
Le Champenois *(EC2)*
Le Coq d'Argent *(EC3)*
Luc's Brasserie *(EC3)*
Maison Novelli *(EC1)*
Mange 2 *(EC1)*
MPW *(E14)**
Novelli EC1 *(EC1)*
Sheekey's *(EC4)*

CUISINES – EUROPE

Game

Central
Dorchester Grill *(W1)**
The Marquis *(W1)**
Rules *(WC2)*
Wiltons *(SW1)*

West
Monkeys *(SW3)**

German

West
Prost *(W11)*

North
Cosmo *(NW3)*

Greek

Central
Beotys *(WC2)*
White Tower *(W1)*

West
Café O *(SW3)*
Costa's Grill *(W8)**
Halepi *(W2)*
Kalamaras, Mega *(W2)*
Kalamaras, Micro *(W2)*

North
Daphne *(NW1)*
Greek Valley *(NW8)*
Lemonia *(NW1)*
Nontas *(NW1)**
Vrisaki *(N22)**

East
Kolossi Grill *(EC1)**

Hungarian

Central
Gay Hussar *(W1)*

Italian

Central
L'Altro Soho *(W1)*
L'Arte *(W1)**
Bertorelli's *(W1, WC2)*
Bice *(W1)*
Café Pasta *(WC2)*
Caffè Uno *(W1, WC2)*
Caldesi *(W1)*
La Capannina *(W1)*
Caraffini *(SW1)*
Cecconi's *(W1)*
Como Lario *(SW1)*

Diverso *(W1)*
La Finezza *(SW1)*
La Fontana *(SW1)*
Grissini *(SW1)*
The Halkin *(SW1)*
Hyde Park Hotel
   Park Room *(SW1)*
L'Incontro *(SW1)*
Italian Kitchen *(WC1, WC2)*
Little Italy *(W1)*
Luigi's *(WC2)*
Luna Nuova *(WC2)*
Mimmo d'Ischia *(SW1)*
Neal Street *(WC2)*
Oliveto *(SW1)**
Olivo *(SW1)**
Orso *(WC2)*
Pollo *(W1)*
Ristorante Italiano *(W1)*
Sale e Pepe *(SW1)*
Santini *(SW1)*
Signor Sassi *(SW1)*
La Spighetta *(W1)**
Toto's *(SW1)**
Uno *(SW1)**
Vasco & Piero's Pavilion *(W1)**
Il Vicolo *(SW1)*
Zafferano *(SW1)**
Zilli Fish *(W1)**

West
L'Accento Italiano *(W2)*
Al San Vincenzo *(W2)**
L'Altro *(SW3, SW6, W11)*
Assaggi *(W2)**
Bersagliera *(SW3)*
Bucci *(SW3)*
Café 206 *(W11)*
Café Montpeliano *(SW3)*
Café Pasta *(W4, W8)*
Caffé Uno *(W4)*
Caffè Uno *(SW6, W2, W8)*
Calzone *(SW10, W11)*
Ciabatta *(SW3)*
Cibo *(W14)**
Da Pierino *(SW7)*
Daphne's *(SW3)*
De Cecco *(SW6)**
La Delizia *(SW3, SW5)**
Elistano *(SW3)**
Il Falconiere *(SW7)*
La Famiglia *(SW10)*
Formula Veneta *(SW10)*
The Green Olive *(W9)*
King's Road Café *(SW3)*
Leonardo's *(SW10)**
Luigi's Delicatessen *(SW10)**
Made in Italy *(SW3)*
Mona Lisa *(SW10)*
Montpeliano *(SW7)*

Mr Frascati *(W2)*
Orsino *(W1)*
Osteria Basilico *(W11)**
Osteria del Parco *(W11)*
Osteria Le Fate *(SW3)*
Palio *(W11)*
Paparazzi Café *(SW3)*
Picasso *(SW3)*
The Red Pepper *(W9)**
Riccardo's *(SW3)*
The River Café *(W6)**
Sabatino *(W8)*
Sambuca *(SW3)*
San Frediano *(SW3)*
San Lorenzo *(SW3)*
San Martino *(SW3)*
Sandrini *(SW3)*
Scalini *(SW3)*
Spago *(SW7)*
Tusc *(SW5)*
Ziani *(SW3)*
Zucca *(W11)*

North
A Tavola *(NW8)*
Altro *(NW3)*
Billboard Café *(NW6)*
Café Pasta *(N1, NW3)*
Caffè Uno *(N1, N6, NW1, NW8)*
Calzone *(N1, NW3)*
Casale Franco *(N1)*
Florians *(N8)*
Marine Ices *(NW3)*
Mezzaluna *(NW2)*
La Porchetta Pizzeria *(N4)**
San Carlo *(N6)*
Vegia Zena *(NW1)**
Villa Bianca *(NW3)*

South
Antipasto e Pasta *(SW4)*
Bellinis *(SW13)*
Buona Sera *(SW11)**
Caffè Uno *(SW13)*
Cantina del Ponte *(SE1)*
Del Buongustaio *(SW15)**
Enoteca Turi *(SW15)**
C Notarianni & Sons *(SW11)**
Ost. Antica Bologna *(SW11)**
Prego *(TW9)*
Riva *(SW13)**

East
Alba *(EC1)*
Caravaggio *(EC3)*
The Clerkenwell *(EC1)*
Taberna Etrusca *(EC4)*
Terraza-Est *(EC4)*

Irish

Central
O'Conor Don *(W1)*

Mediterranean

West
Woz *(W10)*

East
The Eagle *(EC1)**

Polish

West
Daquise *(SW7)*
Ognisko Polskie *(SW7)*
Wódka *(W8)*

North
Zamoyski *(NW3)*

Portuguese

South
Café Portugal *(SW8)**

Russian

Central
Kaspia *(W1)**

West
Nikita's *(SW10)*

North
Troika *(NW1)*

Scandinavian

West
South *(W11)*

North
Anna's Place *(N1)*

Steaks & grills

Central
Chez Gérard *(W1, WC2)*
Christopher's *(WC2)*
The Gaucho Grill *(W1)**
The Guinea *(W1)*
Kettners *(W1)*
Quaglino's *(W1)*
Rib Room *(SW1)*
Rowley's *(SW1)*
Smollensky's *(W1)*
Smollensky's, Strand *(WC2)*
Soho Soho *(W1)*

West
El Gaucho *(SW3)**
Popeseye *(W14)**
Rôtisserie *(W12)*
Rôtisserie Jules *(SW3, SW7, W11)*

North
Camden Brasserie *(NW1)*
Rôtisserie *(N1)*

South
Polygon Bar & Grill *(SW4)**
Le Pont de la Tour Bar &
  Grill *(SE1)*

East
Arkansas Café *(E1)**
Fox & Anchor *(EC1)**
Hope & Sir Loin *(EC1)**
Simpson's of Cornhill *(EC3)*

Spanish

Central
Bar Madrid *(W1)*

West
Albero & Grana *(SW3)*
Albero & Grana, Bar *(SW3)**
Cambio de Tercio *(SW5)*
Galicia *(W10)*
Los Remos *(W2)*

North
Bar Gansa *(NW1)**
Cuba Libre *(N1)*
Don Pepe *(NW8)*
La Finca *(N1)*

South
La Finca *(SE11)*
Meson Don Felipe *(SE1)*
Rebato's *(SW8)**
La Rueda *(SW4)*

East
Barcelona Tapas *(E1, EC3)**
Fuego *(EC3)*
Leadenhall Tapas Bar *(EC3)*

Swiss

Central
St Moritz *(W1)*

International

Central
Balans *(W1)*
Boisdale *(SW1)*
Boulevard *(WC2)*
Brown's *(W1, WC2)*

Café Emm *(W1)*
Cork & Bottle *(WC2)*
Deals *(W1)*
Dôme *(W1, WC2)*
Dover St Wine Bar *(W1)*
Footstool *(SW1)*
Garlic & Shots *(W1)*
Gordon's Wine Bar *(WC2)*
Grumbles *(SW1)*
Hanover Square *(W1)*
Hardy's *(W1)*
Little Bay *(SW1)*
Mackintosh's Brasserie *(SW1)*
Mad Dog Café *(W1)*
Motcomb's *(SW1)*
Oriel *(SW1)*
Pitcher & Piano *(W1, WC2)*
Pomegranates *(SW1)*
Sarastro *(WC2)*
Shampers *(W1)*
Stock Pot *(SW1, W1)*
Vendôme *(W1)*

West
Balans West *(SW5)*
Blakes Hotel *(SW7)*
Brown's *(SW3)*
Café Grove *(W11)*
Chelsea Bun Diner *(SW10)*
Chelsea Kitchen *(SW3)*
Conrad Hotel *(SW10)**
Coopers Arms *(SW3)*
Deals *(SW10, W6)*
Dôme *(SW3, SW5, W8)*
Dove *(W6)*
The Enterprise *(SW3)*
Foxtrot Oscar *(SW3)*
Front Page *(SW3)**
The Gasworks *(SW6)*
Glaisters *(SW10)*
Julie's *(W11)*
Julie's Bar *(W11)*
Mackintosh's Brasserie *(W4)*
Pitcher & Piano *(SW10, SW6, W4)*
PJ's *(SW3)*
The Scarsdale *(W8)*
Sporting Page *(SW10)*
Stock Pot *(SW3)*
The Tuscan *(W11)*
Windsor Castle *(W8)*
Wine Gallery *(SW10)*

North
Banners *(N8)*
Café Delancey *(NW1)*
Caffe Graffiti *(NW3)*
Cosmo *(NW3)*
Dôme *(N1, NW3)*
The Fox Reformed *(N16)*
House on Rosslyn Hill *(NW3)*

The Landmark Hotel *(NW1)*
The Little Bay *(NW6)*
Pitcher & Piano *(N1)*

South
Alma *(SW18)*
Archduke Wine Bar *(SE1)*
Bah Humbug *(SW2)*
Batt. Barge Bistro *(SW8)*
Café Jeune *(SW9)*
Côte à Côte *(SW11)*
Hornimans *(SW4)*
Naked Turtle *(SW14)*
Pitcher & Piano *(SW12)*
The Ship *(SW18)*

East
Al's *(EC1)*
Brasserie Rocque *(EC2)*
Dôme *(EC1, EC4)*
Foxtrot Oscar *(EC3)*
Mustards Brasserie *(EC1)*
Vic Naylors *(EC1)*

'SNACK' FOOD

Afternoon tea

Central
Aurora *(W1)**
Brown's Hotel *(W1)*
Fifth Floor (Café) *(SW1)*
Hyde Park Hotel
  Park Room *(SW1)*
The Lanesborough *(W1)*
Simpsons-in-the-Strand *(WC2)*
Thomas Goode *(W1)*
Villandry *(W1)*
The Waldorf Meridien *(WC2)*

West
Basil St Hotel *(SW3)*
Daquise *(SW7)*
Julie's Bar *(W11)*
Ognisko Polskie *(SW7)*

North
The Landmark Hotel *(NW1)*

Burgers, etc

Central
Capital Radio
  Restaurant *(WC2)*
Deals *(W1)*
Ed's Easy Diner *(W1)**
Fashion Café *(W1)*
Football Football *(SW1)*
Hard Rock Café *(W1)*
Joe Allen *(WC2)*

Planet Hollywood *(W1)*
The Rainforest Café *(W1)*
Wolfe's *(WC2)*

West
Big Easy *(SW3)*
Deals *(SW10, W6)*
Ed's Easy Diner *(SW3)**
Foxtrot Oscar *(SW3)*
Henry J Beans *(SW3)*
Luigi Malones *(SW7)*
Sticky Fingers *(W8)*
Tootsies *(SW6, SW7, W11, W4)*

North
Ed's Easy Diner *(NW3)**
Tootsies *(NW3)*

South
Tootsies *(SW13)*

East
Babe Ruth's *(E1)*

Fish & chips

Central
Fryer's Delight *(WC1)**
Seafresh *(SW1)**

West
Costa's Fish *(W8)**
Geale's *(W8)**

North
Nautilus *(NW6)**
Seashell *(NW1)**
Toff's *(N10)**
Two Brothers *(N3)**
Upper St Fish Shop *(N1)**

South
Brady's *(SW18)**

Ice cream

Central
Häagen-Dazs *(WC2)*

West
Häagen-Dazs *(SW7, W2)*

North
Häagen-Dazs *(NW3)*
Marine Ices *(NW3)*

South
C Notarianni & Sons *(SW11)**

Pizza

Central
Ask *(SW1, W1)*

CUISINES – 'SNACK' FOOD/AMERICAS

Chicago Pizza Pie
  Factory *(W1)*
Gourmet Pizza Co. *(W1)*
Kettners *(W1)*
Luna Nuova *(WC2)*
Oliveto *(SW1)**
Pizza On The Park *(SW1)*
PizzaExpress *(SW1, W1, WC1,
  WC2)*
Pizzeria Condotti *(W1)*

West
Ask *(SW6, SW7, W11, W4)*
Calzone *(SW10, W11)*
Ciabatta *(SW3)*
Da Mario *(SW7)*
La Delizia *(SW3, SW5)**
Paparazzi Café *(SW3)*
Pizza Chelsea *(SW3)*
Pizza Pomodoro *(SW3)*
Pizza the Action *(SW6)*
PizzaExpress *(SW10, SW3, SW6,
  W11, W14, W2, W4, W8)*
Pucci Pizza *(SW3)*
The Red Pepper *(W9)**
Spago *(SW7)*

North
Ask *(N1, NW3)*
Calzone *(N1, NW3)*
Casale Franco *(N1)*
Marine Ices *(NW3)*
PizzaExpress *(N1, NW1, NW3,
  NW8)*
La Porchetta Pizzeria *(N4)**

South
Bellinis *(SW13)*
Buona Sera *(SW11)**
Eco *(SW4)**
Gourmet Pizza Co. *(SE1)*
C Notarianni & Sons *(SW11)**
Pizza Metro *(SW11)**
PizzaExpress *(SE1, SW11, SW14,
  SW15, SW18, SW4)*
Pizzeria Castello *(SE1)**

East
Gourmet Pizza Co. *(E14)*
Pizza Pomodoro *(E1)*
PizzaExpress *(EC2)*

Sandwiches, cakes, etc

Central
Bar Italia *(W1)*
Garden Café *(WC1)*
Maison Bertaux *(W1)**
Pâtisserie Valerie *(W1, WC2)**
Pret A Manger *(SW1, W1, WC1,
  WC2)*
Seattle Coffee Co *(SW1, W1,
  WC2)**

Star Café *(W1)*

West
Café Grove *(W11)*
Coins *(W11)*
Fileric *(SW7)**
King's Road Café *(SW3)*
Lisboa Patisserie *(W10)**
Manzara *(W11)**
Pâtisserie Valerie *(SW3)**
Pret A Manger *(SW3, W6, W8)*
Le Shop *(SW3)*
Troubadour *(SW5)*

North
Pret A Manger *(N1, NW1)*

South
Boiled Egg *(SW11)*
Fileric *(SW8)**

East
Brick Lane Beigel Bake *(E1)**
Pret A Manger *(EC1, EC2, EC4)*

AMERICAS

American

Central
Christopher's *(WC2)*
Joe Allen *(WC2)*
Smollensky's *(W1)*
Smollensky's, Strand *(WC2)*
TGI Friday's *(W1, WC2)*

West
Big Easy *(SW3)*
Chicago Rib Shack *(SW7)*
Montana *(SW6)**
Shoeless Joe's *(SW6)*
TGI Friday's *(W2)*

East
Arkansas Café *(E1)**
Babe Ruth's *(E1)*

Argentinian

Central
The Gaucho Grill *(W1)**

Brazilian

West
Paulo's *(W6)*

Cajun/creole

West
Cactus Blue *(SW3)*

Fats *(W9)*

Mexican/TexMex

Central
Café Pacifico *(WC2)*
Down Mexico Way *(W1)*
La Perla *(WC2)*
Texas Embassy Cantina *(WC2)*

West
Texas Lone Star *(SW7)*

South
Dixie's Bar & Grill *(SW11)*

South American

Central
Bar Madrid *(W1)*
Café Latino *(W1)*

West
Cactus Blue *(SW3)*
El Gaucho *(SW3)**

North
Cuba Libre *(N1)*
La Piragua *(N1)*

South
Fina Estampa *(SE1)**

AFRICA

Afro-Caribbean

Central
Calabash *(WC2)*

West
Fats *(W9)*

North
Cottons *(NW1)*

North African

Central
Momo *(W1)*

West
Adams Café *(W12)**
Pasha *(SW7)*

North
Laurent *(NW2)**

East
Moro *(EC1)**

South African

West
Springbok Café *(W4)*

Sudanese

West
Mandola *(W11)*

Tunisian

West
Adams Café *(W12)**

North
Laurent *(NW2)**

MIDDLE EAST

Egyptian

North
Ali Baba *(NW1)**

Israeli

North
Solly's *(NW11)**

Kosher

North
Nautilus *(NW6)**
Solly's *(NW11)**

Lebanese

Central
Al Bustan *(SW1)**
Al Hamra *(W1)*
Al Sultan *(W1)*
Fakhreldine *(W1)*
Maroush *(W1)**
Ranoush *(W1)**

West
Beirut Express *(W2)**
Ebla *(W6)*
Maroush *(SW3, W2)**
Phoenicia *(W8)**

Middle Eastern

North
Ali Baba *(NW1)**

Persian

West
Alounak *(W14)**
Isfehan *(W2)*

Turkish

Central
Café Sofra *(W1, WC1, WC2)*
Efes Kebab House *(W1)*
Sofra *(W1, WC2)*

West
Manzara *(W11)**

North
Iznik *(N5)**
Pasha *(N1)*
Sarcan *(N1)**

South
Beyoglu *(SW11)**

East
Café Sofra *(EC4)*

ASIA

Afghani

Central
Caravan Serai *(W1)*

North
Afghan Kitchen *(N1)*

Burmese

West
Mandalay *(W2)**

Chinese

Central
China City *(WC2)*
Chuen Cheng Ku *(W1)*
Dorchester, Oriental *(W1)**
Fung Shing *(WC2)*
Golden Dragon *(W1)**
Harbour City *(W1)**
Hunan *(SW1)**
Jenny Lo's *(SW1)*
Ken Lo's Memories *(SW1)**
Mekong *(SW1)*
Mr Chow *(SW1)*
Mr Kong *(WC2)**
New World *(W1)*
Poons *(WC2)*
Poons, Lisle Street *(WC2)**
Princess Garden *(W1)*

Wong Kei *(W1)*
Zen Central *(W1)*
Zen Garden *(W1)*

West
The Four Seasons *(W2)*
Good Earth *(SW3)**
Ken Lo's Memories *(W8)*
Mandarin Kitchen *(W2)**
Mao Tai *(SW6)*
Mr Wing *(SW5)*
Nam Long *(SW5)*
Nanking *(W6)*
New Culture Rev'n *(SW3)*
Park Inn *(W2)*
Royal China *(W2)**
Zen *(SW3)**

North
Cheng Du *(NW1)*
China Blues *(NW1)*
Feng Shang *(NW1)*
Gung-Ho *(NW6)**
New Culture Rev'n *(N1, NW1)*
Singapore Garden *(NW6)**
The Vegetarian
  Cottage *(NW3)*
Yoahan Plaza *(NW9)*
ZeNW3 *(NW3)**

South
Four Regions *(SE1)*
Royal China *(SW15)**

East
Imperial City *(EC3)**
Poons in the City *(EC3)**

Chinese, Dim sum

Central
Chuen Cheng Ku *(W1)*
Dorchester, Oriental *(W1)**
Golden Dragon *(W1)**
Harbour City *(W1)**
New World *(W1)*
Zen Central *(W1)*

West
Royal China *(W2)**
Zen *(SW3)**

South
Royal China *(SW15)**

Indian

Central
Chor Bizarre *(W1)*
Gopal's of Soho *(W1)**
India Club *(WC2)**
Malabar Junction *(WC1)*

Mandeer *(W1)**
La Porte des Indes *(W1)*
Ragam *(W1)*
Red Fort *(W1)*
Salloos *(SW1)**
Soho Spice *(W1)*
Tamarind *(W1)**
Veeraswamy *(W1)**
Woodlands *(SW1, W1)*

West

Anarkali *(W6)*
Bombay Brasserie *(SW7)**
Bombay Palace *(W2)**
Café Lazeez *(SW7)*
Chutney Mary *(SW10)*
Khan's *(W2)*
Khan's of Kensington *(SW7)**
Khyber Pass *(SW7)*
Legend of India *(SW10)*
Malabar *(W8)**
Mamta *(SW6)**
Nayab *(SW6)**
Noor Jahan *(SW5)**
Standard Tandoori *(W2)*
Star of India *(SW5)**
Tandoori Lane *(SW6)**
Tandoori of Chelsea *(SW3)*
Vama *(SW10)*

North

Anglo Asian Tandoori *(N16)*
Chutneys *(NW1)*
Diwana Bhel-Poori
 House *(NW1)**
Geeta *(NW6)**
Great Nepalese *(NW1)**
Haandi *(NW1)*
Rani *(N3)*
Rasa *(N16)**
Vijay *(NW6)**

South

Battersea Rickshaw *(SW11)*
Bengal Clipper *(SE1)**
Bombay Bicycle Club *(SW12)**
Café Spice Namaste *(SW11)**
Haweli *(SW13)**
Indian Ocean *(SW17)**
Kastoori *(SW17)**
Ma Goa *(SW15)**
Rani *(TW9)*
Shree Krishna *(SW17)**
Zujuma's *(SW19)**

East

Café Indiya *(E1)*
Café Spice Namaste *(E1)**
Lahore Kebab House *(E1)**
Rupee Room *(EC2)*
Sri India *(EC2)*

Indian, Southern

Central

India Club *(WC2)**
Malabar Junction *(WC1)*
Mandeer *(W1)**
Ragam *(W1)*
Woodlands *(SW1, W1)*

West

Mamta *(SW6)**

North

Chutneys *(NW1)*
Diwana Bhel-Poori
 House *(NW1)**
Geeta *(NW6)**
Rani *(N3)*
Rasa *(N16)**
Vijay *(NW6)**

South

Kastoori *(SW17)**
Rani *(TW9)*
Shree Krishna *(SW17)**

Indonesian

South

Enak Enak *(SW11)*

East

Inmala *(EC2)*

Japanese

Central

Ajimura *(WC2)*
Arisugawa *(W1)**
Benihana *(W1)*
Café Sogo *(SW1)*
Hamine *(W1)*
Ikkyu *(W1, WC2)**
Masako *(W1)**
Matsuri *(SW1)**
Mitsukoshi *(SW1)**
Miyama *(W1)**
Nobu *(W1)**
Shogun *(W1)**
Suntory *(SW1)*
Tokyo Diner *(WC2)*
Wagamama *(W1, WC1)**
Yo! Sushi *(W1)*
Yoshino *(W1)**

West

Bar Japan *(SW5)*
Benihana *(SW3)*
Inaho *(W2)**
Sushi Wong *(W8)*
t'su *(SW3)*

CUISINES – ASIA

North
Benihana *(NW3)*
Bu San *(N7)**
Café Japan *(NW11)**
Sushi-Say *(NW2)**
Wakaba *(NW3)**

East
Aykoku-Kaku *(EC4)*
City Miyama *(EC4)**
Japanese Canteen *(EC1)*
Moshi Moshi Sushi *(EC2, EC4)**
Noto *(EC2, EC4)*
Tatsuso *(EC2)**

Japanese, Sushi

Central
Arisugawa *(W1)**
Ikkyu *(W1, WC2)**
Matsuri *(SW1)**
Mitsukoshi *(SW1)**
Miyama *(W1)**
Nobu *(W1)**
Shogun *(W1)**
Suntory *(SW1)*
Yo! Sushi *(W1)*
Yoshino *(W1)**

West
Inaho *(W2)**
Sushi Wong *(W8)*
t'su *(SW3)*

North
Café Japan *(NW11)**
Sushi-Say *(NW2)**
Wakaba *(NW3)**

East
City Miyama *(EC4)**
Moshi Moshi Sushi *(EC2, EC4)**
Tatsuso *(EC2)**

Japanese, Teppan-yaki

Central
Benihana *(W1)*
Matsuri *(SW1)**
Miyama *(W1)**
Suntory *(SW1)*

West
Benihana *(SW3)*
Sushi Wong *(W8)*

North
Benihana *(NW3)*

East
Tatsuso *(EC2)**

Korean

North
Bu San *(N7)**

Malaysian

Central
Melati *(W1)**
Singapura *(WC2)*

West
Jim Thompson's *(SW6)*
Mawar *(W2)**

North
Singapore Garden *(NW6)**

East
Café Spice Namaste *(E1)**
Singapura *(EC3, EC4)*

Misc oriental

Central
Mongolian Barbecue *(WC2)*
Wok Wok *(W1)*

West
Bonjour Vietnam *(SW6)*
Mongolian Barbecue *(SW6, SW7, W4)*
Sash *(SW6)*
Tiger Lil's *(SW3)*
Wok Wok *(SW10)*

North
Gecko *(NW1)*
Mongolian Barbecue *(NW1)*
Tiger Lil's *(N1)*
Yoahan Plaza *(NW9)*

South
Tiger Lil's *(SW4)*

East
East One *(EC1)*
Tao *(EC4)*

Thai

Central
Bahn Thai *(W1)*
Blue Jade *(SW1)*
Chiang Mai *(W1)**
Manorom *(WC2)*
Mondo *(W1)*
Silks & Spice *(W1)**
Sri Siam *(W1)**
Thai Pot *(WC2)*

West
Bangkok *(SW7)**

Bedlington Café *(W4)**
Ben's Thai *(W9)**
Blue Elephant *(SW6)**
Busabong Too *(SW10)**
Busabong Tree *(SW10)**
Café 209 *(SW6)*
Chaba *(SW10)*
Churchill *(W8)**
Dove *(W6)*
Esarn Kheaw *(W12)**
Fat Boy's *(W4)*
Jim Thompson's *(SW6)*
Khun Akorn *(SW3)*
Krungtap *(SW10)*
Latymers *(W6)**
S&P Patara *(SW3)**
Sabai Sabai *(W6)**
Sash *(SW6)*
Tawana *(W2)**
Thai Bistro *(W4)**
Thai on the River *(SW10)*
Topsy-Tasty *(W4)**
Tui *(SW7)**

North
Tuk Tuk *(N1)*
Yum Yum *(N16)**

South
Chada *(SW11)*
The Pepper Tree *(SW4)*
Phuket *(SW11)*
Thailand *(SE14)**

East
Sri Siam City *(EC2)**
Sri Thai *(EC4)**

Vietnamese

Central
Mekong *(SW1)*

West
Nam Long *(SW5)*

AREA OVERVIEWS

CENTRAL

Soho, Covent Garden & Bloomsbury
(Parts of W1, all WC2 and WC1)

Price	Name	Cuisine	Rating
£60+	Savoy Grill	*British, Traditional*	④❷❷
	Café Royal Grill	*French*	– – –
	Savoy River Restaurant	"	④❸❷
£50+	Neal Street	*Italian*	④④④
£40+	Alastair Little	*British, Modern*	❸④⑤
	Atlantic Bar & Grill	"	④⑤❷
	Café de Paris	"	⑤⑤④
	The Ivy	"	❷❶❶
	Mezzo	"	⑤④❸
	Rules	*British, Traditional*	❸❷❷
	Simpsons-in-the-Strand	"	④❸④
	Sheekey's	*Fish & seafood*	④④④
	Zilli Fish	"	❷❸❸
	The Criterion	*French*	❸④❶
	Quo Vadis	"	❸❸④
	Luigi's	*Italian*	④④④
	Christopher's	*American*	❸④❷
£35+	Atelier	*British, Modern*	❸❸④
	Bank	"	❸④❸
	Circus	"	– – –
	dell'Ugo	"	④⑤❸
	Manzi's	*Fish & seafood*	❷❷④
	Au Jardin des Gourmets	*French*	④❷❸
	L'Escargot	"	❷❷❸
	Orso	*Italian*	④④④
	Red Fort	*Indian*	❸❸④
£30+	Alfred	*British, Modern*	❸④④
	Café du Jardin	"	❸④❸
	French House	"	④④❸
	Gabriel	"	❸④④
	Hodgson's	"	④④❸
	Saint	"	④④❷
	Stephen Bull	"	❷❷❸
	Mezzonine	*East/West*	⑤④④
	Beotys	*French*	④❶❸
	Bistrot Soho	"	④④④
	L'Estaminet	"	❸❶④
	Magno's Brasserie	"	⑤❸④
	Mon Plaisir	"	❷❷❶
	Le Palais du Jardin	"	❷❸❷
	Pélican	"	④❸❸

	Soho Soho	"	④④❸
	Gay Hussar	Hungarian	❸❷❶
	Bertorelli's	Italian	④④④
	La Capannina	"	❸❷④
	Vasco & Piero's Pavilion	"	❷❶❸
	Fashion Café	Burgers, etc	⑤⑤⑤
	Planet Hollywood	"	⑤④❸
	Joe Allen	American	④❸❷
	Fung Shing	Chinese	❷④⑤
	Ajimura	Japanese	❸④⑤
	Singapura	Malaysian	❸❸④
£25+	Belgo Centraal	Belgian	④④❷
	Blues	British, Modern	❸❷❷
	The Lexington	"	❸❸❸
	Museum St Café	"	❷❷❸
	Café Bohème	French	❸❸❶
	Café Flo	"	④④❸
	Chez Gérard	"	④❸❸
	Townhouse Brasserie	"	❸❸❸
	Italian Kitchen	Italian	❸❷❷
	Little Italy	"	④❷❸
	Luna Nuova	"	④❸④
	St Moritz	Swiss	❸❷❸
	Balans	International	❸❷❸
	Boulevard	"	❸❸❸
	Brown's	"	④❸❸
	Deals	"	④④④
	Garlic & Shots	"	④❸④
	Sarastro	"	⑤⑤❶
	Shampers	"	❸❸④
	Capital Radio Restaurant	Burgers, etc	④❷❸
	The Rainforest Café	"	④❸❷
	Wolfe's	"	❸④④
	Smollensky's, Strand	American	④④❸
	TGI Friday's	"	⑤④❸
	Café Pacifico	Mexican/TexMex	❸④❷
	Texas Embassy Cantina	"	④❸❸
	Harbour City	Chinese	❷④⑤
	Gopal's of Soho	Indian	❶④❸
	Ikkyu	Japanese	❶④❸
	Bahn Thai	Thai	❸⑤⑤
	Chiang Mai	"	❷⑤④
	Mondo	"	❸④❷
	Sri Siam	"	❷❷❸
£20+	All Bar One	British, Modern	❸④❸
	Andrew Edmunds	"	❸❷❶
	Hujo's	"	❸❶❷
	Plummers	"	❸❷④

			Ratings
	Porters	British, Traditional	④⑤⑤
	Café Rouge	French	⑤⑤④
	Randall & Aubin	"	❸④❸
	Café Pasta	Italian	④❷❸
	Caffè Uno	"	④❸④
	Café Emm	International	❸④❸
	Cork & Bottle	"	❸❸❷
	Dôme	"	④④❸
	Pitcher & Piano	"	④❸❷
	The Waldorf Meridien	Afternoon tea	④❷❷
	Ed's Easy Diner	Burgers, etc	❷❷❷
	Kettners	Pizza	④④❷
	La Perla	Mexican/TexMex	❸❸④
	Café Latino	South American	❸❷❷
	Calabash	Afro-Caribbean	❸④⑤
	Sofra	Turkish	❸❸④
	China City	Chinese	❸④④
	Chuen Cheng Ku	"	④④④
	Golden Dragon	"	❶④④
	Mr Kong	"	❷④⑤
	New World	"	④⑤④
	Malabar Junction	Indian	❸❷❷
	Soho Spice	"	❸❸❷
	Yo! Sushi	Japanese	④❷❷
	Melati	Malaysian	❷④④
	Mongolian Barbecue	Misc oriental	⑤④④
	Wok Wok	"	❸❸❸
	Manorom	Thai	❸❸④
	Thai Pot	"	❸❸④
£15+	Aurora	British, Modern	❷❸❷
	PizzaExpress	Pizza	❸❸❸
	Pâtisserie Valerie	Sandwiches, cakes, etc	❷❷❷
	Star Café	"	❸④❸
	Cranks	Vegetarian	④④④
	Mildreds	"	❷❷❸
	Poons	Chinese	❸❸④
	Poons, Lisle Street	"	❷❸④
	India Club	Indian	❷❷④
	Hamine	Japanese	❸④④
	Wagamama	"	❷❷❸
£10+	Café des Amis du Vin	French	❷❸④
	Pollo	Italian	④④❸
	Gordon's Wine Bar	International	④❷❶
	Stock Pot	"	④❸❸
	Garden Café	Sandwiches, cakes, etc	❸❸❸
	Food for Thought	Vegetarian	❷❸④
	Café Sofra	Turkish	❸❸④
	Wong Kei	Chinese	❸⑤④

	Tokyo Diner	Japanese	❸❶❸
£5+	Fryer's Delight	Fish & chips	❶❷❸
	Häagen-Dazs	Ice cream	❸④④
	Bar Italia	Sandwiches, cakes, etc	④❸❶
	Maison Bertaux	"	❷❷❷
	Pret A Manger	"	❸❶❸
	Seattle Coffee Co	"	❷④❸

Mayfair & St James's
(Parts of W1 and SW1)

£100+	Oak Room MPW	French	– – –
£80+	Chez Nico	French	❷❸④
	Le Gavroche	"	❷❷❸
£70+	Connaught	British, Traditional	❸❶❷
	Suntory	Japanese	❸❸④
£60+	The Ritz	French	④❷❶
	Le Soufflé	"	❷❷⑤
	Dorchester, Oriental	Chinese	❷❸④
	Mitsukoshi	Japanese	❶❸⑤
£50+	The Square	British, Modern	❷❸❸
	Dorchester Grill	British, Traditional	❷❶❷
	Wiltons	"	④④❸
	Nobu	East/West	❷④❸
	Claridges Restaurant	French	❸❷❷
	Four Seasons	"	❷❷❸
	L'Odéon	"	④④④
	Les Saveurs	"	❸❷④
	Windows on the World	"	④④❸
	Cecconi's	Italian	⑤④④
	Miyama	Japanese	❷❸⑤
	Shogun	"	❷❸❸
£40+	The Avenue	British, Modern	④④❸
	Le Caprice	"	❷❶❶
	Coast	"	❸④④
	The Lanesborough	"	④❷❶
	Nicole's	"	④④④
	Quaglino's	"	④④❷
	33	"	❷❸④
	Thomas Goode	"	⑤❷❸
	Brown's Hotel	British, Traditional	❸❸❷
	Green's	"	❸❷❸
	Greenhouse	"	❸❷❸

	Bentley's	*Fish & seafood*	③②③
	Cave	*French*	②②③
	L'Oranger	*"*	①①②
	Bice	*Italian*	⑤④④
	Diverso	*"*	③②④
	Signor Sassi	*"*	③③③
	Kaspia	*Russian*	②②③
	The Guinea	*Steaks & grills*	③③④
	Rowley's	*"*	⑤④④
	Princess Garden	*Chinese*	④④④
	Zen Central	*"*	③④⑤
	Zen Garden	*"*	③②③
	Benihana	*Japanese*	④③④
	Matsuri	*"*	②②④
£35+	Langan's Brasserie	*British, Modern*	④②❶
	Opus 70	*"*	④③⑤
	Scott's	*"*	③③③
	Dover St Wine Bar	*International*	⑤⑤③
	Vendôme	*"*	③③②
	Al Hamra	*Lebanese*	③④③
	Fakhreldine	*"*	③④④
£30+	The Marquis	*British, Modern*	②❶④
	Café Fish	*Fish & seafood*	③④④
	The Gaucho Grill	*Steaks & grills*	②③②
	Momo	*North African*	③③❶
	Al Sultan	*Lebanese*	③④④
	Chor Bizarre	*Indian*	③④③
	Tamarind	*"*	❶②②
	Veeraswamy	*"*	②②②
£25+	Sotheby's Café	*British, Modern*	③②③
	Zinc	*"*	④②④
	Boudin Blanc	*French*	③③②
	Café Flo	*"*	④④③
	Chez Gérard	*"*	④③③
	Ristorante Italiano	*Italian*	③③③
	Il Vicolo	*"*	③②④
	Brown's	*International*	④③③
	Hanover Square	*"*	③③④
	Hard Rock Café	*Burgers, etc*	③②❶
	Smollensky's	*American*	④④③
	Yoshino	*Japanese*	❶④③
£20+	All Bar One	*British, Modern*	③④③
	L'Artiste Musclé	*French*	④②②
	Caffè Uno	*Italian*	④③④
	Chicago Pizza Pie Factory	*Pizza*	④③④
	Gourmet Pizza Co.	*"*	③④③

	Down Mexico Way	*Mexican/TexMex*	⑤③②
	Sofra	*Turkish*	③③④
	Woodlands	*Indian*	③④④
	Café Sogo	*Japanese*	③③④
£15+	Ask	*Pizza*	③③③
	PizzaExpress	"	③③③
	Pizzeria Condotti	"	③③②
£10+	Stock Pot	*International*	④③③
	Wren at St James's	*Vegetarian*	④④④
	Café Sofra	*Turkish*	③③④
£5+	Pret A Manger	*Sandwiches, cakes, etc*	③①③
	Seattle Coffee Co	"	②④③

**Fitzrovia & Marylebone
(Part of W1)**

£50+	Interlude	*French*	③③④
	Pied à Terre	"	①②③
	Masako	*Japanese*	②②③
£40+	La Porte des Indes	*Indian*	③④③
£35+	Stephen Bull	*British, Modern*	②②③
	Elena's L'Etoile	*French*	②②②
	Le Muscadet	"	③③④
	Nico Central	"	③③④
	Villandry	"	– – –
	Arisugawa	*Japanese*	②④④
£30+	Oceana	*British, Modern*	③④④
	The Union Café	"	④④④
	Zoe	"	④④④
	Odin's	*French*	③①①
	White Tower	*Greek*	③③③
	Bertorelli's	*Italian*	④④④
	Maroush	*Lebanese*	②②④
£25+	Justin de Blank	*British, Modern*	③②④
	Café Flo	*French*	④④③
	Langan's Bistro	"	④③④
	Caldesi	*Italian*	③②④
	O'Conor Don	*Irish*	③②②
	Hardy's	*International*	③③③
	Caravan Serai	*Afghani*	③③②
	Ikkyu	*Japanese*	①④③
£20+	All Bar One	*British, Modern*	③④③
	Café Rouge	*French*	⑤⑤④

AREA OVERVIEWS

	L'Arte	*Italian*	❶❸④
	Caffè Uno	"	④❸④
	La Spighetta	"	❷④❸
	Mad Dog Café	*International*	④❸④
	Efes Kebab House	*Turkish*	❸❷❸
	Sofra	"	❸❸④
	Mandeer	*Indian*	❷❷❷
	Woodlands	"	❸④④
	Silks & Spice	*Thai*	❷❸❷
£15+	Bar Madrid	*Spanish*	④④❷
	Ask	*Pizza*	❸❸❸
	PizzaExpress	"	❸❸❸
	Pâtisserie Valerie	*Sandwiches, cakes, etc*	❷❷❷
	Cranks	*Vegetarian*	④④④
	Ragam	*Indian*	❸④⑤
£10+	Stock Pot	*International*	④❸❸
	Ranoush	*Lebanese*	❶④④
	Café Sofra	*Turkish*	❸❸④
£5+	Pret A Manger	*Sandwiches, cakes, etc*	❸❶❸
	Seattle Coffee Co	"	❷④❸

Belgravia, Victoria & Pimlico
(SW1, except St James's)

£50+	The Halkin	*Italian*	❸❸❸
	L'Incontro	"	④⑤⑤
	Santini	"	⑤④④
£40+	Atrium	*British, Modern*	④⑤④
	The Fifth Floor	"	④❸❸
	Vong	*East/West*	❷❸❷
	La Finezza	*Italian*	❸❸④
	La Fontana	"	❸❸④
	Mimmo d'Ischia	"	❸❸❸
	Toto's	"	❷❷❷
	Rib Room	*Steaks & grills*	❸❷④
	Ken Lo's Memories	*Chinese*	❷❷④
	Mr Chow	"	⑤④④
	Salloos	*Indian*	❷④⑤
£35+	Drones	*British, Modern*	④❸❷
	Tate Gallery	"	④❸❷
	La Poule au Pot	*French*	④❸❶
	Simply Nico	"	❷❷⑤
	Grissini	*Italian*	❸❷❸
	Sale e Pepe	"	❸❸❶
	Zafferano	"	❶❷❷

	Boisdale	*International*	③②②
	Motcomb's	*"*	③②②
	Pomegranates	*"*	④④③
	Al Bustan	*Lebanese*	②②④
£30+	Ebury Street Wine Bar	*British, Modern*	③④③
	Fifth Floor (Café)	*"*	③④②
	The Foundation	*"*	④⑤⑤
	Grenadier	*British, Traditional*	⑤③❶
	Shepherd's	*"*	③②③
	The Chelsea Restaurant	*French*	②③④
	Entrecote	*"*	④③④
	Caraffini	*Italian*	③②③
	Como Lario	*"*	④③③
	Olivo	*"*	②③③
	Footstool	*International*	⑤④③
	Oliveto	*Pizza*	②③③
£25+	Grumbles	*International*	④③③
	Oriel	*"*	④④②
	Hunan	*Chinese*	❶②④
£20+	Uno	*Italian*	②③③
	Mackintosh's Brasserie	*International*	④③②
	Football Football	*Burgers, etc*	⑤③④
	Blue Jade	*Thai*	③③④
£15+	Hyde Park Hotel		
	Park Room	*Afternoon tea*	③②②
	Seafresh	*Fish & chips*	②③④
	Ask	*Pizza*	③③③
	Pizza On The Park	*"*	③③②
	PizzaExpress	*"*	③③③
	Jenny Lo's	*Chinese*	④③④
	Mekong	*Vietnamese*	③④③
£10+	Little Bay	*International*	④④③
£5+	Pret A Manger	*Sandwiches, cakes, etc*	③❶③
	Seattle Coffee Co	*"*	②④③

211

WEST

Chelsea, South Kensington, Kensington, Earl's Court & Fulham (SW3, SW5, SW6, SW7, SW10 & W8)

£80+	Blakes Hotel	*International*	④④❶
£60+	Capital Hotel	*French*	❷❸④
	La Tante Claire	"	❶❶❸
£50+	Aubergine	*French*	❶❷❷
	Bibendum	"	❸❸❸
	Chavot	"	– – –
	Turner's	"	❸④❸
	San Lorenzo	*Italian*	⑤⑤④
£40+	The Canteen	*British, Modern*	❷❸❷
	Clarke's	"	❶❶❸
	The Collection	"	④④❸
	English Garden	"	❸❷❷
	English House	"	❸❷❷
	Hilaire	"	❷❷❸
	Launceston Place	"	❷❷❶
	Shaw's	"	❸❷❸
	The Tenth	"	❸❸❸
	Poissonnerie de l'Avenue	*Fish & seafood*	❷❸❸
	Monkeys	*French*	❷❷❸
	Daphne's	*Italian*	❸④❷
	Montpeliano	"	④❸❸
	Sabatino	"	④❷④
	Scalini	"	❸❸❷
	Albero & Grana	*Spanish*	④④❷
	Zen	*Chinese*	❷❷❸
	Bombay Brasserie	*Indian*	❷❸❷
	Benihana	*Japanese*	④❸④
	Blue Elephant	*Thai*	❷❷❶
£35+	Arcadia	*British, Modern*	④❷❷
	Belvedere	"	⑤④❷
	Bluebird	"	④❸❷
	Boyd's	"	❷❸④
	Dan's	"	④❷❶
	Fables	"	④⑤⑤
	Joe's Café	"	❸④❷
	Kensington Place	"	❷❸❷
	Simply Nico Chelsea	"	❷❶❸
	Stratford's	*Fish & seafood*	❷❷④
	La Belle Epoque	*French*	④④❸
	Brasserie St Quentin	"	❸❷❷

	Lou Pescadou	"	②④❸
	Le Suquet	"	②④②
	La Famiglia	Italian	❸④②
	Osteria Le Fate	"	⑤⑤❸
	San Martino	"	④❸❸
	Sandrini	"	❸❸❸
	Nikita's	Russian	④❸②
	Conrad Hotel	International	②❷❸
	Montana	American	❷❸②
	Ken Lo's Memories	Chinese	④❸④
	Chutney Mary	Indian	❸❸❸
	Khun Akorn	Thai	④④④
£30+	The Abingdon	British, Modern	❸❸❸
	Bar Central	"	④④❸
	Bistrot 190	"	❸④②
	Charco's	"	❸④④
	Kartouche	"	④④❸
	192	"	④⑤❸
	755	"	❷❷⑤
	606 Club	"	④❸②
	Basil St Hotel	British, Traditional	❸❷②
	Maggie Jones's	"	④❸❶
	Bibendum Oyster Bar	Fish & seafood	❶❷②
	Chezmax	French	❶❶❸
	La Ciboulette	"	❷❷④
	L'Escargot Doré	"	❸❷④
	Grill St Quentin	"	④④④
	Novelli W8	"	④④④
	Thierry's	"	④❸②
	Formula Veneta	Italian	④❸❸
	Sambuca	"	❸❶④
	San Frediano	"	⑤④④
	Ziani	"	④❸❸
	Wódka	Polish	④❸❸
	The Enterprise	International	❸❸②
	PJ's	"	⑤④❸
	Maroush	Lebanese	❷❷④
	Phoenicia	"	❷❶④
	Good Earth	Chinese	❷❷❸
	Mao Tai	"	❷❷❸
	Mr Wing	"	❸❸❶
	Café Lazeez	Indian	④❸❸
	Star of India	"	❷④②
	Tandoori of Chelsea	"	④❸❸
	Vama	"	④❷④
	Busabong Tree	Thai	❷❸❸
	Nam Long	Vietnamese	❸④❶
£25+	Brinkley's	British, Modern	④❸②

Name	Cuisine	Ratings
Café Med	"	④❸❷
Chelsea Ram	"	❶❸❷
Chelsea Square	"	④❸❸
The Cross Keys	"	④❸❷
Goolies	"	❷❷❸
James R	"	④④④
Joe's Brasserie	"	❸❸❸
Le Metro	"	❸❸❸
The Parson's Nose	"	❸❸④
The Pen	"	❸❸❷
Ghillies	Fish & seafood	❸❸❸
Au Bon Accueil	French	④❶❷
La Bouchée	"	④❺❷
La Brasserie	"	④④❷
Café Flo	"	④④❸
Café O	Greek	❸❶④
Bersagliera	Italian	❸❷❸
Bucci	"	❸❷❸
De Cecco	"	❷❸❷
Elistano	"	❷❷❸
Il Falconiere	"	❸❶❸
Leonardo's	"	❷❷❸
Paparazzi Café	"	④❸❷
Tusc	"	④④④
Ognisko Polskie	Polish	❸❸❷
Cambio de Tercio	Spanish	④❸❸
Balans West	International	❸❷❸
Brown's	"	④❸❸
Deals	"	④④④
Foxtrot Oscar	"	④❸❸
The Gasworks	"	❺❸❷
Glaisters	"	④❺❸
Wine Gallery	"	❸④❷
Big Easy	American	④④❸
Chicago Rib Shack	"	④❸④
Shoeless Joe's	"	❺④❷
Cactus Blue	South American	④④❷
Malabar	Indian	❷❷❸
Nayab	"	❷❸④
Sushi Wong	Japanese	❸❸④
t'su	"	❸❸❸
Jim Thompson's	Malaysian	④❺❶
Bangkok	Thai	❷❸④
Busabong Too	"	❷❸④
S&P	"	❷❷④
S&P Patara	"	❷❷④
Thai on the River	"	❸④❸
Tui	"	❶❸❺
£20+ All Bar One	British, Modern	❸④❸

	Name	Cuisine	Ratings
	The Crescent	"	④❸④
	Ffiona's	"	❸②②
	Gilbert's	"	⑤❸⑤
	Vingt-Quatre	"	❷❸❸
	Café Rouge	French	⑤⑤④
	Emile's	"	❸①❸
	Francofill	"	❷❷④
	Café Montpeliano	Italian	❸❸②
	Café Pasta	"	④❷❸
	Caffè Uno	"	④❸④
	Da Pierino	"	❸❸④
	Made in Italy	"	❸❸❸
	Riccardo's	"	❸⑤④
	Spago	"	❸④④
	Albero & Grana, Bar	Spanish	❷④❷
	Dôme	International	④④❸
	Front Page	"	❷❸❷
	Pitcher & Piano	"	④❸❷
	The Scarsdale	"	④❸❷
	Sporting Page	"	❸❸❷
	Ed's Easy Diner	Burgers, etc	❷❷❷
	Henry J Beans	"	④❸❸
	Luigi Malones	"	④❷❷
	Sticky Fingers	"	④❸❸
	Tootsies	"	④❸④
	Geale's	Fish & chips	❷④⑤
	Ciabatta	Pizza	❸④❸
	Da Mario	"	❸④④
	La Delizia	"	❷④❸
	Pizza Chelsea	"	❸④④
	Pizza Pomodoro	"	④④❶
	Texas Lone Star	Mexican/TexMex	⑤⑤❸
	El Gaucho	South American	❷④❸
	Khan's of Kensington	Indian	❷❸④
	Legend of India	"	❸❷❸
	Noor Jahan	"	❷❸④
	Tandoori Lane	"	❷❶❷
	Bonjour Vietnam	Misc oriental	④⑤④
	Mongolian Barbecue	"	⑤④④
	Tiger Lil's	"	④❸❷
	Wok Wok	"	❸❸❸
	Chaba	Thai	❸❸④
£15+	Calzone	Italian	❸❸❸
	King's Road Café	"	④❷④
	Picasso	"	❸❸❸
	Daquise	Polish	④❸❸
	Rôtisserie Jules	Steaks & grills	④❸④
	Chelsea Bun Diner	International	❸❸❸
	Coopers Arms	"	❸❷❷

	Windsor Castle	"	③④❶
	Ask	Pizza	❸❸❸
	Pizza the Action	"	❸❷❸
	PizzaExpress	"	❸❸❸
	Pucci Pizza	"	④④❶
	Pâtisserie Valerie	Sandwiches, cakes, etc	❷❷❷
	Le Shop	"	❸❸❸
	New Culture Rev'n	Chinese	❸④④
	Khyber Pass	Indian	❸❸④
	Mamta	"	❷❷⑤
	Bar Japan	Japanese	❸❸❸
	Sash	Misc oriental	❸④❸
	Krungtap	Thai	❸❸❸
£10+	Costa's Grill	Greek	❷❶❷
	Luigi's Delicatessen	Italian	❶④❸
	Mona Lisa	"	❸❷④
	Chelsea Kitchen	International	④❷④
	Stock Pot	"	④❸❸
	Costa's Fish	Fish & chips	❷❷④
	Troubadour	Sandwiches, cakes, etc	④⑤❶
	Café 209	Thai	④❷❸
	Churchill	"	❷④❸
£5+	Häagen-Dazs	Ice cream	❸④④
	Fileric	Sandwiches, cakes, etc	❷❸④
	Pret A Manger	"	❸❶❸

Notting Hill, Holland Park, Bayswater, North Kensington & Maida Vale (W2, W9, W10, W11)

£60+	I Thai	East/West	④④④
£50+	Halcyon Hotel	British, Modern	❷❸❷
	Leith's	"	④❸❸
£40+	Al San Vincenzo	Italian	❶❷④
	Julie's	International	④❸❶
£35+	Alastair Little	British, Modern	❸❸④
	Beach Blanket Babylon	"	⑤⑤❷
	First Floor	"	⑤④❷
	Jimmy Beez	"	❸④❸
	The Sugar Club	"	❷❷❷
	Jason's	Fish & seafood	❶❸❸
	Chez Moi	French	❸❷❸
	Assaggi	Italian	❶❶❸
	Mr Frascati	"	④❸④

			Rating
	Orsino	"	④❸❷
£30+	Anonimato	British, Modern	❷❶❸
	W11	"	④④❷
	The Green Olive	Italian	❸❸❸
	Palio	"	⑤④❸
	Zucca	"	❸❸❷
	Woz	Mediterranean	❸❷❷
	South	Scandinavian	④④❸
	Maroush	Lebanese	❷❷④
	Bombay Palace	Indian	❷❷❸
£25+	Café Med	British, Modern	④❸❷
	The Cow	"	❷❷❷
	Mas Café	"	❷④❷
	Veronica's	British, Traditional	❸❷❸
	Brass. du Marché	French	❷❶❷
	La Pomme d'Amour	"	❸❶❷
	Prost	German	❸❷④
	Halepi	Greek	❸❷④
	Kalamaras, Mega	"	④❸❷
	L'Accento Italiano	Italian	❸④❸
	Café 206	"	— — —
	Osteria Basilico	"	❷❸❶
	Osteria del Parco	"	❸❸❷
	The Red Pepper	"	❷④❸
	Julie's Bar	International	❸❸❶
	The Tuscan	"	④❸❸
	TGI Friday's	American	⑤④❸
	Mandarin Kitchen	Chinese	❶④④
	Park Inn	"	❸❷④
	Royal China	"	❶❸❸
	Inaho	Japanese	❶④❸
£20+	The Ladbroke Arms	British, Modern	❸❸❸
	Raoul's Café	"	❷❸❸
	The Westbourne	"	❸⑤❷
	Café Rouge	French	⑤⑤④
	Caffè Uno	Italian	④❸④
	Galicia	Spanish	❸④❸
	Los Remos	"	❸❸④
	Tootsies	Burgers, etc	④❸④
	Fats	Cajun/creole	❸④④
	Mandola	Sudanese	❸⑤❸
	Isfehan	Persian	❸❷❸
	The Four Seasons	Chinese	❸⑤⑤
	Ben's Thai	Thai	❷❸❸
	Tawana	"	❷④④
£15+	The Prince Bonaparte	British, Modern	❸④❸
	Kalamaras, Micro	Greek	❸④④

	Calzone	*Italian*	**3 3 3**
	Rôtisserie Jules	*Steaks & grills*	**4 3 4**
	Café Grove	*International*	**4 4 2**
	Ask	*Pizza*	**3 3 3**
	PizzaExpress	*"*	**3 3 3**
	Beirut Express	*Lebanese*	**2 2 3**
	Manzara	*Turkish*	**2 3 3**
	Mandalay	*Burmese*	**2 1** 4
	Khan's	*Indian*	**3 5 3**
	Standard Tandoori	*"*	**3 3** 4
	Mawar	*Malaysian*	**2 3** 5
£10+	Coins	*Sandwiches, cakes, etc*	**3** 4 **3**
£5+	Häagen-Dazs	*Ice cream*	**3** 4 4
	Lisboa Patisserie	*Sandwiches, cakes, etc*	**1 3 3**

Hammersmith, Shepherd's Bush
Chiswick & Olympia
(W4, W5, W6, W12, W14)

£40+	Cibo	*Italian*	**2 3** 4
	The River Café	*"*	**1 3 2**
£35+	Chinon	*French*	**1** 4 4
	La Dordogne	*"*	**2 1 2**
£30+	Noughts 'n' Crosses	*British, Modern*	4 4 **3**
	Snows on the Green	*"*	**3 3** 4
	Springbok Café	*South African*	**3 3** 4
£25+	Blythe Road	*British, Modern*	**3 3 2**
	The Brackenbury	*"*	**2 3 3**
	Brook	*"*	**3** 4 **3**
	Chiswick	*"*	**2 2** 4
	Wilson's	*"*	**3 0 3**
	Popeseye	*Steaks & grills*	**1 3** 4
	Rôtisserie	*"*	**3 3** 4
	Deals	*International*	4 4 4
	Nanking	*Chinese*	**3 3 3**
	Anarkali	*Indian*	**3** 4 4
£20+	All Bar One	*British, Modern*	**3** 4 **3**
	Anglesea Arms	*"*	**2 5 3**
	The Havelock Tavern	*"*	**2 5 3**
	Stone Mason's Arms	*"*	**2 2 3**
	Café Rouge	*French*	5 5 4
	Café Pasta	*Italian*	4 **2 3**
	Caffè Uno	*"*	4 **3** 4
	Mackintosh's Brasserie	*International*	4 **3 2**

	Name	Cuisine	Ratings
	Pitcher & Piano	"	4 3 2
	Tootsies	Burgers, etc	4 3 4
	Blah! Blah! Blah!	Vegetarian	3 4 4
	The Gate	"	1 2 3
	Paulo's	Brazilian	3 2 3
	Adams Café	Tunisian	2 2 4
	Ebla	Lebanese	3 2 4
	Mongolian Barbecue	Misc oriental	5 4 4
	Esarn Kheaw	Thai	1 4 4
	Fat Boy's	"	3 3 3
	Sabai Sabai	"	2 2 4
	Topsy-Tasty	"	1 2 4
£15+	Dove	International	3 3 2
	Ask	Pizza	3 3 3
	PizzaExpress	"	3 3 3
	Alounak	Persian	1 3 3
	Bedlington Café	Thai	1 4 4
	Latymers	"	2 3 5
	Thai Bistro	"	2 3 4
£5+	Pret A Manger	Sandwiches, cakes, etc	3 1 3

NORTH

Hampstead, West Hampstead, St John's Wood, Regent's Park, Kilburn & Camden Town (NW postcodes)

£40+	The Landmark Hotel	*International*	③④②
	Benihana	*Japanese*	④③④
	Wakaba	"	②③④
£35+	Odette's	*British, Modern*	③②①
	L'Aventure	*French*	②②①
	Oslo Court	"	①①③
	China Blues	*Chinese*	④④③
£30+	The Blenheim	*British, Modern*	④④④
	Bradley's	"	③②②
	Café des Arts	"	④③②
	Gresslin's	"	②③⑤
	Quincy's	"	②①②
	Mezzaluna	*Italian*	③③④
	Villa Bianca	"	④③②
	House on Rosslyn Hill	*International*	④④②
	Cheng Du	*Chinese*	③②③
	Feng Shang	"	③③②
	ZeNW3	"	②③③
£25+	Belgo Noord	*Belgian*	④④②
	Byron's	*British, Modern*	④④③
	Cucina	"	③②③
	The Engineer	"	③④②
	The Vine	"	③⑤③
	Café Flo	*French*	④④③
	La Cage Imaginaire	"	④③③
	Camden Brasserie	"	③②③
	A Tavola	*Italian*	④④②
	Vegia Zena	"	①③③
	Café Delancey	*International*	④④②
	Caffe Graffiti	"	③③③
	Cottons	*Afro-Caribbean*	④④②
	Solly's	*Israeli*	②④③
	Gung-Ho	*Chinese*	②②②
	Sushi-Say	*Japanese*	②②④
	Singapore Garden	*Malaysian*	②③④
£20+	All Bar One	*British, Modern*	③④③
	The Chapel	"	③④③
	Crown & Goose	"	③④③
	Lansdowne	"	③⑤②
	Café Rouge	*French*	⑤⑤④
	Daphne	*Greek*	③②③

	Greek Valley	"	③③④
	Lemonia	"	③②②
	Billboard Café	Italian	④②③
	Café Pasta	"	④②③
	Caffè Uno	"	④③④
	Marine Ices	"	③③③
	Don Pepe	Spanish	③②③
	Cosmo	International	③②④
	Dôme	"	④④③
	Ed's Easy Diner	Burgers, etc	②②②
	Tootsies	"	④③④
	Nautilus	Fish & chips	②③④
	Seashell	"	①③④
	Manna	Vegetarian	②③④
	Laurent	Tunisian	①②⑤
	Great Nepalese	Indian	②③⑤
	Café Japan	Japanese	②②④
	Gecko	Misc oriental	④③③
	Mongolian Barbecue	"	⑤④④
£15+	Czech Club	Czech	③④④
	Nontas	Greek	②③④
	Calzone	Italian	③③③
	Zamoyski	Polish	④③②
	Troika	Russian	③③③
	Bar Gansa	Spanish	②③②
	Ask	Pizza	③③③
	PizzaExpress	"	③③③
	Ali Baba	Egyptian	②②④
	New Culture Rev'n	Chinese	③④④
	The Vegetarian Cottage	"	③③③
	Chutneys	Indian	③④③
	Haandi	"	③③④
	Vijay	"	②③④
£10+	The Little Bay	International	④④③
	Diwana B.-Poori Hs	Indian	②③④
	Geeta	"	②③⑤
£5+	Häagen-Dazs	Ice cream	③④④
	Pret A Manger	Sandwiches, cakes, etc	③①③
	Yoahan Plaza	Misc oriental	③③⑤

AREA OVERVIEWS

Islington, Highgate, Crouch End, Stoke Newington, Finsbury Park, Muswell Hill & Finchley (N postcodes)

£35+	Frederick's	*French*	❸❷❷
£30+	Euphorium	*British, Modern*	– – –
	Granita	*"*	❷❸④
	Lola's	*"*	❸❸④
	Fisk	*Fish & seafood*	④④④
	Village Bistro	*French*	❸❸❸
	The White Onion	*"*	❷❷❷
	Casale Franco	*Italian*	❸⑤❸
	San Carlo	*"*	❸❷❸
	Anna's Place	*Scandinavian*	❸❷❷
£25+	Jindivick	*British, Modern*	❷❷❷
	Kavanagh's	*"*	❸❷❷
	Chez Liline	*Fish & seafood*	❶❸⑤
	Café Flo	*French*	④④❸
	Soulard	*"*	❷❷❷
	Florians	*Italian*	❸❷❸
	Rôtisserie	*Steaks & grills*	❸❸④
	Toff's	*Fish & chips*	❶❷④
	Cuba Libre	*South American*	④❸❸
£20+	All Bar One	*British, Modern*	❸④❸
	The Lord Palmerston	*"*	❸❷❷
	Mesclun	*"*	❸❷④
	Café Rouge	*French*	⑤⑤④
	Vrisaki	*Greek*	❷❸④
	Café Pasta	*Italian*	④❷❸
	Caffè Uno	*"*	④❸④
	Banners	*International*	④④❷
	Dôme	*"*	④④❸
	The Fox Reformed	*"*	❸❸❷
	Pitcher & Piano	*"*	④❸❷
	Two Brothers	*Fish & chips*	❶❷④
	Pasha	*Turkish*	❸❷❸
	Rani	*Indian*	❸❷④
	Bu San	*Korean*	❷❸⑤
	Tiger Lil's	*Misc oriental*	④❸❷
	Tuk Tuk	*Thai*	❸❸⑤
	Yum Yum	*"*	❷❷❸
£15+	Le Mercury	*French*	⑤④❸
	Le Sacré-Coeur	*"*	❸❸❷
	Calzone	*Italian*	❸❸❸
	La Porchetta Pizzeria	*"*	❷❷❷
	La Finca	*Spanish*	❸④❸
	Upper St Fish Shop	*Fish & chips*	❷④④

	Ask	*Pizza*	❸❸❸
	PizzaExpress	*"*	❸❸❸
	La Piragua	*South American*	❸❷❷
	Iznik	*Turkish*	❷❷❶
	Sarcan	*"*	❷❸❸
	New Culture Rev'n	*Chinese*	❸④④
	Anglo Asian Tandoori	*Indian*	❸❸❸
	Rasa	*"*	❶❶❸
£10+	Afghan Kitchen	*Afghani*	❸④❸
£5+	Pret A Manger	*Sandwiches, cakes, etc*	❸❶❸

SOUTH

**South Bank
(SE1)**

£50+	Le Pont de la Tour	*British, Modern*	③④②
£40+	Oxo Tower	*British, Modern*	④④②
	The Butlers Wharf Chop-house	*British, Traditional*	③③③
£35+	Blue Print Café	*British, Modern*	③④②
	The People's Palace	*"*	④③④
	Cantina del Ponte	*Italian*	⑤⑤④
£30+	Bar Central	*British, Modern*	④④③
	Livebait	*Fish & seafood*	①②④
	Le Pont de la Tour Bar & Grill	*Steaks & grills*	③③②
	Bengal Clipper	*Indian*	②③④
£25+	The Apprentice	*British, Modern*	②④⑤
	Mezzanine	*"*	③③③
	RSJ	*"*	②②③
	Bistrot 2 Riverside	*East/West*	②②②
	Archduke Wine Bar	*International*	③③③
	Fina Estampa	*South American*	②②④
	Four Regions	*Chinese*	③③③
£20+	Three Little Pigs	*British, Modern*	⑤④⑤
	The Waterloo Fire Station	*"*	④④③
	Café Rouge	*French*	⑤⑤④
	Meson Don Felipe	*Spanish*	③④②
	Gourmet Pizza Co.	*Pizza*	③④③
£15+	PizzaExpress	*Pizza*	③③③
	Pizzeria Castello	*"*	②②②

**Battersea, Clapham, Wandsworth,
Barnes, Putney, Brixton & Lewisham
(All postcodes south of the river except SE1)**

£40+	Putney Bridge	*British, Modern*	⑤⑤③
£35+	Belair House	*British, Modern*	③④②
	Chez Bruce	*"*	①①②
	Lobster Pot	*Fish & seafood*	①②②
£30+	Bar Central	*British, Modern*	④④③
	Buchan's	*"*	④③④

	Name	Cuisine	Ratings
	The Cook House	"	③②④
	Phoenix	"	③②③
	Ransome's Dock	"	②②②
	Redmond's	"	③②②
	Sonny's	"	②②②
	The Stepping Stone	"	②①③
	Le Gothique	French	③③③
	Monsieur Max	"	②③③
	Antipasto e Pasta	Italian	③②③
	Del Buongustaio	"	①②②
	Enoteca Turi	"	②②③
	Prego	"	④④③
	Riva	"	②③④
	Bombay Bicycle Club	Indian	②③③
	Thailand	Thai	②②③
£25+	The Depot	British, Modern	④③②
	Glaisters	"	④⑤③
	On the Rise	"	③③④
	S Bar	"	③③③
	Valhalla	"	④③③
	Ghillies	Fish & seafood	③③③
	Le Bouchon Bordelais	French	④④②
	La Bouffe	"	③③②
	Le P'tit Normand	"	③②④
	Ost. Antica Bologna	Italian	②④②
	Café Portugal	Portuguese	①③④
	Polygon Bar & Grill	Steaks & grills	②③②
	La Rueda	Spanish	③②②
	Naked Turtle	International	④②②
	The Ship	"	③③②
	Royal China	Chinese	②③③
	Café Spice Namaste	Indian	①②②
	Zujuma's	"	②②③
	Enak Enak	Indonesian	③④③
	Chada	Thai	③③④
£20+	Helter Skelter	British, Modern	③⑤④
	The Lavender	"	③④②
	The Mason's Arms	"	②④②
	Scoffers	"	③②②
	The Stable	"	③④③
	Vincent's	"	③②④
	Café de la Place	French	③④③
	Café Rouge	"	⑤⑤④
	Emile's	"	③①③
	Gastro	"	②③②
	Buona Sera	Italian	②③②
	Caffè Uno	"	④③④
	Rebato's	Spanish	②①②

225

	Name	Cuisine	Ratings
	Alma	*International*	③④③
	Bah Humbug	*"*	⑤③①
	Café Jeune	*"*	③④③
	Hornimans	*"*	③④③
	Pitcher & Piano	*"*	④③②
	Tootsies	*Burgers, etc*	④③④
	Eco	*Pizza*	①④③
	Pizza Metro	*"*	①①③
	Battersea Rickshaw	*Indian*	③③③
	Haweli	*"*	②③④
	Indian Ocean	*"*	②②④
	Ma Goa	*"*	②②④
	Rani	*"*	③②④
	Tiger Lil's	*Misc oriental*	④③②
£15+	White Cross Hotel	*British, Modern*	③④②
	La Finca	*Spanish*	③④③
	Batt. Barge Bistro	*International*	④③②
	Côte à Côte	*"*	⑤④③
	Brady's	*Fish & chips*	②③④
	Bellinis	*Pizza*	③③③
	C Notarianni & Sons	*"*	②④④
	PizzaExpress	*"*	③③③
	Boiled Egg	*Sandwiches, cakes, etc*	③④③
	Dixie's Bar & Grill	*Mexican/TexMex*	⑤④②
	Beyoglu	*Turkish*	①③④
	Kastoori	*Indian*	①①④
	Shree Krishna	*"*	①④④
	The Pepper Tree	*Thai*	③②③
	Phuket	*"*	③②④
£5+	Fileric	*Sandwiches, cakes, etc*	②③④

EAST

Smithfield & Farringdon (EC1)

£40+	Maison Novelli	French	— — —
£35+	Bubb's	French	③④④
	Mange 2	"	③③④
£30+	The Fence	British, Modern	④③③
	The Quality Chop House	"	③③③
	St John	"	④③④
	Stephen Bull Bistro	"	②③④
	Rudland & Stubbs	Fish & seafood	④④④
	Café du Marché	French	②③①
	Hope & Sir Loin	Steaks & grills	②②④
£25+	Abbaye	Belgian	③④④
	The Peasant	British, Modern	③③④
	Bleeding Heart	French	②②②
	Novelli EC1	"	— — —
	Alba	Italian	③③④
	The Clerkenwell	"	③③④
	Mustards Brasserie	International	④③③
	Moro	North African	②③③
	East One	Misc oriental	③③③
£20+	Fox & Anchor	British, Traditional	②③②
	The Eagle	Mediterranean	②④③
	Dôme	International	④④③
	Vic Naylors	"	⑤⑤③
	Carnevale	Vegetarian	②②③
£15+	Kolossi Grill	Greek	②②③
	Al's	International	③⑤③
	Japanese Canteen	Japanese	④④⑤
£5+	Pret A Manger	Sandwiches, cakes, etc	③①③

The City & East End (All E and EC postcodes, except EC1)

£60+	Tatsuso	Japanese	①③④
£50+	City Miyama	Japanese	②②④
£40+	City Brasserie	British, Modern	④④③
	City Rhodes	"	①②③
	Gladwins	"	③②③
	Beauchamp's	Fish & seafood	④④④

AREA OVERVIEWS

	Name	Cuisine	Rating
	Le Champenois	*French*	④③④
	Caravaggio	*Italian*	④④③
	Aykoku-Kaku	*Japanese*	③④④
£35+	Searcy's Brasserie	*British, Modern*	③④④
	Whittington's	*"*	④④④
	Aquarium	*Fish & seafood*	③④③
	Gow's	*"*	③③④
	Sheekey's	*"*	⑤③④
	Ashtons	*French*	④④③
	Brasserie Rocque	*International*	④④③
£30+	Leith's at the Institute	*British, Modern*	④⑤④
	Sweetings	*Fish & seafood*	②②②
	Luc's Brasserie	*French*	③③③
	MPW	*"*	②②④
	Taberna Etrusca	*Italian*	④④③
	Imperial City	*Chinese*	②②②
	Inmala	*Indonesian*	③③④
	Singapura	*Malaysian*	③③④
	Tao	*Misc oriental*	④④③
	Sri Siam City	*Thai*	②②④
	Sri Thai	*"*	②④④
£25+	The Bar	*British, Modern*	③④⑤
	Canteloupe	*"*	③②②
	Frocks	*"*	③③②
	Hothouse Bar & Grill	*"*	④④④
	The Bow Wine Vaults	*British, Traditional*	③③③
	George & Vulture	*"*	④②③
	Café Flo	*French*	④④③
	Terraza-Est	*Italian*	③③④
	Foxtrot Oscar	*International*	④③③
	Babe Ruth's	*American*	④④③
	Café Spice Namaste	*Indian*	①②②
	Rupee Room	*"*	③③④
£20+	All Bar One	*British, Modern*	③④③
	Simpson's of Cornhill	*British, Traditional*	③③③
	Café Rouge	*French*	⑤⑤④
	Fuego	*Spanish*	③④②
	Dôme	*International*	④④③
	Gourmet Pizza Co.	*Pizza*	③④③
	Pizza Pomodoro	*"*	④④①
	Futures	*Vegetarian*	③③③
	Café Indiya	*Indian*	③③③
£15+	Reynier	*British, Traditional*	③②③
	Arkansas Café	*Steaks & grills*	②③④
	Barcelona Tapas	*Spanish*	②③③
	Leadenhall Tapas Bar	*"*	④③③

	PizzaExpress	*Pizza*	❸❸❸
	Lahore Kebab House	*Indian*	❷⑤⑤
	Moshi Moshi Sushi	*Japanese*	❷❷❸
	Noto	*"*	❸❸④
£10+	The Place Below	*Vegetarian*	❷❷❸
	Café Sofra	*Turkish*	❸❸④
	Poons in the City	*Chinese*	❷❷④
£5+	Pret A Manger	*Sandwiches, cakes, etc*	❸❶❸
	Futures	*Vegetarian*	❷❸ –
£1+	Brick Lane Beigel Bake	*Sandwiches, cakes, etc*	❷❶④

MAPS

MAP I – LONDON OVERVIEW

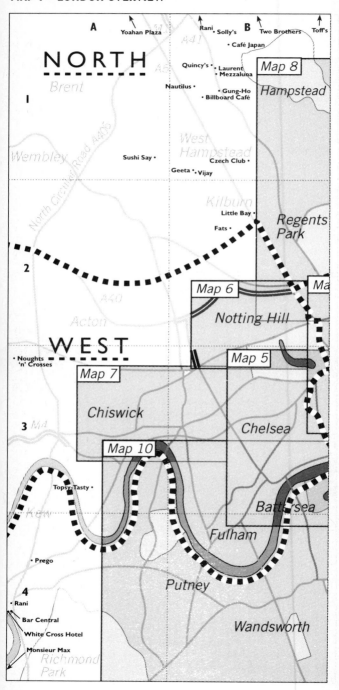

MAP 1 – LONDON OVERVIEW

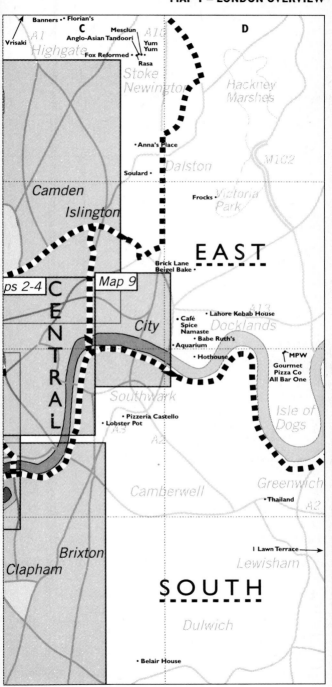

Vrisaki • | A1 | Banners • | • Florian's
Highgate | C | Mesclun | A10 | D
Anglo-Asian Tandoori | Yum Yum
Fox Reformed • | • Rasa

Stoke Newington

Hackney Marshes

• Anna's Place

Dalston | M102

Soulard •

Camden

Islington | Frocks • | *Victoria Park*

EAST

ps 2-4 | C | Map 9

Map 9

Brick Lane
Beigel Bake •

• Lahore Kebab House

C | • Café | *Docklands* | A13
E | Spice
N | Namaste
T | • Babe Ruth's
R | • Aquarium
A | • Hothouse | ↑ MPW
L | | Gourmet
City | Pizza Co
All Bar One

Southwark | *Isle of Dogs*

• Pizzeria Castello
• Lobster Pot | A3 | A2

Camberwell | *Greenwich*

• Thailand | A2

1 Lawn Terrace →

Brixton | *Lewisham*

Clapham | **SOUTH**

Dulwich

• Belair House

MAP 2 – WEST END OVERVIEW

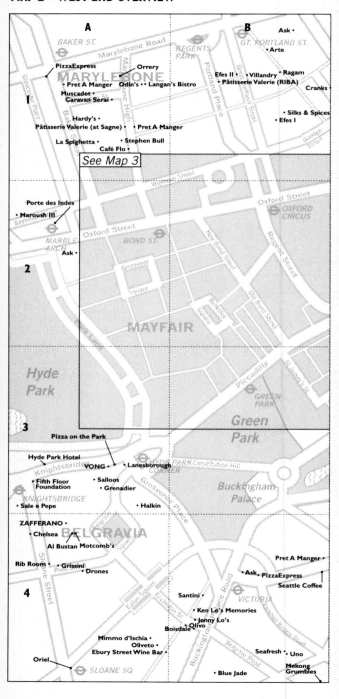

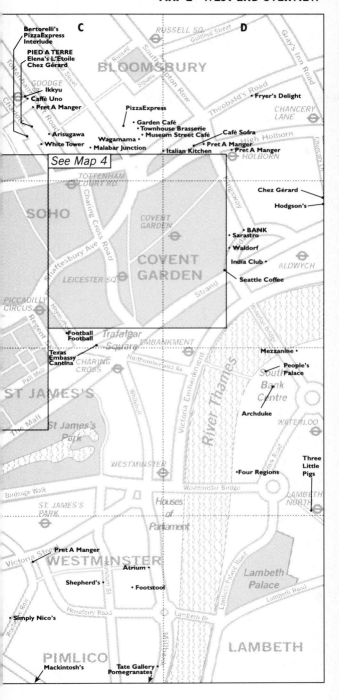

MAP 2 –WEST END OVERVIEW

C

RUSSELL SQ.

Bertorelli's
PizzaExpress
Interlude

PIED A TERRE
Elena's L'Etoile
Chez Gérard

BLOOMSBURY

D

GOODGE

• Fryer's Delight

Ikkyu

CHANCERY
LANE

• Caffè Uno

• Pret A Manger

PizzaExpress

• Garden Café
• Townhouse Brasserie
• Museum Street Café

Café Sofra

• Arisugawa

Wagamama

• Pret A Manger

• White Tower

Malabar Junction

• Italian Kitchen

• Pret A Manger

HOLBORN

See Map 4

TOTTENHAM
COURT RD.

Chez Gérard

SOHO

Charing Cross Road

COVENT
GARDEN

Hodgson's

COVENT
GARDEN

• BANK
• Sarastro

LEICESTER SQ.

• Waldorf

India Club •

ALDWYCH

PICCADILLY
CIRCUS

Seattle Coffee

Strand

•Football
Football

Trafalgar
Square

EMBANKMENT

Mezzanine •

Texas
Embassy
Cantina

CHARING
CROSS

Northumberland Av.

**South
Bank
Centre**

People's
Palace

ST JAMES'S

Whitehall

Archduke

WATERLOO

The Mall

St James's
Park

River Thames

Three
Little
Pigs

WESTMINSTER

•Four Regions

LAMBETH
NORTH

Bridge Walk

ST. JAMES'S
PARK

Westminster Bridge

Houses
of
Parliament

Lambeth
Palace

• Pret A Manger

Victoria St.

WESTMINSTER

Atrium •

Shepherd's •

• Footstool

Lambeth Palace Road

• Simply Nico's

Horseferry Road

Lambeth Br.

LAMBETH

PIMLICO

Mackintosh's

Tate Gallery
Pomegranates

Millbank

MAP 3 – MAYFAIR, ST JAMES'S & WEST SOHO

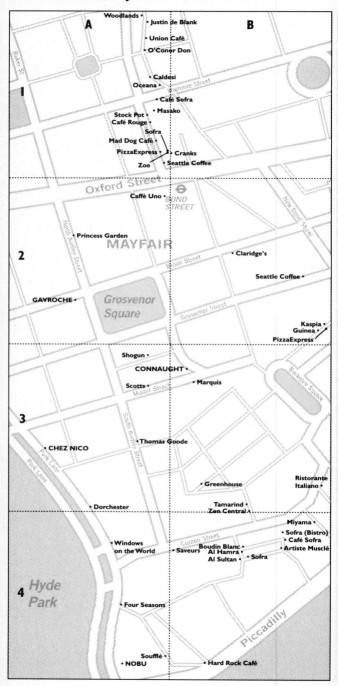

A **B**

Woodlands •
• Justin de Blank
• Union Café
• O'Coner Don

• Caldesi
Oceana •
• Café Sofra
• Masako
Stock Pot •
Café Rouge •
• Sofra
Mad Dog Café •
PizzaExpress • • Cranks
Zoe • • Seattle Coffee

1

Baker St

Wigmore Street

Oxford Street

Caffè Uno •
○ *BOND STREET*

MAYFAIR

• Princess Garden

North Audley Street

Brook Street

• Claridge's

Seattle Coffee •

GAVROCHE •

Grosvenor Square

New Bond Street

Kaspia •
Guinea •
PizzaExpress •

2

Grosvenor Street

Shogun •
CONNAUGHT •
Scotts • • Marquis

Mount Street

South Audley Street

Berkeley Square

3

• **CHEZ NICO**
• Thomas Goode

Park Lane

• Greenhouse

Ristorante Italiano •

• Dorchester
Tamarind •
Zen Central •

Miyama •
• Sofra (Bistro)
• Café Sofra
• **Artiste Musclé**

• Windows on the World
• Saveurs
Boudin Blanc •
Al Hamra •
• Sofra
Al Sultan •

Curzon Street

4

Hyde Park

• Four Seasons

Soufflé •
• **NOBU**
• Hard Rock Café

Piccadilly

MAP 3 – MAYFAIR, ST JAMES'S & WEST SOHO

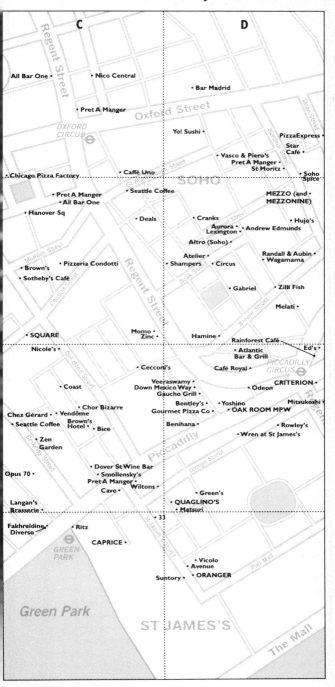

MAP 4 – EAST SOHO, CHINATOWN & COVENT GARDEN

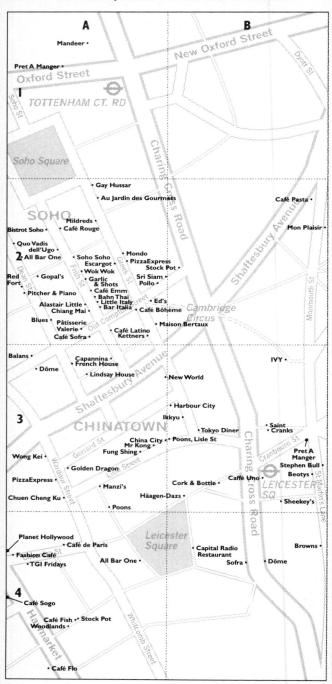

MAP 4 – EAST SOHO, CHINATOWN & COVENT GARDEN

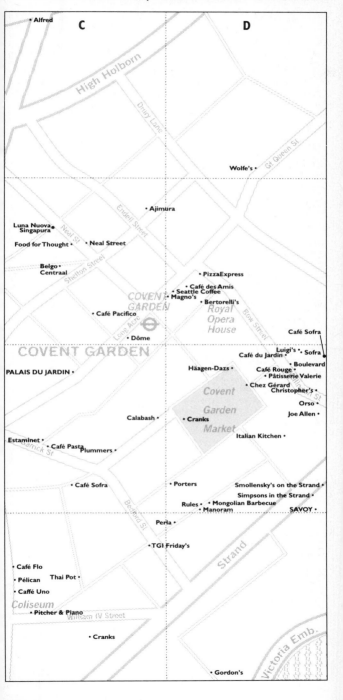

MAP 5 – KNIGHTSBRIDGE, CHELSEA & SOUTH KENSINGTON

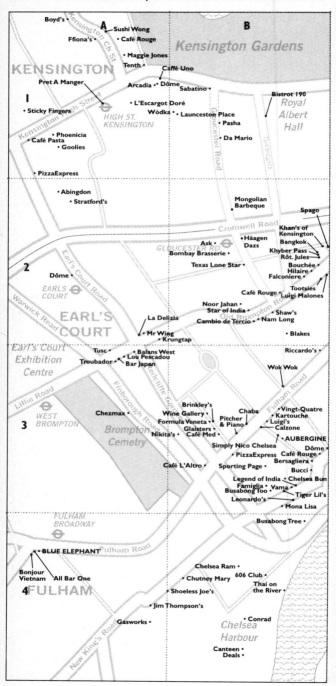

KENSINGTON

Boyd's

Sushi Wong — A
Ffiona's •
• Café Rouge
• Maggie Jones
Tenth •
• Caffè Uno
• Dôme
Pret A Manger
Arcadia • • Sabatino
L'Escargot Doré
Wòdka • • Launceston Place
• Sticky Fingers
HIGH ST. KENSINGTON
• Pasha
• Da Mario
• Phoenicia
• Café Pasta
• Goolies
• PizzaExpress
• Abingdon
• Stratford's

B
Kensington Gardens
Bistrot 190
Royal Albert Hall

Mongolian Barbeque •
Cromwell Road
Spago
Khan's of Kensington
• Häagen Dazs
Bangkok
Ask •
Bombay Brasserie •
Khyber Pass
Rôt. Jules •
Texas Lone Star •
Bouchée
Hilaire
Falconiere
Dôme •
Café Rouge •
• Tootsies
• Luigi Malones
Noor Jahan •
Star of India •
• Shaw's
La Delizia
Cambio de Tercio •
• Nam Long
• Mr Wing
• Blakes
• Krungtap

EARLS COURT
EARL'S COURT
Earl's Court Exhibition Centre
Riccardo's •
Tusc •
• Balans West
• Lou Pescadou
Troubador •
Bar Japan
Wok Wok •

WEST BROMPTON
Brinkley's •
Chezmax •
Wine Gallery •
Formula Veneta •
Chaba •
• Vingt-Quatre
• Kartouche
Pitcher & Piano
• Luigi's
Glaisters •
• Calzone
Brompton Cemetery
Nikita's •
• Café Med
Simply Nico Chelsea •
• AUBERGINE
• PizzaExpress
Dôme •
Café Rouge •
Café L'Altro •
Bersagliera •
Sporting Page •
• Bucci
Legend of India •
• Chelsea Bun
Famiglia •
Busabong Too •
• Vama
Leonardo's •
• Tiger Lil's
• Mona Lisa
Busabong Tree •

FULHAM BROADWAY
BLUE ELEPHANT
Bonjour Vietnam •
All Bar One
FULHAM
Chelsea Ram •
• 606 Club
Chutney Mary •
Thai on the River •
Shoeless Joe's •
Jim Thompson's •
Gasworks •
• Conrad
Chelsea Harbour
Canteen •
Deals •

MAP 5 – KNIGHTSBRIDGE, CHELSEA & SOUTH KENSINGTON

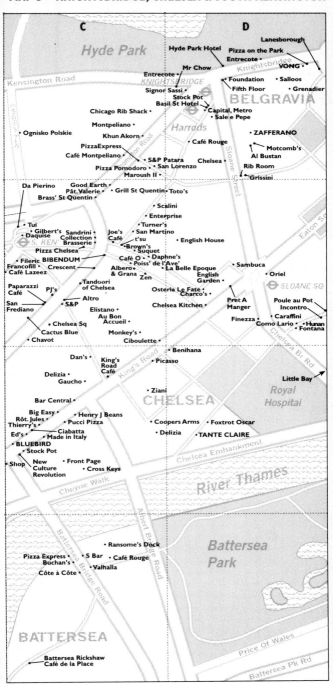

C

D

Lanesborough

Hyde Park

Hyde Park Hotel

Pizza on the Park

Entrecote •

VONG •

Kensington Road

Mr Chow

Knightsbridge

• Foundation • Salloos

Entrecote •

KNIGHTSBRIDGE

Fifth Floor • Grenadier

Signor Sassi •

BELGRAVIA

Stock Pot

Basil St Hotel •

Chicago Rib Shack

• Capital, Metro

• Sale e Pepe

Harrods

Montpeliano •

ZAFFERANO •

Khun Akorn •

• Café Rouge

Motcomb's •

Ognisko Polskie •

Al Bustan

PizzaExpress

Chelsea

Rib Room

Café Montpeliano •

• S&P Patara

Pizza Pomodoro • • San Lorenzo

Grissini •

Maroush II •

• Da Pierino

Good Earth

Pât. Valerie

• Grill St Quentin • Toto's

Brass' St Quentin •

• Scalini

• Enterprise

• Tui

• Turner's

• Gilbert's Sandrini

• San Martino

• Daquise Collection Joe's

t'su

Brasserie Café

• English House

Pizza Chelsea

• Brown's

• Suquet

• Fileric

Café O • Daphne's

Francofill •

Poiss' de l'Ave'

Crescent Albero

• La Belle Epoque

Café Lazeez

& Grana Zen

• Sambuca

English

Paparazzi

Garden •

• Oriel

Café

• Tandoori

Osteria Le Fate

SLOANE SQ

PJ's

of Chelsea

Charco's •

San

Altro

Chelsea Kitchen •

Pret A

Poule au Pot

Frediano

• S&P

Manger

Incontro

Elistano •

• Caraffini

Au Bon

Finezza •

Como Lario • • Hunan

• Chelsea Sq

Accueil •

• Fontana

Cactus Blue

Monkey's •

Chavot

• Ciboulette

Chelsea Br Rd

• Benihana

Dan's • King's

Road

Delizia • Café • Picasso

Little Bay

Gaucho •

Royal

• Ziani

CHELSEA

Hospital

Bar Central •

Big Easy •

• Henry J Beans

Rôt. Jules • • Pucci Pizza

• Coopers Arms • Foxtrot Oscar

Thierry's •

• Ciabatta

Ed's •

• Made in Italy

• Delizia

TANTE CLAIRE

• BLUEBIRD

Chelsea Embankment

• Stock Pot

• Shop New

• Front Page

Culture

• Cross Keys

Revolution

Cheyne Walk

River Thames

Battersea

Park

• Ransome's Dock

Pizza Express •

• S Bar

• Café Rouge

Buchan's •

Côte à Côte •

• Valhalla

BATTERSEA

Price Of Wales

• Battersea Rickshaw

Café de la Place

Battersea Pk Rd

MAP 6 – NOTTING HILL & BAYSWATER

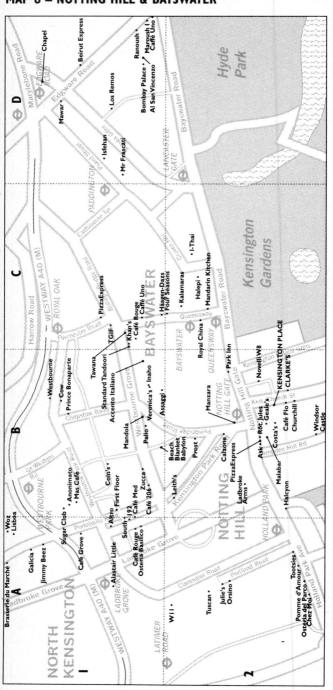

MAP 7 – HAMMERSMITH & CHISWICK

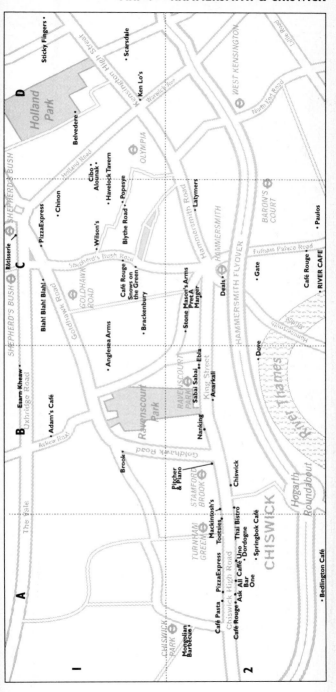

MAP 8 – HAMPSTEAD, CAMDEN TOWN & ISLINGTON

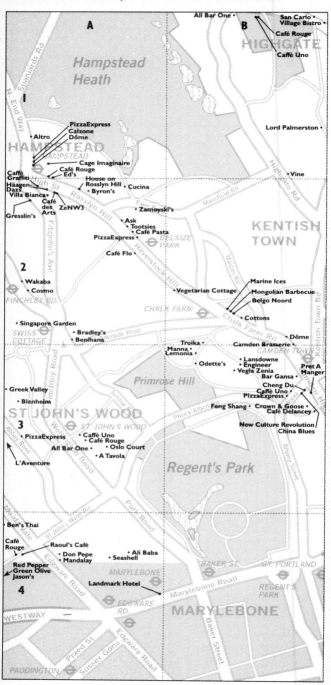

A

B

Hampstead Heath

All Bar One •

San Carlo •
Village Bistro •
Café Rouge •

HIGHGATE

Caffè Uno •

1

PizzaExpress •
Calzone
Dôme

Lord Palmerston •

HAMPSTEAD
HAMPSTEAD

• Altro

Cage Imaginaire •

• Vine

Caffè
Graffiti
Ed's •
Café Rouge •
House on •
Rosslyn Hill
• Cucina

Haägen-
Dazs •
Villa Bianca •
Café des
Arts •
ZeNW3
Byron's •

Gresslin's •

• Zamoyski's

KENTISH
TOWN

• Ask
• Tootsies
• Café Pasta
PizzaExpress •

BELSIZE
PARK

2

• Café Flo

• Wakaba
• Cosmo

Marine Ices •
• Vegetarian Cottage
Mongolian Barbecue •
Belgo Noord •

FINCHLEY RD.

CHALK FARM

• Cottons

• Singapore Garden

SWISS
COTTAGE

• Bradley's
• Benihana

Chalk Farm Rd.

• Dôme

Camden Brasserie •

CAMDEN TOWN

Troika •
Manna •
Lemonia •

Lansdowne •
• Engineer
• Vegia Zenia

Pret A
Manger

• Odette's

Bar Gansa •

Cheng Du •

• Greek Valley
• Blenheim

Primrose Hill

Caffè Uno •
PizzaExpress •

Feng Shang •
Crown & Goose •
Café Delancey •

ST JOHN'S WOOD
ST. JOHN'S WOOD

New Culture Revolution
China Blues

3

• PizzaExpress

• Caffè Uno
• Café Rouge
All Bar One •
• Oslo Court
• A Tavola

L'Aventure

Regent's Park

• Ben's Thai

Café
Rouge •
• Raoul's Café
• Don Pepe
• Mandalay
• Ali Baba
• Seashell

BAKER ST.
GT. PORTLAND

Red Pepper
Green Olive
Jason's •

MARYLEBONE

REGENT'S
PARK

4

Landmark Hotel •

Marylebone Road

EDGWARE
RD.

MARYLEBONE

WESTWAY

PADDINGTON

MAP 8 – HAMPSTEAD, CAMDEN TOWN & ISLINGTON

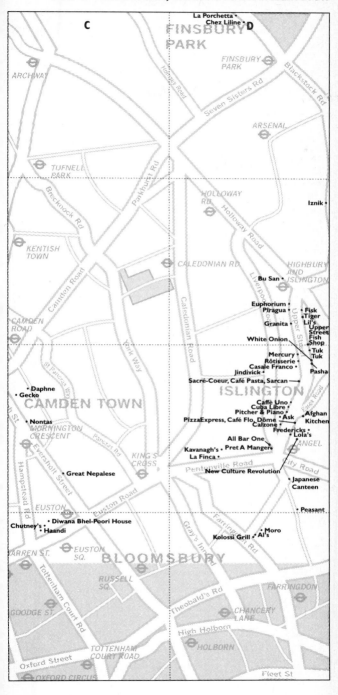

C

D

La Porchetta •
• Chez Liline

FINSBURY PARK

FINSBURY PARK

ARCHWAY

Seven Sisters Rd

Blackstock Rd

ARSENAL

TUFNELL PARK

Brecknock Rd

Parkhurst Rd

HOLLOWAY RD

Holloway Road

Iznik •

KENTISH TOWN

Camden Road

CALEDONIAN RD.

Caledonian Road

HIGHBURY AND ISLINGTON

Liverpool Rd

Bu San •

CAMDEN ROAD

York Way

Euphorium •
Pirague •

• Fisk
•Tiger

Granita •

Lil's
Upper
Street
Fish
Shop

White Onion •

St Pancras Way

Mercury •
Rôtisserie •
Casale Franco •
Jindivick •

•Tuk
Tuk

• Pasha

Sacré-Coeur, Café Pasta, Sarcan ▸

• Daphne
• Gecko

ISLINGTON

CAMDEN TOWN

Caffé Uno •
Cuba Libre •
Pitcher & Piano •

• Nontas

Pancras Rd

PizzaExpress, Café Flo, Dôme •
Calzone •

• Ask

Afghan
Kitchen

MORNINGTON CRESCENT

Eversholt Street

Fredericks •

Essex Road

• Lola's

All Bar One •

ANGEL

Hampstead Rd

KING'S CROSS

Kavanagh's •
La Finca •

Pret A Manger •

City Road

• Great Nepalese

Pentonville Road

New Culture Revolution •

EUSTON

Euston Road

Gray's Inn Road

• Japanese
Canteen

Chutney's •
• Diwana Bhel-Poori House
• Haandi

Farringdon Road

• Peasant

WARREN ST.

EUSTON SQ.

BLOOMSBURY

• Moro

Kolossi Grill •

• Al's

RUSSELL SQ.

Theobald's Rd

FARRINGDON

GOODGE ST.

Tottenham Court Rd

CHANCERY LANE

High Holborn

TOTTENHAM COURT ROAD

Oxford Street

HOLBORN

OXFORD CIRCUS

Fleet St

MAP 9 – THE CITY

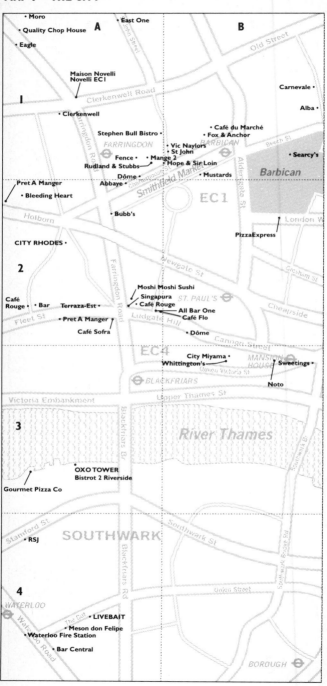

- Moro
- Quality Chop House
- Eagle

A

- East One

B

Old Street

Maison Novelli
Novelli EC1

Clerkenwell Road

1

- Clerkenwell

Carnevale •

Alba •

Stephen Bull Bistro •

FARRINGDON

- Café du Marché
- Fox & Anchor

BARBICAN

• Vic Naylors
• St John

Beech St

• Searcy's

• Fence   • Mange 2
Rudland & Stubbs •   • Hope & Sir Loin

Barbican

Dôme •

Aldersgate St

Abbaye •

• Mustards

Smithfield Market

EC1

Pret A Manger •

• Bleeding Heart

Holborn

London Wall

• Bubb's

CITY RHODES •

PizzaExpress

Newgate St

2

Gresham St

Café
Rouge •   • Bar

Terraza-Est •

Farringdon Road

Moshi Moshi Sushi
Singapura
• Café Rouge

ST. PAUL'S

Cheapside

Fleet St

• Pret A Manger
Café Sofra

Ludgate Hill

All Bar One
Café Flo

• Dôme

Cannon Street

EC4

City Miyama •

MANSION
HOUSE

• Whittington's •

Queen Victoria St

• Sweetings •

BLACKFRIARS

Noto •

Victoria Embankment

Upper Thames St

Blackfriars Br

River Thames

3

Southwark Br

OXO TOWER
Bistrot 2 Riverside

Gourmet Pizza Co •

Stamford St

SOUTHWARK

Southwark St

• RSJ

Blackfriars Rd

Southwark Bridge Rd

4

Union Street

WATERLOO

The Cut

• **LIVEBAIT**
• Meson don Felipe
• Waterloo Fire Station

Waterloo Road

• Bar Central

BOROUGH

MAP 9 – THE CITY

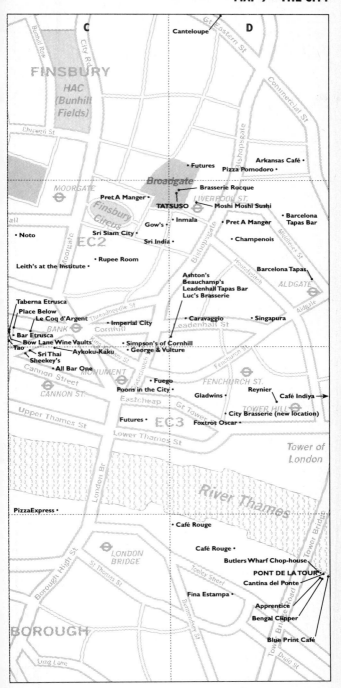

FINSBURY
HAC (Bunhill Fields)

Canteloupe

MOORGATE

Broadgate

• Futures
Pizza Pomodoro •
Arkansas Café •

Brasserie Rocque
Pret A Manger •
Finsbury Circus
TATSUSO
Moshi Moshi Sushi

LIVERPOOL ST.

• Noto

Gow's •
• Inmala
• Pret A Manger
Barcelona Tapas Bar •

EC2
Sri Siam City •
Sri India •
• Champenois

• Rupee Room
Barcelona Tapas
Leith's at the Institute •
ALDGATE

Ashton's
Beauchamp's
Leadenhall Tapas Bar
Luc's Brasserie

Taberna Etrusca
Place Below
Le Coq d'Argent
• Caravaggio
• Singapura

• Imperial City
Leadenhall St.

• Bar Etrusca
Cornhill
• Simpson's of Cornhill
Bow Lane Wine Vaults
Tao
Aykoku-Kaku
• George & Vulture

• Sri Thai
Sheekey's
BANK
MONUMENT
• All Bar One

Cannon Street
• Fuego
FENCHURCH ST.

CANNON ST.
Poons in the City •
Eastcheap
Gladwins •
Reynier
Café Indiya →

Upper Thames St.
Futures •
EC3
City Brasserie (new location)
Foxtrot Oscar •
TOWER HILL

Lower Thames St.

Tower of London

River Thames

PizzaExpress •

LONDON BRIDGE

• Café Rouge

Café Rouge •

Butlers Wharf Chop-house

PONT DE LA TOUR

Cantina del Ponte

Fina Estampa •

Apprentice

Bengal Clipper

BOROUGH

Blue Print Café

Lung Lane

Tower Bridge

MAP 10 – SOUTH LONDON (AND FULHAM)

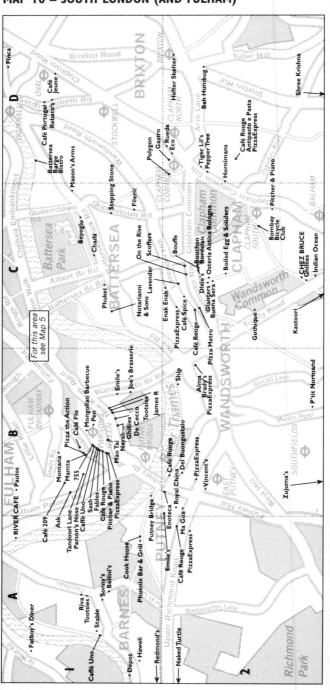

Finca
Café Portugal
Rebato's
Café Jeune
Brixton Road
Tulse Hill
Shree Krishna

Battersea Barge Bistro
Mason's Arms
Polygon
Gastro
Rueda
Eco
Helter Skelter
Bah Humbug
Tiger Lil's
Pepper Tree
Hornimans
Café Rouge
Antipasto e Pasta
PizzaExpress

Stepping Stone
Fileric
Beyoglu
Chada
Phuket
Notarianni & Sons
On the Rise
Scoffers
Lavender
Bouffe
Bouchon Bordelais
Dixie's
Osteria Antica Bologna
Boiled Egg & Soldiers
Bombay Bicycle Club
CHEZ BRUCE
Ghillies
Indian Ocean

Café Spice
Enak Enak
PizzaExpress
Café Rouge
Pizza Metro
Glaisters
Buona Sera
Gothique
Kastoori

Emile's
Joe's Brasserie
Mongolian Barbecue
Pen
Ghillies
De Cecco
James R
Alma
Brady
PizzaExpress
Ship
P'tit Normand

Pizza the Action
Café Flo
Mamta
Montana
755
Ask
Café 209
Tandoori Lane
Parson's Nose
Caffè Uno
Sash
Fables
Café Rouge
Pitcher & Piano
PizzaExpress
Mao Tai
Nayab
Café Rouge
Royal China
Del Buongustaio
Vincent's
PizzaExpress
Zujuma's

RIVER CAFE
Paulos
Enoteca
Emile's
Ma Goa
Café Rouge
PizzaExpress
Putney Bridge
Cook House
Phoenix Bar & Grill

Fatboy's Diner
Riva
Tootsies
Stable
Sonny's
Bellini's
Café Uno
Depot
Haweli
Redmond's
Naked Turtle

For this area see Map 5

NOTES